Strategies of Inclusion and Exclusion in online and offline Interaction

ŁÓDŹ STUDIES IN LANGUAGE

Edited by Barbara Lewandowska-Tomaszczyk and Łukasz Bogucki

VOLUME 74

Emanuela Campisi / Ester Di Silvestro /
Marco Venuti (eds.)

Strategies of Inclusion and Exclusion in online and offline Interaction

PETER LANG

Berlin - Bruxelles - Chennai - Lausanne - New York - Oxford

Bibliographic Information published by the Deutsche Nationalbibliothek
The Deutsche Nationalbibliothek lists this publication in the Deutsche Nationalbibliografie; detailed bibliographic data is available online at http://dnb.d-nb.de.

Library of Congress Cataloging-in-Publication Data
A CIP catalog record for this book has been applied for at the Library of Congress.

The publication of the present volume was supported by the PRIN project 'Designing effective policies for Politically Correct: A rhetorical/pragmatic model of total speech situation' Prot. 201794A3F2_001.

ISSN 1437-5281
ISBN 978-3-631-85214-9 (Print)
E-ISBN 978-3-631-91356-7 (E-PDF)
E-ISBN 978-3-631-91357-4 (E-PUB)
DOI 10.3726/b21485

Published by Peter Lang GmbH, Berlin, Deutschland

info@peterlang.com - www.peterlang.com

Table of Contents

Introduction

Identity is a crucial concept in the (self-)definition and (self-)representation of every human being. This concept is not stable, and it is continually formed, shaped, and negotiated through the interaction with others (Seargeant & Tagg, 2014, p. 5). Identity is characterised by both *sameness* and *distinctiveness* (Jacobson-Widding, 1983, p. 13) that influence not only personal identity but also collective identity (Jacobson-Widding, 1983, p. 13). Indeed, the construction of personal identity cannot be separated from the collective one and its social and cultural background (Erikson, 1968, p. 20; Jacobson-Widding, 1983, p. 14). More precisely, Erikson (1968, p. 19) focused on the *continuity* of personal identity defining *sameness* as sameness with oneself (Jacobson-Widding, 1983, p. 13). At the same time, sameness clearly refers also to collective identity because people that belong to a group must share some features (Jacobson-Widding, 1983, p. 13). On the other hand, *distinctiveness* concerns both personal and collective identity because it indicates the distinctions among groups of people (Jacobson-Widding, 1983, p. 13). It is also important to specify that in-group identity is often perceived as heterogeneous – since in-group social actors care about their self-identity and the differentiation from others –, while out-group identity is perceived as homogeneous (Brewer, 1993). The representation of in-group and out-group identities is linked to the processes of inclusion and exclusion. For instance, people who highly identify within a group will reinforce even more this attitude when there is an out-group threat that jeopardises their in-group identity (Branscombe et al., 1993, p. 382; Wilder & Shapiro, 1984). As a result, in-group and out-group identities are connected to the processes of inclusion and exclusion because these processes are crucial in the construction of both personal and collective identities. According to Brewer's (1993) model of "optimal distinctiveness":

> [...] an individual's sense of self is shaped by opposing needs for assimilation and differentiation between self and others. Assimilation is the inclusion of self and others in social categories defined by shared features or common interests. Differentiation is the exclusion of others from the definition of self (Brewer, 1993, p. 157).

Consequently, assimilation supports the process of inclusion and especially the sense of belonging to a group of people with common interests and features. Instead, differentiation involves both the exclusion of in-group people – since social actors preserve their distinctiveness – and especially the exclusion of out-group entities. Indeed, even the concept of *community* – from a psychological perspective – is pervaded by both positive and negative outcomes (Fisher & Sonn, 2007, p. 26) of inclusionary and exclusionary practices. The community's dynamics involve supportive and positive feelings connected to the inclusion process (Fisher & Sonn, 2007, p. 26). At the same time, these dynamics can encourage the rise of negative feelings and actions – linked to the exclusion process – towards people who do not belong to the community such as stigmatisation and vilification (Fisher & Sonn, 2007, p. 26). For this reason, the existence of a community is based on the processes of inclusion and exclusion since there is the necessity to determine who can or cannot be considered a member of that group (Fisher & Sonn, 2007, p. 26).

Nowadays the processes of inclusion and exclusion – and consequently even the formation of personal and collective identities – are deeply interwoven with social media interaction because these online platforms provide new spaces for identity construction (Seargeant & Tagg, 2014). Specifically, in the current globalised world the processes concerning the formation of identity – such as inclusion and exclusion – are supported, increased, and extended to a large number of individuals since social media allows the creation of online communities that are formed by people in spite of their geographical locations (Seargeant & Tagg, 2014). For example, social media have been crucial in the (online) debate and in the spread of social movements such as #metoo (Mendes et al., 2018) and Thunberg's Fridays for Future (Brünker et al., 2019; Soler i Martí et al., 2020). In addition, social media can be defined as *eco chambers* (Sunstein, 2007; Pariser, 2011) where discourses – especially political discourses – can be polarised (Barberá et al., 2015). The polarisation of discourses can lead to an enhancement of the in-group identity (Gillani et al., 2018) extremising the in-group positions (Cinelli et al., 2021) and to the exclusion of social actors who do not share those positions. The processes of inclusion and exclusion are similar in online and offline interactions but, as mentioned before, in online interaction they are enhanced by social media's characteristics such as its free accessibility (Flew & Iosifidis, 2019, p. 9) that allows to a lot of people – who do not even know each other in real life – to gather and to create bonds (Fuchs, 2014, p. 35; Murthy, 2013, p. 3).

For instance, on social media (e.g., Twitter, Facebook and Instagram) hashtags play a crucial role in connecting different people who do not necessarily share common values (Seargeant & Tagg, 2014, p. 142). Furthermore, hashtags are particularly useful in the organisation of online discourses (Scott, 2018; Zappavigna, 2015). According to Zappavigna, hashtags contribute to the *searchability* of online discourses facilitating the rise of new forms of social bonding (Zappavigna, 2015, p. 16). More precisely, hashtags have three main functions that contribute to searchability. Firstly, the interpersonal function facilitates the construction of relationships through evaluative stances (Zappavigna, 2015, p. 6). Secondly, the experiential function defines the posts' discourses as being part of a particular kind of experience (Zappavigna, 2015, p. 6). Thirdly, the textual function organises the post textually since hashtags are metadata (Zappavigna, 2015, p. 6).

In addition, identity and its construction are connected to language (Tabouket-Keller, 2017) and its performativity (Austin, 1962; Butler, 1997) in both offline and online interactions. According to Tabouret-Keller (2017, p. 315):

> The language spoken by somebody and his or her identity as a speaker of this language are inseparable: This is surely a piece of knowledge as old as human speech itself. Language acts are acts of identity.

Moreover, it should be specified that the process of communication involves the interactive participation of social actors who cooperate disseminating traces of their (social) identity (Gumperz, 1983, p. 111). Linguistic analyses have influenced – and intersected with – many fields of study such as anthropology, psychology and sociology (Gumperz, 1983, p. 112). In this regard, some Discourse Studies disciplines (e.g., Critical Discourse Analysis) – that are generally interdisciplinary fields of study – focus on *language in use* (van Dijk, 1997, p. 2) and perceive language as a social practice. This means that language is the product of social practices but, at the same time, it represents a tool capable to shape society and social order (Angermuller et al., 2014, p. 3). For this reason, linguistic behaviour should be considered and interpreted in the social context in which it is reproduced (Bhatia et al., 2008, p. 1). The Critical Discourse Analysis (CDA) approach provides a clear example to understand how the processes of inclusion and exclusion – and consequently even the in-group and out-group identity formation – can be strategically performed through language. CDA pays particular attention to the relationship among language, power and ideology (Machin & Mayr, 2012) since language – as a form of social practice – can legitimise specific ideologies and normalise power inequalities (Machin & Mayr, 2012). The enhancement of the in-group identity can be achieved through specific linguistic strategies that represent the out-group entities as otherness and as dangerous threats. The out-group entities can be dehumanised, represented as threats that jeopardise social order, or they can even be suppressed through a rich variety of linguistic strategies (e.g., metaphorical representations, representational strategies, transitivity etc.). For instance, these inclusionary and exclusionary linguistic practices are currently relevant and visible in right-wing politicians' populist discourses (Wodak, 2015). Although the boundaries of a community are the product of social and cultural practices, (far) right-wing politicians often present the community and its boundaries – based on ethnic identity (Meeus et al., 2010, p. 307) – as a fixed order that cannot and should not be changed. Furthermore, this fixed social order is strengthened by these politicians through the construction of *otherness* that is formed by out-group threats such as immigrants – who threaten the in-group cultural and religious identity (Meeus et al., 2010, p. 306) –, feminist movements and the LGBTQ+ community that strongly destabilise the social status quo (e.g., the concept of traditional family and traditional gender roles) (Mudde, 2019). However, the polarised and common dichotomy *us versus them* is not limited to the social actors already mentioned (e.g., immigrants), but it can be also generally extended to every out-group entity that opposes to an in-group identity.

This volume aims to introduce different – and even less common – perspectives on identity construction as an interactional practice focusing on the analysis of communicative practices that may either facilitate or hinder effective online and offline interaction.

Chapter 2 by Francesca Ervas starts with the assumption that social networks communities can be described as "imagined communities" with "liquid" borders between the real and the imagined, characterised by "deferred rationality", "epistemic bubbles" and misinterpretation. Ervas analyses two case studies of multimodal metaphors in a Facebook group (Italian political elections in March 2018 and the pro-vaccination versus anti-vaccination dispute on herd immunity) to show that even the multimodal and especially visual nature of communication, usually a powerful epistemic and persuasive device, may enhance and reinforce the epistemic bubbles in these communities.

In Chapter 3, Emanuela Campisi and Marco Venuti investigate how the label "politically correct" is used by Italian Twitter users, especially in contexts of offence and exclusion, by means of a corpus of Italian tweets containing the hashtags #politicamentecorretto and #politicallycorrect. The results show that, as for other countries, in Italy the label is used mainly with the purpose of offending somebody because of her/his attempt to use or promote an inclusive language. The findings are discussed with special reference to the lack of consensus around the importance of language as a tool to increase equality, and to the actual efficacy of PC practices as they have been implemented so far.

Chapter 4 too, by Ester di Silvestro, draws on a corpus of Italian tweets, with the goal of investigating the Italian far-right populist discourse. More precisely, the analysis focuses on a case-study about Matteo Salvini, in order to highlight which linguistic strategies are used to exclude or include immigrants. The results of the analysis show that Matteo Salvini combines several strategies (e.g., opposition strategy, aggregation strategies and metaphorical representations) to dehumanise immigrants and legitimise their (physical) exclusion.

Contemporary society – defined as a complex ecosystem in which culture and technology cohabit – and ingroup identity construction are the focus of Davide Bennato's Chapter 5. Two opposite views are discussed: transhumanism, an optimistic ideology in which the digital is a means to achieve and overcome the individual and social limits, and neo-Luddism, which claims that technological development is not synonymous with technological progress, and that technology will lead to undesirable outcomes. Bennato provides some case studies to spell out the neo-luddist identity, in order to show how this emerging stance leads unavoidably to the exclusion of its supporters from a technologically mediated community and, as a consequence, from contemporary society as well.

In Chapter 6, Alessandra Micalizzi provides evidence in favour of the idea that nowadays personal and social identity is increasingly defined by dietary choices ("we are what we don't eat"). The paper analyses a corpus of narratives coming from vegetarian and vegan Italians, together with some online conversations in some famous Italian food-blogs. The results show that especially junior vegs underline the presence of social barriers in maintaining their diet, suggesting interesting dynamics of inclusion/exclusion among veg-people with a neat difference (in perception, practices, and languages) between vegetarians and vegans.

That narratives are a valuable source when it comes to exclusion is shown also in Paolo Donadio's Chapter 7. Specifically, the aim of this chapter is to investigate the construction of migrants' identity through spontaneous discursive representation, in particular through the narration of migration experiences and cultural clashes. Through the narrative reformulation and the analysis of its discursive components, Donadio shows how subjects construct, during the conversation, multiple identities for themselves and the "characters" of their story; in this way, it is possible to compare different cultures and approaches to the host community and to identify the spaces for a real integration.

Stavros Assimakopoulos and Rebecca Vella Muskat, in Chapter 8, present the analysis of online comments made in reaction to news reports pertaining to migrant and LGBTIQ issues. Online communities use different strategies in the negotiation of both positive and negative attitudes debating pro- and anti- migrant and LGBTIQ ideological positioning. The analysis focuses on the presence of explicit and implicit discursive strategies in the communication of the two opposing stances. The results show that while indirectness is the main weapon of choice for believers of both social inclusion and exclusion of the relevant minority groups, explicitness is used more in defences of social inclusion as well as in the context of responses to comments with an opposing view.

In Chapter 9, Federica Formato presents the debate on gendered forms in interactions among speakers on social media and provides a comprehensive overview of what goes wrong (and what goes right) when discussing gendered language. She does so in the Italian context, where women are still stereotyped as belonging to the private sphere and believed to be unsuitable for the institutional public one. The main focus of the chapter is on the institutionalised and structural imbalance and on the simplistic shortcuts put forward by speakers in order to explain how some terms are used or perceived. Drawing on recent events, for example the FIFA Women World Cup, Formato shows how personal and social perspectives are strictly intertwined and explores degrees of ego identity.

Gendered discourses on the social networking service Twitter are at the core of Chapter 10 by Stefania Maci. This study investigates the phenomenon of mansplaining, a neologism recently popularised on social media, and used to indicate men speaking to women in a patronising manner. Drawing on the (multimodal)analysis of tweets containing #mansplain, the analysis assesses to what extent the hashtag is actually used to identify effective politically (in) correct communication. The aim of the chapter is to detect whether #mansplain measures societal beliefs on the basis of which people assume how men and women should or should not talk to each other, or whether it has become an ideological weapon through which the processes of identity building can be elaborated and revealed via ingroup/outgroup linguistic strategies.

Ashleigh Feltmate, in Chapter 11, analyses alignment and solidarity within a group of tweets related to the #whyIdidntreport hashtag that became trending in relation to the accusations of sexual assault moved against the Supreme Court nominee Brett M. Kavanaugh. Thirty-one tweets were selected and coded for turn-taking organisation, on- and off-record politeness strategies, engagement formulations, alignment, solidarity, face-threatening acts, and emoji modulation. The analysis highlights how Twitter participants – those who push for change and those who resist it – use dialogically contractive formulations in their messages to exclude others with counter positions from engaging in the conversation of the thread; the contractive formulations also do important work for victims of sexual assault as they create a safe space for reporting events that are all too frequently denied or ignored when communicated in face-to-face interactions.

The last Chapter 12 by Marco Mazzone provides an overview of political correctness norms (PCNs), here regarded as an emblematic example of failed policy in support of inclusive language use. In details, it is suggested to consider

PCNs norms – that is, the norms intended to regulate linguistic behaviour to avoid ideological positioning and the exclusion of minorities and – as a special case of tabooing, reviewing some relevant anthropological literature in search of a framework to understand the faith in the magical power of words. The chapter ends with the discussion of the developmental psychological model proposed by Erik Erikson, in order to theoretically frame the phenomenon under consideration not only in this chapter, but in the book as a whole.

References

Angermuller, J., Maingueneau, D., & Wodak, R. (2014). The Discourse Studies Reader: An Introduction. In J. Angermuller, D. Maingueneau & R. Wodak (Eds.), *The Discourse Studies Reader: Main Currents in Theory and Analysis* (pp. 1–14). Amsterdam: John Benjamins.

Austin, J. L. (1962). *How to Do Things with Words*. Oxford: Oxford University Press.

Barberá, P., Jost, J. T., Nagler, J., Tucker, J. A., & Bonneau, R. (2015). Tweeting From Left to Right: Is Online Political Communication More Than an Echo Chamber? *Psychological Science*, 26(10), 1531–1542.

Bhatia, V. K., Flowerdew, J., & Jones, R. H. (2008). Approaches to Discourse Analysis. In V. K. Bhatia, J. Flowerdew & R. H. Jones (Eds.), *Advances in Discourse Studies* (pp. 1–18). London: Routledge.

Branscombe, N. R., Wann, D. L., Noel, J. G., & Coleman, J. (1993). In-Group or Out-Group Extremity: Importance of the Threatened Social Identity. *Personality and Social Psychology Bulletin*, 19(4), 381–388.

Brewer, M. B. (1993). Social Identity, Distinctiveness, and in-Group Homogeneity. *Social Cognition*, 11(1), 150–164.

Brünker, F., Deitelhoff, F., & Mirbabaie, M. (2019). Collective Identity Formation on Instagram – Investigating the Social Movement Fridays for Future. In *Proceedings of the 30th Australasian Conference on Information Systems (ACIS 2019)* (pp. 304–310). Perth: Australia.

Butler, J. (1997). *Excitable Speech: A Politics of the Performative*. New York: Routledge.

Cinelli, M., De Francisci Morales, G., Galeazzi, A., Quattrociocchi, W., & Starnini, M. (2021). The Echo Chamber Effect on Social Media. *Proceedings of the National Academy of Sciences*, 118(9), e2023301118.

Erikson, E. H. (1968). *Identity: Youth and Crisis*. New York: Norton Company.

Fisher, A., & Sonn, C. (2007). Sense of Community and Dynamics of Inclusion-Exclusion by Receiving Communities. *Australian Community Psychologist*. 19(2), 26–34.

Flew, T., & Iosifidis, P. (2019). Populism, Globalisation and Social Media. *The International Communication Gazette*. 82(1), 7–25.

Fuchs, C. (2014). *Social Media: A Critical Introduction*. London: SAGE.

Gillani N., Yuan, A., Saveski, M., Vosoughi, S., & Roy, D. (2018). Me, My Echo Chamber, and I: Introspection on Social Media Polarization. In *Proceedings of the 2018 World Wide Web Conference (WWW '18)* (pp. 823–831) International World Wide Web Conferences Steering Committee, Republic and Canton of Geneva, CHE.

Gumperz, J. J. (1983). Communication and Social Identity. In A. Jacobson-Widding (Ed.). *Identity: Personal and Socio-Cultural. A Symposium* (pp. 111–122). Acta Univ. Ups. Uppsala Studies in Cultural Anthropology. Almqvist & Wiksell International.

Jacobson-Widding, A. (1983). Introduction. In A. Jacobson-Widding (Ed.). *Identity: Personal and Socio-Cultural. A Symposium* (pp. 13–32). Acta Univ. Ups. Uppsala Studies in Cultural Anthropology. Almqvist & Wiksell International.

Machin, D., & Mayr, A. (2012). *How to Do a Critical Discourse Analysis. A Multimodal Introduction*. London: SAGE.

Meeus, J., Duriez. B., Vanbeselaere, N., & Boen, F. (2010). The Role of National Identity Representation in the Relation between In-Group Identification and Out-Group Derogation: Ethnic Versus Civic representation. *The British Journal of Social Psychology*, 49(2), 305–320.

Mendes, K., Ringrose, J., & Keller, J. (2018). #MeToo and the Promise and Pitfalls of Challenging Rape Culture Through Digital Feminist Activism. *European Journal of Women's Studies*, 25(2), 236–246.

Mudde, C. (2019). *The Far-Right Today*. Cambridge: Polity Press.

Murthy, D. (2013). *Twitter: Social Communication in the Twitter Age*. Cambridge: Polity Press.

Pariser, E. (2011). *The Filter Bubble: What the Internet Is Hiding From You*. London: Viking.

Scott, K. (2018). 'Hashtags Work Everywhere': The Pragmatic Functions of Spoken Hashtags. *Discourse, Context & Media*, 22, 57–64.

Seargeant P., & Tagg C. (2014). Introduction: The Language of Social Media. In P. Seargeant, & C. Tagg (Eds.), *The Language of Social Media: Identity and Community on the Internet* (pp. 1–20). London: Palgrave Macmillan.

Soler i Martí, R., Ferrer-Fons, M., & Terren, L. (2020). The Interdependency of Online and Offline Activism: A Case Study of Fridays for Future-Barcelona in the Context of the COVID-19 Lockdown. *Hipertext.net*, 21, 105–114.

Sunstein, C. R. (2007). *Republic.com 2.0*. Princeton: Princeton University Press.

Tabouret-Keller, A. (2017). Language and Identity. In F. Coulmas (Eds.), *The Handbook of Sociolinguistics* (pp. 315–326). Oxford: Blackwell Publishing.

van Dijk, T. A. (1997). The Study of Discourse. In T. A. van Dijk (Eds.), *Discourse as Structure and Process. Discourse Studies: A Multidisciplinary Introduction* (pp. 1–34). London: SAGE.

Wilder, D. A., & Shapiro, P. N. (1984). Role of Out-Group Cues in Determining Social Identity. *Journal of Personality and Social Psychology*, 47(2), 342–348.

Wodak, R. (2015). *The Politics of Fear. What Right-Wing Populist Discourses Mean*. London: SAGE.

Zappavigna, M. (2015). Searchable Talk: The Linguistic Functions of Hashtags. *Social Semiotics*, 25(3), 274–291.

Francesca Ervas
University of Cagliari, Italy
ervas@unica.it

Chapter 1 Imaginary communities: Multimodal reasoning on vaccination in social networks

Abstract: Social networks communities are "imagined communities" characterised by "deferred rationality" and "epistemic bubbles". Two case studies of multimodal metaphors in a Facebook group are analysed to show that the visual nature of communication may enhance and reinforce the epistemic bubbles in these communities.

Keywords: social network communities, multimodal metaphor, deferred rationality, epistemic bubbles.

1. Introduction

Language plays a fundamental role in the understanding of both the connection and the disconnection of the self to the social world. Language can also track the passages from our social online ("coupled") and offline ("decoupled") states of connection to the others. Recently, the term *languaging* has been coined to refer to the specific way we connect to others, making sense of the social world. Languaging is a *participatory sense-making* coming from the dynamic interaction of coupling with the environment (Cuffari et al., 2015). Cuffari and colleagues define languaging as "a form of social agency involving a double regulation of self and interaction that integrates the tensions inherent in dialogical organization and participation genres" (Cuffari et al., 2015, p. 1092, emphasis in the text).

The participatory sense-making is essentially *dialogical* and *dynamic*, as it is "a practice that transcends the self-other boundary and enables agents to regulate self and other as well as interaction couplings" (Cuffari et al., 2015, p. 1089). From this perspective, languaging cannot be reduced to language *tout court*, as it includes all the ways we interact with others and make sense of our connection to others, which cannot be reduced to the sole verbal modality[1]. In this chapter, I will therefore look at the participatory sense-making as *a multimodal process*,

---

1 Within cognitive linguistics the various ways in which we express ourselves are defined as *modalities* of expression (visual, verbal, etc.), while within the semiotics they are

which employs different modalities in social interaction (Forceville, 2020). Though in the past the hegemony of the verbal modality over other modalities has guided philosophical research on social interaction, nowadays it is time to overcome such hegemony and consider different modalities as a source for social interaction (Ervas, 2019a).

The chapter will focus on multimodal interaction in social networks, which are the means by which we can "decouple" ourselves from reality and real social communities we belong to, but at the same time also the means by which we "couple" with a virtual reality and online communities. In this view, social networks can be conceived as "imagined communities" (Anderson, 1983; Arfini, 2019), which are based on real communities but at the same time go beyond their limits, thus favouring decoupled processes from social reality (Section 2). Such processes are responsible for the creation of *imaginary communities*, when communities are no more coupled with real communities and where the interaction with others is "solipsistic" rather than "participatory" (Section 3). I will use the notion of *multimodal narrative practice* (Gallagher, 2003; Gallagher & Hutto, 2008; Hutto, 2007, 2008), to make clear the specific mechanisms that can lead reasoning in the collective virtual environment of social networks to be disembodied and detached from real communities (Section 4).

Finally, two case studies of multimodal narrative practice in social networks are discussed, focusing on public institutional pages promoting vaccination on Facebook (Section 5). Anti-vaccination communities easily become *epistemic bubbles* or even *echo chambers* when the community members' reasoning is decoupled from others' reasoning, without possibility of recoupling. The problem of vaccine hesitancy is quite recurrent in the history of medicine, as well as the challenge to reach group immunity despite anti-vaccination movements (Grignolio, 2018). Institutional communication is thus crucial to reach patients' compliance in pro-vaccination campaigns and metaphors have been widely used to this aim (Ervas, 2018). Nowadays, social networks are the new frontier of health communication and the phenomenon of imaginary communities, where reasoning suffers from a missed alignment in the processes of coupling and recoupling with others, urgently needs to be investigated.

---

defined as *modes*. The terminology – I will use in the chapter especially when defining the images – is therefore dependent on the discipline in which such phenomena will be discussed. Thanks to a conference participant for having pointed out this distinction.

2. Social networks as imagined communities

The idea of languaging as a participatory sense-making is connected to a specific philosophical and cognitive view of the identities who participate in making sense of the world. This view is known as the enactive approach to (social) cognition, which relates the human activities of sense-making "to self-produced identities and to the regulation of coupling with environmental domains that support those identities" (Cuffari et al., 2015, p. 1092). In this view, identity is the outcome of the dynamic self-produced and self-sustained processes of coupling with the environment and with other identities. Also *decoupling processes* are fundamental to "self-produced identities" (De Bruin & Kästner, 2012; De Bruin & De Haan, 2012). Anyway, the decoupling processes should lead to a process of recoupling with reality, to avoid a disembodied experience of the social world. Indeed, in the processes of decoupling and recoupling with others, the subjects can acquire a new, personal way of interacting with them (Baird et al., 2012).

Imagination can be considered a process of decoupling from reality, by which we re-couple with reality in a new and creative way. We can imagine ourselves, the others and ourselves in relation to the others, based on our previous experience, but at the same time in a new and different way, when compared to our previous experience. Imagination – conceived as a process of decoupling and recoupling with reality – can work in both real and virtual communities, but via different mechanisms. For instance, one of the main tenets of Anderson's concept of *nation* is that imagination plays a central role in shaping the identity of a community of people, "regardless of the actual inequality and exploitation that may prevail in each" (Anderson, 1983, p. 7). Imagination is the cement that keeps a community together, as the members of the community cannot see all each other, but they do own an image of their community as a whole. Given the size of a nation as a community, imagination is needed to go beyond the limits of the individuals' actual experience to grasp the collective experience: a nation is indeed imagined "because the members of even the smallest nation will never know most of their fellow-members, meet them, or even hear of them, yet in the minds of each lives the image of their communion" (Anderson, 1983, p. 6).

Imagining the other members of a community is not completely different from seeing them: some properties we attribute to them in the process of imagination may be the same we attributed to them in the process of seeing them and recovered from memory. However, as in every process of imagination, we also select from memory and sometimes even invent some properties of theirs that we believe to be the most important or salient to be considered as a member of that community. In the process of selecting the relevant properties of the members for the identity of the community, some other properties – which the members do not share – are neglected, as Ernest Renan warned: “The essence of a nation is that all individuals have a lot in common, but also that all of them have forgot a lot” (my translation from French: “Or l’essence d’une nation est que tous les individus aient beaucoup de choses en commun, et aussi que tous aient oublié bien des choses”) (Renan, 1947, p. 892).

A nation is imagined as *limited*, “because even the largest of them, encompassing perhaps a billion living human beings, has finite, if elastic, boundaries, beyond which lie other nations” (Anderson, 1983, p. 7). It is imagined as *sovereign* because, being aware of the pluralism of identities, it dreams to be free: it is “the gage and emblem of freedom” (Anderson, 1983, p. 7). It is imagined as a *community*, because it is “always conceived as a deep, horizontal comradeship” (Anderson, 1983, p. 7). As in the case of a nation, a community in a social network, such as Facebook (FB), can also be defined as limited and sovereign, and as a community characterised by a horizontal comradeship. Each FB group has a limited (even though extensible) number of members sharing the same interests and/or beliefs, opinions, and so forth, but it is also aware of the existence of other groups characterised by other interests and/or beliefs, opinions, and so forth. Each FB member and each FB group are free, because everyone can sign up, navigate and post images, verbal or audio-visual messages, and so forth, and answer to other members’ posts by posting images, verbal or audio-visual messages, and so forth, following some shared rules, accepted by the members of the FB group (Caers et al., 2013). Finally, social relations on FB groups are characterised by a similar “horizontal comradeship”: each member’s contacts are called “friends”.

In polemical contraposition to Ernest Gellner (1964), Anderson really cares to make clear that nations are not “imagined” in the sense that they are completely “illusory” and decoupled from reality:

> With a certain ferocity Gellner makes a comparable point when he rules that “Nationalism is not the awakening of nations to self-consciousness: it *invents* nations where they do not exist” (Gellner, 1964, p. 169. italics added). […] He assimilates ‘invention’ to ‘fabrication’ and ‘falsity’, rather than to ‘imagining’ and ‘creation’. In this way he implies that ‘true’ communities exist which can be advantageously juxtaposed to nations. In fact, all communities larger than primordial villages of face-to-face contact (and perhaps even these) are imagined (Anderson, 1983, p. 6).

It follows from Anderson’s statement that an imagined community can be a village or an entire continent, or even – independent from its geographical extension – a social network community such as an FB group. This does not mean that the imagined communities have no roots in real communities: despite few “fake profiles", the great majority of profiles are created by "real" people. Therefore, the imagination process has nothing to do with falsity, as all the community members imagine the community on the basis of a shared background in real communities. For instance, previous literature showed that, in FB communities, 70 % of shared news comes from "real" friends or even members of the family, that is people already known in the "real community" (Oeldorf-Hirscha & Sundar, 2015) and that, even though each profile has a limit of 5000 contacts or friends, FB members prefer to manage 150/200 contacts (Dunbar, 2016), that is the number of contacts of a face-to-face community.

In Anderson's view, communities are not to be distinguished by their falsity versus genuineness, but rather "by *the style in which they are imagined*" (Anderson, 1983, p. 6, italics added). Indeed, each community imagines itself through its metaphors and myths, and more generally, through the languages it creates and the memories it shares via its technologies. Language itself creates the shared beliefs and identity of the imagined community. When compared to the technology the communities had in the past, social network communities have a new technology (computer and internet connection) to send and share messages in a variety of (combined) formats (verbal messages, audio, video, images). FB members can comment and discuss online, in a (re) interpretation process of multimodal messages connected by some threads to a post. As each imagined community is identified by the specific style in which it is imagined, the style in which social networks communities are imagined may be described as a *multimodal narrative practice*, that is a process of participatory sense-making having a multimodal nature and made possible by a technology which allows members a live dialogue. However, I shall argue that precisely the imagination style of social networks communities has made the borders between real, imagined and imaginary communities more *liquid* and prone to alter the processes of coupling, decoupling and recoupling with the others. Social network imagined communities can easily become *imaginary communities*, when the members are more prone to forget what makes them different from each other, focusing just on the common interests and beliefs as members of the same community.

3. Reasoning in social networks

In "real communities" people can dialogue with other members, providing reasons, opinions, comments, explanations, and waiting for the others' answers, which might in their turn modulate or anyway influence the following requests, opinions, comments, explanations, and so forth. Disagreement is indeed the food of personal and collective growth, as we need it to find reasons in order to defend our ideas, to revise, to improve and to refine our system of beliefs. In "virtual communities", as those we can find in Facebook's groups, there is the technology for a live dialogue, but the interlocutor is not in front of us and there is always the possibility s/he will answer later or never ever, deferring *ad libitum* the exchange of reasons. Therefore, on the one hand we can be always coupled with the others via the new technology of the social networks, but on the other hand we can be always decoupled with the others, because in principle nobody could answer or look at our profile. It might be claimed that this can happen in real communities too, but in virtual communities we have no way to timely feel the continuous dynamic process of coupling, decoupling and recoupling with the others. The very structure of the social networks has changed and even distorted our ability to anticipate possible (and sometimes welcome) disagreements.

Moreover, we are supposed to be contacted by everyone on every possible topic: there is in principle no limit on *who* can contact us and on *what* topic. As Mercier and Sperber pointed out (2017, pp. 249–250):

> Before the invention of the printing press and the advent of modern media, people were typically made aware that somebody in their own group had opinions different from theirs thanks to interactions with that person. Finding out about *differences of opinion* and trying to resolve them commonly occurred through repeated exchanges of arguments that could be anticipated and mentally rehearsed. Nowadays we are inundated with the *opinions of people we will never meet*: editorialists, anchormen, bloggers. We are also *expected to have an opinion on different topics* – from politics to music to food – and to be able to defend this opinion when challenged, giving us reasons to *prepare for a variety of debates that might never occur.*

Reasoning in anticipation of a disagreement, which might not come, can lead communication via social networks to be "solitary" rather than "participatory". There is nothing bad with "solitary" reasoning anticipating a dialogue, as long as the dialogue will take place (Mercier & Sperber, 2017), but "solitary" reasoning can be problematic if it remains "solitary", thus hindering the growth of creative and cooperative communities (John-Steiner, 2000).

The lack of dialogic anticipation easily brings to individualistic reasoning, which tends to erase the differences of disagreement with others. While in a live dialogue the disagreement anticipation allows to anchor reasoning to the dynamic process of coupling and decoupling with others, the lack of disagreement anticipation is the mechanism that brings social network communities to more easily forget those differences among members that can produce disagreement itself. In Renan's terms (1947), social network communities, conceived as imagined communities, can more easily forget those differences which can produce disagreement as the food of personal and collective growth of the communities themselves. Every imagined community is not constituted only by the commonalities between members but also by the differences among them. In social network communities, it is easier for a member of the imagined community to forget the differences and imagine the other members as people who can be different and can entertain different opinions from oneself, though sharing some interests or beliefs.

When the members of an imagined community do not feel anymore the need to let the possibility of disagreement open and/or to figure out possible reasons to dissent, the imagined community can become an *imaginary community*. An imagined community becomes an imaginary community precisely when reasoning not only remains solitary, but also prone to the illusion of collective reasoning. Paradoxically, FB groups are prone to the risk of becoming big solitary reasoning entities: from this point of view, the social network is not really *social*, as it might be defined as a network of individual reasoners who can be always connected with the others without knowing whether the others will ever continue the dialogue. Instead of a dynamic process of coupling/decoupling from others, the relationship to others via social network will be prone to become solipsistic and disembodied. The social construction of the FB members can easily become a "dialogue with themselves" (Tappan, 1997): in a sense, the members of imaginary communities can always be coupled to others, but are *de facto* always decoupled with others, as they are not in need to recouple with the others in a dialogic relation.

Imaginary communities paradoxically reason like a huge solitary individual and are therefore exposed to the same *confirmation bias* of individualistic reasoning (Mercier & Sperber, 2011), but at a collective level, precisely because the participatory dimension is undermined by the possible lack of recoupling processes with others. Individualistic reasoning is indeed influenced by a confirmation bias, that is people's tendency to validate their prior decisions (Nickerson, 1998; Correia, 2011). Individualistic reasoning and its confirmation bias have been seen as a natural and incisive strategy within a perspective that considers *persuasion* as the final outcome of reasoning. However, when considering argumentation rather than persuasion, collective reasoning has proven to improve the argumentative exchange and, generally, to have more inclusive outcomes in reasoning, especially when reasoning is performed in peer groups in a live cooperation setting (Moshman & Geil, 1998; Laughlin et al., 2006; Milch et al., 2009).

When compared to "traditional" imagined communities, it is more likely that a member of a social network community overestimates the commonalities with the other members of the community and think the others as having the same beliefs, interests, desires, and so forth. In imaginary communities, even the irritation coming from a real disagreement is lacking and their members experience the illusion of owning the relevant knowledge on important issues of the public life in "real" communities, without really owning it (Arfini et al., 2017), or the worst, using it as a valid tool to manage real communities. In social network communities, the members can play the role of "produsers" (Bruns & Highfield, 2012), who are neither consumers nor producers of new contents, as they share information produced by another source as it were their own. As pointed out (Arfini & Bertolotti, 2018, pp. 15–16):

> User-generated elaborations of news and the sharing activities on the network are proven to boost the "sense of agency" of users, the feeling that the agents have some control on the information they share. And this belief may be not utterly wrong, since the important thing about a content shared on an on-line community is who shared it, not what has been shared. In this sense, the feeling of agency and control over the information shared on on-line media can be experienced as "epistemological power" over that information in that particular community. The emergence of "produsers" gave birth also to the phenomenon of self-proclaimed experts, who are the acclaimed leaders in social driven networks.

As I shall discuss in the next section, an example is the anti-vaccination movement which largely exploits the social networks to spread misinterpretation and create polarised imaginary communities whose leaders are often self-proclaimed experts commenting against the public institutional FB pages (Ervas, 2018, 2019b).

The missed dynamic process of coupling and decoupling can therefore be at the origin of "epistemic bubbles" (Woods, 2005) or, the worst, "echo chamber" (Thi Nguyen, 2020) in social networks, which might let misinterpretation, self-isolation and even exclusion or group polarization spread across communities. *Epistemic bubbles* can be defined as social epistemic structure where "other relevant voices" have been accidentally or anyway not-intentionally left out, as if they were "not heard", while in echo chambers "other relevant voices have been actively excluded and discredited", because systematically undermined (Thi Nguyen, 2020, p. 141). The missed alignment in the process of coupling and recoupling with others has indeed important consequences for how we construct sociality. Previous studies showed that, when using social network, our attention is only half-directed at the other co-present people while the other half is directed to the social network activity (Vanden Abeele et al., 2019), thus entering a mental state of "absent presence" and diminishing the quality of both dialogues (Gergen, 2002). Feelings of affiliation and intimacy also decrease when people involved in the FB conversation do not pay enough attention to their interlocutors (Turkle, 2011), making them feel "alone together".

4. Multimodal reasoning in social networks

The phenomena we described are made possible by the specific technology used in social networks, influencing not only the interaction of the single FB members with other members of the community, but also their way of knowing and communicating. However, I shall argue, the narrative practice (Gallagher, 2003; Gallagher & Hutto, 2008; Hutto, 2007, 2008) adopted by imagined communities in social networks has another crucial feature influencing reasoning: *multimodality*. Indeed, in social networks verbal communication is quite reduced and always combined with other modalities. Therefore, in the case of imagined communities in social networks, "the style in which they are imagined" (Anderson, 1983, p. 6) is a *multimodal narrative practice*, which makes use of different modalities, and especially the visual modality, to convey a point in the participatory sense-making of the community.

In social networks, visual communication prevails over verbal and audio communication (Patel, 2016; Jakus, 2018)[2]. Verbal texts are very short (for instance, Twitter members had a maximum number of 140 characters, then extended to 280 characters in 2017), while images do not «waste» characters, and also provide the possibility to simultaneously represent different elements in a single content. The visibility of a message or a post is also increased by "vivid" elements as visual ones (De Vries et al., 2012), dynamic elements (animations), colors and, above all images, thus representing a good way to attract other members' attention, to reinforce the position and the expectations toward the member who send the message and to have more possibilities to actually receive an answer by the other members (Fortin & Dholakia, 2005; Lohtia et al., 2003). Indeed, as previously argued (Mitchell, 1986; Goodman, 1978), images have many effects in communication as they are meant to metaphorically create new worlds and/or produce new perceptions and views of the real world.

These effects are amplified by the presence of "metaphorical" images, which do not represent reality as it is, but let the members imagine the actual message. Metaphor can be a useful communicative device to let people imagine an unknown target domain in light of a known source domain (Ervas, 2019a), which provides

2 As pointed out, in social media 84 % of communication is visual (Jakus, 2018) and community members prefer to deactivate other modalities to exclusively enjoy the visual one: for instance, 85 % of FB videos are seen without audio (Patel, 2016).

a perspective (or a "frame") under which to understand the target (Semino et al., 2016; Burgers et al., 2016). In the interpretation process, some properties of the source are attributed to the target, while other properties are ignored as simply recognised as non-relevant to understand the target and/or its properties. This is the reason why metaphor is never neutral, and it can instead be described as a framing device with an "ignorance-preserving" trait (Arfini et al., 2018). The selection of the relevant properties and the ignorance of other properties can seriously affect reasoning (Thibodeau & Borodisky, 2011, 2013, but see Steen et al., 2014 for criticism). In social network communities, metaphors are very widespread in their visual modality, where the source domain, the target domain or both the domains are visually represented (Forceville, 1994, 1996, 2008). An example of visual metaphor is provided in Figure 1.1, where we need to imagine the pregnant belly of the mother to understand that the tree represents "Mother Nature" and thus to get the point of the social campaign for the environmental day. The text ("Mother Nature too needs care and protection. Show her you care. By caring for her trees. Love trees… Love nature…") accompanying the image makes it a *multimodal pictorial metaphor*.

Figure 1.1. Example of multimodal metaphor (Credits: World Environment Day, Creative agency: Valappila Communication, India)

Previous studies show that visual and multimodal pictorial metaphors are more persuasive than verbal ones (Bulmer & Buchanan-Oliver, 2006), as well as more memorable and pleasant (Sopory & Dillard, 2002). In marketing studies, they proved to increase the perceived credibility of the brand (Jeong, 2008), the appreciation of the ad (Chang & Yen, 2013) and trust of the consumer toward the brand (Phillips & McQuarrie, 2009). However visual metaphors interpretation is heavily constrained by the perceptual, visual features of the metaphor, and the viewer can experience a lack of directionality in metaphor interpretation (Indurkhya & Ojha, 2017). To understand a visual metaphor, the viewer needs to go through a reasoning path which consists in solving three problems (Forceville, 1994, 2008): (a) identifying the conceptual domains in the image (what domains are represented in the images); (b) understanding the directionality of the metaphor (what domain is the metaphor source and what domain is the metaphor target); (c) attributing some properties of the source to the target. Precisely in solving these problems, visual metaphor acts as a reasoning device, which might resort to mental imagery and/or to imagination (see Arcangeli, 2020 for a distinction) to recover not only specific properties to attribute to the target, but also entire objects and/or actions (Ervas, 2019a; Cavazzana & Bolognesi, 2020). The texts in multimodal pictorial metaphors instead provide a "verbal anchoring" which may facilitate the interpretation process.

However, the multimodal and especially visual nature of communication via social networks does not help: for instance, multimodal metaphors are powerful epistemic and persuasive devices (Forceville & Urios-Aparisi, 2009), which do not necessarily involve a belief or an attitude change. Metaphor is responsible for a "framing effect", which filters people's perceptions and concepts, providing a specific perspective which can be changed just with conscious effort, especially in the case of the conventional metaphors widespread in a community. Moreover, visual details in multimodal metaphors might limit (instead of promoting) imagination, anchoring imagination to perceptual features that are irrelevant for the reasoning process. Indeed, multimodal metaphors direct the audience's attention towards certain visual properties, possibly leading to risky inferences, in line with the idea of the visual impedance effect (Knauff & Johnson-Laird, 2002). The context and knowledge of the viewer may affect the interpretation of the images, as well as prototypical effects due to the constraints of our perceptual system (Pylyshyn, 2002) and imagination (Johnson, 1987). These are some of the reasons why the style in which social networks communities are imagined can easily bring them to go astray thus becoming imaginary communities.

5. Imaginary communities: Two case studies on vaccination

Previous studies pointed out that visual communication, metaphors included, cannot count as a form of argumentation, questioning the very existence of visual arguments (Fleming, 1996; Blair, 1996; Johnson, 2003). We could wonder whether visual metaphors can be considered as a sort of condensed and implicit argument guiding the network community along a path of inferences to a conclusion, attributing to the target the relevant properties of the source, as it has already argued in the case of verbal metaphor (Oswald & Rihs, 2014; Wagemans, 2016; Ervas et al., 2018). As for other kinds of visual, some metaphors may simply be *flags*, just having the aim of increasing visibility and interactivity, that is they only catch our attention and directs us to a verbal message (Birdsell & Groarke, 2007). Some other metaphors are instead *argumentative* (Tseronis & Forceville, 2017), in the sense that they give us a reason to conclude that we should think what the other member of the community wants us to think (Birdsell & Groarke, 2007).

An example of *visual flag* can be the multimodal metaphor of the flower the Italian Ministry of Health used in its official FB page to promote vaccination in 2021 (see Figure 1.2)[3].

Figure 1.2. FB Multimodal metaphor on the FB page of the Italian Ministry of Health

3 The figure with the visual metaphor of the flower and the comments posted by FB members are fully accessible at the official FB page of the Italian Ministry of Health (Ministero della Salute) at the following link: www.facebook.com/MinisteroSalute/photos/a.750222061822286/1728774317300384 (last visit: 08/01/2021).

The visual part of the metaphor is meant to direct the attention of the FB members to the verbal message: "Italy revives with a flower: anti-Covid 19 vaccination" (in Italian in Figure 1.2: "L'Italia rinasce con un fiore: vaccinazione anti-covid 19"). The metaphor is not used as an argument or as part of an argument, as no property of the source is used to specifically promote vaccination. A flower could indeed represent whatever revival and even the verbal message could have used other lexical items, as for instance the verb "sprout out" ("germogliare" in Italian) to better connect the visual and the verbal parts of the multimodal metaphor to achieve the communicative intent.

Most comments of the FB members shows either (1) that other irrelevant visual details are inappropriately used in the ongoing conversation, without possibility for the interlocutor to keep the conversation on the same topic, or (2) that the metaphor itself is used against the FB member who posted the message, without possibility to further argue in a constructive way. As an example of the case (1), the comment "The South of Italy, doesn't it exist?" (in Italian in the FB page: "Il sud non esiste???") polemically refers to the fact that the south of Italy is not represented in the image (Figure 1.2), which was intended to represent the whole Italy, as if the South of Italy were considered "less important" by the Ministry of Health. As an example of the case (2), the comment "In 2030, we will be all dead or all vaccinated" (in Italian in the FB page: "Nel 2030 saremo tutti vaccinati o morti") hints to the fact that, different from the life of a flower, the procedure for collective vaccination against Covid-19 is so slow that other 10 years are needed to reach the collective immunity, but in that timeframe we will all dead instead of revived. Some other FB members even used other metaphors, as for instance in the comment: "A drop in the middle of the sea…" (in Italian in the FB page: "Una goccia in mezzo al mare…"), with the same aim, that is to argue against the message of the Ministry of Health that the procedure for collective vaccination was too slow and thus useless.

Other visual metaphors for vaccination can instead be *argumentative*, as they are not just a flag to attract people's attention, but rather they exploit some properties of the visual to make a point (Ervas, 2019b). This is the case of the umbrella metaphor for vaccination (Figure 1.3)[4] posted in the public FB page "Italy United for Science" ("Italia Unita per la Scienza") in 2016 and titled "Vaccination: it works".

4 Post available at the following FB address: www.facebook.com/IUXLS/posts/941433429272813 (last visit: 08/01/2021). For the same visual metaphor, where a member of the community commented "Rubella umbrella", joking with the words rhyme, see the post at: twitter.com/redpenblackpen/status/613067020414918656/photo/1 (last visit: 08/01/2021). (twitter.com/redpenblackpen/status/613067020414918656/photo/1) should be a link as is indicated the link to the facebook post

Figure 1.3. FB Multimodal metaphor on the FB page "Italy United for Science"

The creative metaphor of an umbrella for vaccination is argumentative because the properties of the source can be used to favor analogical reasoning on vaccination, connecting the visual part of the multimodal metaphor to its verbal part: "What are you doing with those umbrellas? I don't even feel any rain! Close them, they're bad for your arms!" (in Italian in the FB post: "Cosa fate con quegli ombrelli? Io pioggia non ne sento! Abbassateli, vi faranno venire male alle braccia!"). Indeed, umbrellas protect from rain (contagious diseases in the target domain), and they protect not only those who have it (vaccinated people), but also those who do not have it (non-vaccinated people), those who cannot have it (people that cannot be vaccinated for some health reasons) and even those who do not want to have it (the anti-vaccination advocates).

Some FB members misinterpreted the metaphor by imagining details irrelevant for the argumentative point of the message, finally seeking ad hoc confirmation for their own point of view instead of cooperation with the interlocutors, and presenting themselves as experts against the "real" expert of the official FB group "Italy United for Science". For instance, a FB member commented on the post, pointing out that there exist different kinds of rains and different kinds of umbrellas, sold to people even though they are "holed, rusty and fake"[5]. The umbrellas depicted in the image are either not holed or rusty, and there is no way to verify whether they are intended to be fake, but the FB member intentionally proposed imagined details completely irrelevant or unrelated to the argumentative metaphor to argue against the message and finally against vaccination as a collective health good for real communities. The science communicator responded to the comment, further clarifying the argumentative frame created by the metaphor, but the interlocutor continued the "solitary reasoning" without considering the expert's advice as a way to recouple with the others in the online dialogue.

6. Conclusion

Social networks have made the borders among real, imagined and imaginary communities "liquid" and easier to overcome. The social network communities can easily become "epistemic bubbles" or even "echo chambers", when collective reasoning becomes committed to the same confirmation bias of individualistic reasoning. This is the offspring of the "solitary reasoning" coming from the continuous missed alignment of coupling and recoupling processing with the other members of the social network community. In the case of epistemic bubbles, the reasons of people who disagree and, in some cases, of "real" experts, are not considered instead of being anticipated, thus preserving the epistemic bubbles and reinforcing imaginary communities. This represents a new challenge

5 The comment was as follows: "If the rain were always the same, an umbrella would be enough. It's a pity that they sell you holed, rusty and fake umbrellas. They make you open the umbrellas when it's sunny instead of when it's raining. And they always make you point the umbrella in the same direction as if all rains were the same. On the contrary, there are light rains, heavy rains, it rains with the wind, sometimes it hails... Should I go around with 50 open umbrellas waiting for rain? For which one? The rain that hasn't arrived for two centuries?" (my translation from Italian into English of the comment posted on January 17, 2016 at the following link: www.facebook.com/IUXLS/posts/941433429272813; last visit: 08/01/2021).

for institutional communication focusing on vital issues for real collective life, as for instance vaccination.

The *multimodal nature of the style* – in which the social network communities are imagined – provides them with a powerful argumentative and persuasive device. Multimodal metaphors, widely used in social network communication, entail a framing effect which influences the community members' reasoning and conversations. However, visual details of the metaphors can limit imagination instead of empowering it and/or be used just to confirm prior ideas and beliefs, impeding a process of recoupling with other members of the imagined community. In the process, the perceptual elements of visual communication can lead to risky or even faulty inferences, bringing the members astray from the path of the cooperative process needed in group argumentation. Two case studies concerning vaccination showed that the interpretation of multimodal pictorial metaphors can focus on irrelevant properties of the source or even details not provided by the image, especially when the social network members remain in the epistemic bubble of their imaginary community, rather than recoupling with the other members of the imagined community in a cooperative dialogue.

Acknowledgement

The author is very grateful to the organisers and the participants to the conference "Strategies of inclusion and exclusion in social media interaction", University of Catania, September 16–17, 2019, where a first version of this paper was presented, for all the helpful comments and suggestions. Conversations with Andrea Grignolio, Rachele Fanari, Elisabetta Gola, Elisabetta Lalumera, and Pietro Salis on the problem of vaccine hesitancy were extremely helpful. The author kindly acknowledges the financial support of the project "Oltre l'orizzonte – Contro-narrazioni dai margini al centro", OLTRE_ISFP-812584, co-funded by the European Union's ISF-P program under Grant Agreement No. 812584.

References

Anderson, B. (1983). *Imagined Communities: Reflections on the Origin and Spread of Nationalism*. London: Verso.

Arcangeli, M. (2020). The Two Faces of Mental Imagery. *Philosophy and Phenomenological Research*, 101, 304–322.

Arfini, S. (2019). *Ignorant Cognition: A Philosophical Investigation of the Cognitive Features of Not-Knowing*. Cham: Springer.

Arfini S., & Bertolotti T. (2018). Citizens, Experts and the Limits of Science Communication. In P. Barrotta & G. Scarafile (Eds.), *Science and Democracy: Controversies and Conflicts* (pp. 71–86). Amsterdam: John Benjamins.

Arfini, S., Bertolotti, T., & Magnani, L. (2017). Online Communities as Virtual Cognitive Niches. *Synthèse*, 196, 377–397.

Arfini, S., Casadio, C., & Magnani, L. (2018). Ignorance-preserving Mental Models Thought Experiments as Abductive Metaphors. *Foundations of Science*, 24(2), 391–409.

Baird, B., Smallwood, J., Mrazek, M. D., Kam, J. W. Y., Franklin, M. S., & Schooler, J. W. (2012). Inspired by Distraction, Mind Wandering Facilitates Creative Incubation. *Psychological Science*, 23, 1117–1122.

Birdsell, D. S., & Groarke, L. (2007). Outlines of a Theory of Visual Argument. *Argumentation and Advocacy*, 43(3–4), 103–113.

Blair, J. A. (1996). The Possibility and Actuality of Visual Argument. *Argumentation and Advocacy*, 33(1), 23–39.

Bruns, A., & Highfield, T. (2012). Blogs, Twitter, and Breaking News: The Produsage of Citizen Journalism. In R. A. Lind (Ed.), *Produsing Theory in a Digital World: The Intersection of Audiences and Production in Contemporary Theory* (pp. 15–32). New York: Peter Lang Publishing Inc.

Bulmer, S., & Buchanan-Oliver, M. (2006). Visual Rhetoric and Global Advertising Imagery. *Journal of Marketing Communications*, 12, 9–61.

Burgers, C., Konijn, E. A., & Steen, G. J. (2016). Figurative Framing: Shaping Public Discourse Through Metaphor, Hyperbole, and Irony. *Communication Theory*, 26, 410–430.

Caers, R., De Feyter, T., De Couck, M., Stough, T., Vigna, C., & Du Bois, C. (2013). Facebook: A Literature Review. *New Media & Society*, 15, 982–1002.

Cavazzana, A., & Bolognesi, E. (2020). Uncanny Resemblance. Words, Pictures, and Conceptual Representations in the Field of Metaphor. *Cognitive Linguistic Studies*, 7(1), 31–57.

Chang, C., & Yen, C. (2013). Missing Ingredients in Metaphor Advertising: The Right Formula of Metaphor Type, Product Type, and Need for Cognition. *Journal of Advertising*, 42, 80–94.

Correia, V. (2011). Biases and Fallacies: The Role of Motivated Irrationality in Fallacious Reasoning. *Cogency*, 3, 107–126.

Cuffari, E. C., Di Paolo, E., & De Jaegher, H. (2015). From Participatory Sense-Making to Language: There and Back Again. *Phenomenology and the Cognitive Sciences*, 14(4), 1089–1125.

De Bruin, L., & de Haan, S. (2012). Enactivism & Social Cognition: In Search of the Whole Story. *Journal of Cognitive Semiotics*, 4(1), 225–250.

De Bruin, L. C., & Kästner, L. (2012). Dynamic Embodied Cognition. *Phenomenology and the Cognitive Sciences*, 11(4), 541–563.

De Vries, L., Gensler, S., & Leeflang, P. S. H. (2012). Popularity of Brand Posts on Brand Fan Pages. *Journal of Interactive Marketing*, 26, 83–91.

Dunbar, R. I. M. (2016). Do Online Social Media Cut through the Constraints that Limit the Size of Offline Social Networks? *Royal Society Open Science*, 3(1).

Ervas, F. (2018). From the "Garrison" to the "Beehive". Metaphors and Framing Strategies in Vaccine Communication. *Politeia*, 130, 28–37.

Ervas, F. (2019a). Metaphor, Ignorance and the Sentiment of (Ir)rationality. *Synthèse*.

Ervas, F. (2019b). Metafore visive, comunità immaginate e razionalità differita. *Sistemi Intelligenti*, 31(3), 413–438.

Ervas, F., Ledda, A., Ojha, A., Pierro, G. A., & Indurkhya, B. (2018). Creative Argumentation: When and Why People Commit the Metaphoric Fallacy. *Frontiers in Psychology*, 9, 1815.

Fleming, D. (1996). Can Pictures be Arguments? *Argumentation and Advocacy*, 33(1), 11–22.

Forceville, C. (1994). Pictorial Metaphor in Advertisements. *Metaphor and Symbol*, 9(1), 1–29.

Forceville, C. (1996). *Pictorial Metaphor in Advertising*. London: Routledge.

Forceville, C. (2008). Metaphor in Pictures and Multimodal Representations. In R. W. Gibbs (Ed.), *The Cambridge Handbook of Metaphor and Thought* (pp. 462–482). Cambridge: Cambridge University Press.

Forceville, C. (2020). *Visual and Multimodal Communication. Applying the Relevance Principle*. Oxford: Oxford University Press.

Forceville, C., & Urios-Aparisi, E. (Eds.). (2009). *Multimodal Metaphor*. Berlin: De Gruyter.

Fortin, D. R., & Dholakia, R. (2005). Interactivity and Vividness Effects on Social Presence and Involvement with a Web-Based Advertisement. *Journal of Business Research*, 58, 387–396.

Gallagher, S. (2003). Self-narrative, Embodied Action, and Social Context. In A. Wiercinski (Ed.), *Between Suspicion and Sympathy: Paul Ricoeur's Unstable Equilibrium* (pp. 409–423). Toronto: The Hermeneutic Press.

Gallagher, S., & Hutto, D. (2008). Understanding Others through Primary Interaction and Narrative Practice. In J. Zlatev, T. Racine, C. Sinha, & E.

Itkonen (Eds.), *The Shared Mind: Perspectives on Intersubjectivity* (pp. 17–38). Amsterdam: John Benjamins.

Gellner, E. (1964). *Thought and Change*. Chicago: University of Chicago Press.

Gergen, K. J. (2002). The Challenge of Absent Presence. In J. E. Katz & M. A. Aakhus (Eds.), *Perpetual Contact: Mobile Communication, Private Talk, Public Performance* (pp. 227–241). Oxford: Oxford University Press.

Goodman, N. (1978). *Ways of Worldmaking*. Indianapolis: Hackett Publishing Company.

Grignolio, A. (2018). *Vaccines: Are They Worth a Shot?* Cham: Springer.

Hutto, D. (2007). The Narrative Practice Hypothesis: Origins and Applications of Folk Psychology. In D. Hutto (Ed.), *Narrative and Understanding Persons* (pp. 43–68). Cambridge: Cambridge University Press.

Hutto, D. (2008). Limited Engagements and Narrative Extensions. *International Journal of Philosophical Studies*, 16(3), 419–44.

Indurkhya, B., & Ojha, A. (2017). Interpreting Visual Metaphors: Asymmetry and Reversibility. *Poetics Today*, 38, 93–121.

Jakus, D. (2018). Visual Communication in Public Relations Campaigns. *MINIB*, 27, 25–36.

Johnson, M. (1987). *The Body in the Mind: The Bodily Basis of Meaning, Imagination, and Reason*. Chicago: University of Chicago Press.

Johnson, R. H. (2003). Why 'Visual Arguments' Aren't Arguments. *Informal Logic*, 25, 1–13.

John-Steiner, V. (2000). *Creative Collaboration*. Oxford: Oxford University Press.

Knauff, M., & Johnson-Laird, P. N. (2002). Visual Imagery can Impede Reasoning. *Memory & Cognition*, 30, 363 371.

Laughlin, P. R., Hatch, E. C., Silver, J. S., & Boh, L. (2006). Groups Perform Better than the Best Individuals on Letters-to-Numbers Problems: Effects of Group Size. *Journal of Personality and Social Psychology*, 90(4), 644–651.

Lohtia, R., Donthu, N., & Hershberger, E. K. (2003). The Impact of Content and Design Elements on Banner Advertising Click-through Rates. *Journal of Advertising Research*, 43, 410–418.

Mercier, H., & Sperber, D. (2011). Why Do Humans Reason? Arguments for an Argumentative Theory. *Behavioral and Brain Sciences*, 34(2), 57–74.

Mercier, H., & Sperber, D. (2017). *The Enigma of Reason. A New Theory of Human Understanding*. Cambridge, MA: Harvard University Press.

Milch, K. F., Weber, E. U., Appelt, K. C., Handgraaf, M. J. J., & Krantz, D. H. (2009). From Individual Preference Construction to Group Decisions: Framing

Effects and Group Processes. *Organizational Behavior and Human Decision Processes*, 108(2), 242–255.

Mitchell, W. J. T. (1986). *Iconology: Image, Text, Ideology*. Chicago: University of Chicago Press.

Moshman, D. & Geil, M. (1998). Collaborative Reasoning: Evidence for Collective Rationality. *Thinking and Reasoning*, 4(3), 231–248.

Nickerson, R. S. (1998). Confirmation Bias: A Ubiquitous Phenomenon in Many Guises. *Review of General Psychology*, 2, 175–220.

Oeldorf-Hirscha, A., & Sundar, S. S. (2015). Posting, Commenting, and Tagging: Effects of Sharing New Stories on Facebook. *Computers in Human Behavior*, 44, 240–249.

Oswald, S., & Rihs, A. (2014). Metaphor as Argument: Rhetorical and Epistemic Advantages of Extended Metaphors. *Argumentation*, 28, 133–159.

Patel, S. (2016). 85 Percent of Facebook Videos Is Watched without Sound. *Digiday UK*, digiday.com/media/silent-world-facebook-video.

Phillips, B., & McQuarrie, E. F. (2009). Impact of Advertising Metaphor on Consumer Belief. *Journal of Advertising*, 38, 35–48.

Pylyshyn, Z.W. (2002). Mental Imagery: In Search of a Theory. *Behavioral and Brain Sciences*, 25, 157–237.

Renan, E. (1947). *Œuvres Completes*. Paris: Calmann-Lévy.

Semino, E., Demjen, Z., & Demmen, J. (2016). An Integrated Approach to Metaphor and Framing in Cognition, Discourse and Practice. *Applied Linguistics* 39(5), 1–22.

Sopory, P., & Dillard, J. (2002). The Persuasive Effects of Metaphor. *Human Communication Research*, 28, 382–419.

Steen, G. J., Reijnierse G., & Burgers, C. (2014). When Do Natural Language Metaphors Influence Reasoning? A Follow-Up Study to Thibodeau and Boroditsky (2013). *PLoS ONE*, 9(12), e113536.

Tappan, M. B. (1997). Language, Culture, and Moral Development: A Vygotskian Perspective. *Developmental Review*, 17, 78–100.

Thi Nguyen, C. (2020). Echo Chambers and Epistemic Bubbles. *Episteme*, 17(2), 141–161.

Thibodeau, P. H., & Boroditsky, L. (2011). Metaphors We Think with: The Role of Metaphor in Reasoning. *PLoS ONE*, 6, e16782.

Thibodeau, P. H., & Boroditsky, L. (2013). Natural Language Metaphors Covertly Influence Reasoning. *PLoS ONE*, 8, e52961.

Tseronis, A., & Forceville, C. (Eds.). (2017). *Multimodal Argumentation and Rhetoric in Media Genres*. Amsterdam: John Benjamins.

Turkle, S. (2011). *Alone Together: Why We Expect More from Technology and Less from Each Other*. New York, NY: Basic Books.

Vanden Abeele, M. M. P., Hendrickson, A. T., Pollmann, M. M. H., & Ling, R. (2019). Phubbing Behavior in Conversations and its Relation to Perceived Conversation Intimacy and Distraction: An Exploratory Observation Study. *Computers in Human Behavior*, 100, 35–47.

Wagemans, J. (2016). Analysing Metaphor in Argumentative Discourse. *Rivista italiana di filosofia del linguaggio*, 2, 79–94.

Woods, J. (2005). Epistemic Bubbles. In S. Artemov, H. Barringer, A. Garcez, L. Lamb & J. Woods (Eds.), *We Will Show Them: Essay in Honour of Dov Gabbay* (Vol. II. pp. 1–39). London: College Publications.

Emanuela Campisi, Marco Venuti
University of Catania, Italy
emanuela.campisi@unict.it, marco.venuti@unict.it

Chapter 2 "L'ipocrisia dell'inclusività": A corpus-based study on the Italian debate around political correctness on Twitter[1]

Abstract: How is the label "politically correct" used by Italian Twitter users? A corpus of Italian tweets containing the hashtags #politicamentecorretto and #politicallycorrect is analysed. The results show that, as for other countries, also in Italy the label is used with a negative connotation, mainly to condemn the use of inclusive language.

Keywords: political correctness, inclusive language, social media, Corpus Assisted Discourse Studies.

1. Introduction

Is it ok to address the members of your audience as "guys", even when women are present? Can you call somebody "faggot" adding that you did not mean it as an offense, your new black acquaintance "sis" as an attempt to bond with her, or your Chinese friend as "Asian"? These issues fall nowadays under the label "Political correctness" (henceforth PC), a term used to indicate the massive attempt, started within American colleges, to remove from public language use all the forms that could be considered offensive, racist, or gender-biased (Fairclough, 2003; Lukianoff & Haidt, 2015). The debate around PC has become particularly fierce, first in the USA and then in Europe as well: on the one hand, a substantial amount of guidelines and prescriptions about how to avoid offensive terms has been produced and imposed by institutions and organisms; on the other hand, and with the same strength, many people have grown more and more irritable towards this attitude, viewed as a limitation of the freedom of speech, to the

1 This study is part of the project "Politically correct? Language, identity and online communities: in between pragmatics and ideology", funded by the Department of Humanities, of University of Catania (see Mazzone, this volume).

point that some politicians have grounded their entire election campaigns on its disregard.

Interestingly, this debate has changed dramatically – both in the US and in Europe – when it moved from the relatively small circles of academics, politicians and activists to social media platforms. It became clear, in fact, that each country was dealing with PC in different ways, depending on its political climate, on the amount and social rank of the people using those platforms, and on the degree of maturation of the public debate around what are considered the "hottest" topics related to PC, such as immigration, feminism, and gender. Unfortunately, very few studies have been conducted in order to investigate how social media users of different countries talk about PC.

In this paper, we focus on how Italians discuss about PC on Twitter. Following Fairclough (2003), claiming that PC is not a label you give yourself but a way to mark somebody else, usually with a negative connotation, we are especially interested in investigating if, in Italy too, the label is used mainly with the purpose of offending somebody because of her/his attempt to use or promote an inclusive language. For this purpose, we draw on a corpus of Italian Tweets containing the hashtags *#politicamentecorretto* and *#politicallycorrect*. Due to our focus on the attitude towards PC, the main aim of the analysis will be to highlight dynamics of offense and exclusion, as they are displayed in the Tweets containing these hashtags.

2. Discourses about political correctness

2.1. The controversy about political correctness

The negotiation of both individual and group identity is nowadays a crucial topic in sociolinguistics, especially in research about language variation. The reason for this interest is that it has become more and more clear that an "essentialist" definition of identity (i.e., the explanation of an individual behaviour by means of a pre-stablished, fixed and uniform social or ethnic group) is misleading and needs to be replaced with a more dynamic and multiform one. In this perspective, identity is nowadays better defined as "the active negotiation of an individual's relationship with larger social constructs, in so far as this negotiation is signalled through language and other semiotic means" (Mendoza-Denton, 475). In other words, one cannot investigate identity negotiation without looking at the discourses in which this negotiation takes place.

With the goal of spreading and consolidating this dynamic and multiform definition of identity, in the last thirty years, public figures and institutions have carried out a massive attempt to remove all the forms of language use that could be considered offensive, racist (especially when minorities are involved), or gender-biased (Fairclough, 2003; Lukianoff & Haidt, 2015, among others). The underlying assumption in this campaign is that "changes of discourses are not mainly re-labelling but shifts to different spheres of values" (Fairclough 2003, 22–23). For example, even if in many languages it is grammatically correct to use masculine forms to refer both to men and women, many studies show that the grammatical gender of the words we use influence the comprehension of the narrative, encouraging an imagery in which men are powerful and active, and women weak and invisible (Hamilton, 1985; Konishi, 1993, among many). Therefore, in order to avoid such an ideological positioning and its consequences on minorities, people have been encouraged to use a neutral or, even better, inclusive forms.

> Cultural interventions directed at changing representations, values and identities, and doing so in part through changing language (discourse), are actually pervasive in contemporary social life (Fairclough, 2003, p. 20).

The attempt to promote inclusive language has started in the USA, and particularly in American colleges, which have issued a substantial number of guidelines and prescriptions about how to avoid such terms, replacing them with more or less equivalent but "neutral" ones (i.e., "person with a disability" instead of "handicapped", "human beings" instead of "mankind"). Many students and scholar circles have embraced these prescriptions and have actively fought for their circulation, hoping that paying more attention in what they say would help people paying more attention in how they behave. However, at the same time and with the same strength, some people have become increasingly irritable toward this attitude, both inside and outside the campuses.

We can (over)simplify the debate about PC in the following terms: according to the supporters, discourses reflect sphere of values and therefore some expressions (i.e., the ones presented in the introduction) are intrinsically offensive or threatening. It is simply not possible for the speaker to use them without a bad intention, nor for the addressee to receive them without feeling offended. Therefore, it is necessary to stop using them altogether and replacing them with more neutral ones. On the other hand, according to the detractors, first of all words are "just" words, that is they don't have any power *per se*, and sometimes terms that seem offensive or not inclusive enough are just the results of "harmless" habits or traditions. For example, to call a woman *ministro* or *presidente* is not necessarily an attempt to offend her or to hide her feminine identity, but merely a result of the fact that in Italian these terms have only been attested in the masculine form. Furthermore, the concern about an excessive application of PC norms has gone so far that many scholars believe that the attempt to condemn someone for his/her language choices is dangerous especially for young generations, which can become chronically stressed by the exposure to possibly aggressive verbal behaviour and, ultimately, incapable of standing up against opposite values and ideas (Haidt & Lukianoff, 2017).

The debate about PC has many relevant implications not only on language studies, but also on politics, social sciences and pedagogy: while nobody would disagree that a in truly democratic society it is necessary to use respectful and inclusive language forms, in fact, it should not be denied that PC norms, when taken to their extreme and imposed from institutions – without a broader civic education encouraging inclusion outside discourses as well – can might turn out not only useless, but also dangerous. It is maybe in this sense that Fairclough (2003, p. 18) claims that "the PC controversy is, partly, but only partly, controversy over language".

Obviously, a constructive dialogue about these topics presupposes an open-minded attitude and the will to treat the interlocutor as a worthy discussant. Unfortunately, both the sympathy and the hostility toward PC are often expressed with a hostile attitude, led by ideological positioning, leaving no space for a real discussion about the topic. For example, Trump and other politicians both in USA and in Europe (including Italy) have grounded their entire election campaign on its disregard, leaving no space for moderate interpretations of their beliefs ("The big problem this country has is being politically correct. I don't have time for political correctness"; Trump, 2015).

To complicate things further, the debate about PC has changed dramatically both in the US and in Europe when it moved from the relatively small circles of academics, politics, and activists to social media platforms. Thanks to social media, it became crystal-clear that each country has dealt with PC in different ways, depending on the political atmosphere of the moment, on the section of people using social media (i.e. Twitter vs. Facebook), and on the degree of maturation of the public debate around the "hottest" topics related to PC like immigration, feminism, and gender. However, despite these differences have been discussed on the basis of anecdotal evidence, little systematic comparisons have been conducted in order to investigate how social media users of different countries talk about PC.

As a matter of fact, the literature about PC has mainly focused on its cultural-theoretical aspects, as the actual efficacy of the norms and guidelines for inclusive societies and the ethical implications of its acceptance/rejection (Lakoff, 2000). Less is known, however, from a *discourse-analytic perspective* (Suhr & Johnson, 2003, p. 6). And yet, at least two lines of research would be very useful (and relatively easy to undertake): (a) how the debate about PC has affected actual language use (neologisms, restructuring of noun-phrases, use of pronouns) and (b) how the label "political correctness" itself is used. In this paper, we will focus on the latter. Before moving to the description of the dataset and the analysis which have been carried out, we will review some of the available studies on PC with a special focus on Europe and Italy.

2.2. Discourse about political correctness in Europe

Because of its origins and its massive presence in the North-American debates, it is not surprising that the majority of the studies on PC discourses are in English while less is known about other languages and other countries. According to the Financial Times, when it comes to PC there is a "transatlantic gap" between US and Europe, in that even if in Europe too there have been effects on language policies, "European culture wars won't reach American proportions" (Cuper, 2020).

However, the debate about PC *has* moved to Europe, with interesting implications for the pre-existing debates about gender, race and disabilities. Interestingly, PC has been defined as an example of "global/local dialectic", in which a global theme has been discussed in different languages and cultures "disparately inflected by local historical and cultural formations" (Suhr & Johnson, 2003). As a first consequence, there is not such a thing as "the European debate", in that the discussion does not concern the same topics everywhere. For example, in Sweden, one of the most sensitive European countries, the debate about PC concerns mainly immigration: of course, this does not mean that in the last decades there have not been substantial changes in the way in which people talk about other groups (i.e. women or LGBTQ+ members) but simply that these changes have long been accepted by the community and, therefore, are less an issue there compared to other countries, such as Italy, among others. In Italy, instead, equality between men and women is an issue still in need to be addressed at many levels of society (see Formato, this volume): it is not a surprise, therefore, that there are frequent discussions about PC concerning the expression of gender in the language.

Being this the case, one could expect that discourses about PC have different features depending on the country and the language, and that these features could help in better understanding how linguistic choices and discursive practices have changed over time. For example, Johnson and Suhr (2003) have shown that, differently from the US, in German newspapers the label PC was not commonly used until 2000 and that, when used, it had a negative meaning, always implying an "inhibitive force" and "discourse taboos".

2.3. PC in Italy

In Italy, the debate about PC has started more or less after 2010, and it is still ongoing in television, newspapers and social media. As in the US and the other European countries, in Italy too, the main antagonists of PC seem to be far-right politicians and their supporters, who have found in social media a powerful tool to spread their disregard towards the attempts to make Italian a more inclusive language. For example, according to the current leader of the party "Lega – Salvini Premier", Matteo Salvini (see Di Silvestro, this volume), PC can be defined as "*idiozia*" (idiocy) and "*ipocrisia*" (hypocrisy). In the past years, he has used the label "*politicamente corretto*" to attack and mock almost any episode which can be (sometimes vaguely indeed) ascribed to the topic of inclusive language use. Not only do his attacks concern political and social topics such as women and LGBTQ+ rights and immigration, but also everyday column news, such as the singer Mahmood (Italian with Egyptian origins) winning the 2019 edition of *Festival di Sanremo* (the most famous musical Italian TV show) and, more recently, the decision to remove from a chain of Swiss supermarkets a well-known chocolate praline because it is called *Mohrenkopf* (black head).

Figure 2.1. Tweet 11 June 2020. Among censor's cuts to #GonewiththeWind, revocation of the pralines #moretti and demolition of the statues of the racist #CristoforoColombo, I would not be surprised if this will be the next step. Everybody is mad. Take your hands off the excellent and very Italian Amaro #Montenegro

A quick search on the Internet seems to show that, similarly to what happened in the US, in Italy too many have accused PC of being a limitation of freedom of speech. For example, according to the newspaper *Il foglio*, "Nelle sue forme più estreme, il politicamente corretto ha contribuito a uccidere la libertà d'espressione, nella misura in cui ha fatto combaciare il rispetto della diversità con la necessità di rinunciare alla propria identità (Cerasa, 2019)"[2].

However, even if there are some studies investigating PC discourse in some European countries, very few studies have Italian as their target language and, to the best of our knowledge, none concern social media discourses. Indeed, in Italy too, most of the available literature on the topic discusses the history of the phenomenon, mainly referring to the Anglo-Saxon context or generally discussing its ethical implications (i.e. Arcangeli, 2001; Capozzi, 2018).

Among the few studies focusing on the discourse-analytic perspective, Bonnet and Caillault (2014) compare interviews with Dutch, French and Italian police officers questioned about minorities and crime. Their analysis suggests that while Dutch and Italians police officers speak freely about minorities and their attitude toward crime, French officers object strongly to the possibility that race is a factor in crime, showing that they are deeply concerned about avoiding the use of racist talk. Interestingly, according to the authors "Italian respondents are virtually indifferent to a potential accusation of racism, and speak freely about criminal activity of minority" (Bonnet & Caillault, 2014, p.1193): for example, an Italian officer in Milan states openly that while Chinese immigrants are not a problem, Moroccans give a lot of trouble because "it is in their nature". The authors conclude that different countries have different conceptions of what is racist and what is not: therefore, speech norms may be perceived differently. Therefore, Tosi (2001, p. IX) could be right in claiming that "Italy is a country where a great passion for eccentric neologisms and radical manifestations of political correctness cohabits with a widespread tolerance for linguistic sexism and racist connotations in the language of the media."

2.4. Why Twitter

Obviously, the fact that some public figures and institutions use the label with a detractive meaning does not necessarily imply that people would do the same. It seems plausible, however, that they will tend to repeat what their political

2 "in its most extreme forms, political correctness contributed to kill the freedom of speech, in that it has flatten the respect for diversity with the necessity to give up your own identity".

leader or favourite celebrity is saying. As a matter of fact, Twitter encourages this inclination: the possibility to retweet a message written by somebody else increases the chances of spreading the message in question offering at the same time the opportunity to comment on that message, which, at the end, will be strengthened.

There are other features that make this particular platform suitable for studies in corpus linguistics (Sergeant & Tagg, 2014). First of all, it is a valuable source of people's opinion, since users give their opinion about a big variety of topics daily, and it allows the collection of big corpora (Pak & Paroubek, 2010). Second of all, even if in written form, language is informal (and short). Finally, it creates virtual communities: the use of hashtags (#), in fact, allows not only to organise the tweets according to their topic, but also to create hashtags communities, encouraging discussions about common topics of interests (Xiao et al., 2014).

Of course, as for any other corpus, data collected via Twitter may return a partial view of the investigated phenomenon, so one has to keep in mind the limitations of this medium as well. For example, there are substantial differences in the amount and social rank of users in different countries. Moreover, it has been suggested that social media users appear more polarised than in reality (Mounk, 2018). Finally, extended interactions are difficult to recover, so it may not be the ideal place to look at if you are interested in long exchanges. Despite these limitations, Twitter is the perfect pool to draw from for the purpose of this paper, thanks to the use of hashtags.

3. The present study

3.1. Method

According to Fairclough (2003), PC is not a label you give yourself but a way to negatively mark someone else. Similarly, Talbot (2007, p. 755) claims that the main features of PC discourses are characterised by *negativity*, *restriction* and *exaggeration*: "excessiveness or 'going too far' seems to be built into it, as a part of its semantic content". Interestingly, according to the author, these features go beyond traditional concerns about racism and sexism, in that they are applied to every field of social life: among others, she provides examples of loud music in pubs ("If you think that the music's too loud, you're too politically correct!") and cooking shows ("And not only it is delicious, it's also politically correct").

In order to test whether these trends hold in social media interaction and in languages different than English, Suhr and Johnson (2003) suggests that one way to start is to investigate the use of the label PC itself, by investigating the context of use and its collocations. In this way, it is possible to have a first overview of how Italians talk about PC on Twitter. In Italian you can interchangeably use the original English expression *politically correct* and the Italian version *politicamente corretto*; therefore, for the present study we used the Google extension Data Miner to collect a corpus of Tweets including the following hashtags:

#politicallycorrect
#politicamentecorretto

The resulting corpus includes 4416 tweets (from January 2011 to July 2019) and 71690 words. As it is common on Twitter, quite often the Tweets include other related hashtags and/or references to public figures by means of the sign @, and they are accompanied by images, Gif or videos, as in the following example:

Figure 2.2. Tweet 16 April 2015. No to #politically correct; no to #gender ideology. Be #ProFamily & #ProLife

Let your mind fly… Free yourself from political correctness

To provide a detailed description of the corpus, two types of analysis will be presented: a quantitative analysis, mainly focusing on the most common *keywords*, and a qualitative analysis of some of most representative of the collected Tweets, in order to highlight the most common definitions of PC and the topics in which the discussion is carried out. The quantitative analysis has been carried through the software "Sketch Engine", a corpus tool particularly useful because it allows to generate a "word sketch", that is a one-page description of the grammar and the collocations of the word in question (Kilgarriff et al., 2014). Furthermore, Sketch Engine has access to large corpora in different languages, allowing to compare your own corpus with a *reference corpus*, a particularly useful procedure for the extraction of keywords, which are words occurring with unusual frequency in a given corpus. A common tool of analysis in corpus linguistics, according to Scott (1997), keywords reveal the "aboutness", that is the content, of a text. For this study, the keywords have been extracted applying ARF (Average Reduce Frequency) to balance effect size (Hlaváčová, 2006).

3.2. A quantitative analysis: The first 100 keywords

The present analysis focusses on the first 100 keywords, with a special focus on nouns (28), adjectives (19), verbs (12), swearwords (5) and slurs (1). The results of the keywords analysis are summarised in the Tables 2.1–2.4 below.

Table 2.1. Nouns (first 100 words)

Word	ARF	ARF/mill	ARF_ref	ARF_ref/mill	Score
ipocrisia	34	325.6	489	2.1	106.6
buonismo	11	106.5	108	0.5	73.9
dittatura	30	286.8	760	3.2	68.4
idiozia	8	80.1	117	0.5	54.3
censura	23	219.3	974	4.1	43.2
tweet	12	119.8	535	2.3	37.1
conformismo	7	68.3	210	0.9	36.7
razzismo	15	142.3	717	3	35.6
ideologia	15	150.2	1067	4.5	27.5
ridicolo	10	103.9	696	2.9	26.7
stupidità	6	57.8	290	1.2	26.5
insulto	5	53.6	264	1.1	25.8
insulti	7	66.3	533	2.2	20.7
satira	6	61.8	493	2.1	20.4
minoranze	8	82.2	739	3.1	20.2

Table 2.1. Continued

Word	ARF	ARF/mill	ARF_ref	ARF_ref/mill	Score
odio	19	184.1	2183	9.2	18.1
lobby	6	57.4	579	2.4	17
propaganda	11	107.9	1340	5.6	16.4
schifo	7	67	757	3.2	16.2
follia	11	112.1	1444	6.1	16
intolleranza	5	54.9	600	2.5	15.8
genitore	10	101.7	1559	6.6	13.6
twitter	13	132.4	2222	9.4	12.9
schiavi	6	57.8	957	4	11.7
islam	5	48	781	3.3	11.4
manipolazione	5	48.9	965	4.1	9.8
migranti	7	66.6	1403	5.9	9.8
immigrati	8	80.6	1839	7.8	9.3
battuta	9	85.2	2030	8.6	9

Table 2.2. Adjectives (first 100 words)

Word	ARF	ARF/mill	ARF_ref	ARF_ref/mill	Score
correct	17	165.9	101	0.4	116.8
razzista	25	243.4	315	1.3	105
ipocrita	14	137	321	1.4	58.6
ipocriti	8	77.2	138	0.6	49.4
stucchevole	7	66.9	120	0.5	45
gay	20	191.3	1088	4.6	34.4
razzisti	6	57.6	177	0.7	33.6
trans	5	51.6	323	1.4	22.2
idiota	5	48	313	1.3	21.1
scorretto	5	55.7	416	1.8	20.6
offensivo	5	50.6	435	1.8	18.2
omosessuali	7	66.5	677	2.9	17.5
ideologico	5	48.2	579	2.4	14.3
islamico	5	52	687	2.9	13.6
corretto	32	303.6	5400	22.8	12.8
vietato	8	79	1582	6.7	10.4
fascista	5	56.3	1197	5	9.5
Brutta	6	61.7	1413	6	9

Table 2.3. Verbs (first 100 words)

Word	ARF	ARF/mill	ARF_ref	ARF_ref/mill	Score
offendere	12	113.9	341	1.4	47.2
moriremo	5	49.9	48	0.2	42.2
Rotto	19	182	1170	4.9	30.9
Frega	7	70	534	2.3	21.8
sbaglia	5	52.8	646	2.7	14.4
Uccide	5	54.5	842	3.5	12.2
difende	5	52.9	848	3.6	11.8
Dica	6	62.3	1130	4.8	11
imporre	7	70.9	1393	5.9	10.5
Ridere	9	89.4	1871	7.9	10.2
guardate	5	50.3	1016	4.3	9.7
giustificare	5	55.5	1262	5.3	8.9

Table 2.4. Swearwords and slurs

Word	ARF	ARF/mill	ARF_ref	ARF_ref/mill	Score
Froci	7	66	24	0.1	60.7
Cazzo	28	266.9	930	3.9	54.5
coglioni	10	100.8	235	1	51.1
merda	12	120.8	594	2.5	34.8
Palle	16	157.5	881	3.7	33.6
Culo	13	123.3	746	3.1	30

As this overview suggests, in Italy too (at least on Twitter) PC is not a label you give yourself: in fact, in the majority of the Tweets the notion of PC is indeed associated to negative concepts. There is a strong connection with the concept of *hypocrisy*, which seems to suggest that, according to the authors of these Tweets, PC is just a pretence without any true good intention. Many users consider it a form of *dictatorship* by which "strong powers", by means of *censorship*, impose a single line of reasoning. Furthermore, it is often called "the *ideology* of political correctness". All in all, it seems that in Italian, the hashtags *#politicamentecorretto* and *#politicallycorrect* are mainly used to condemn the use of inclusive language, rather than to encourage it. In order to better understand how this is done, in the following section we will provide some qualitative description of some examples, focusing on how PC is defined (Section 3.3) and what are the main topics of the debate (Section 3.4).

3.3. How PC Is defined

A leitmotiv in the analysed Tweets is the idea that PC is a form of censorship, as shown by the following example:

1. *#Youtube*, *#Facebook #Twitter* da agognati regni di libertà si stanno rivelando luoghi di *#censura*, distorsione e manipolazione dell'accesso ai contenuti con igran *#politicallycorrect* quali dati sensibili, contenuti offensivi o violenti, *#fakenews* o presunte violazioni *#copyright*[3].

Not only does this Tweet accuse PC of being a filter imposed on freedom of speech, which social media platforms should promote, but it complains also about the removal of fake news, almost suggesting that this is a form of censorship as well. Similarly, other users accuse PC of damaging satire and humour, sometimes complaining that the filters used by social media are controlled by algorithms and not human beings.

The topic of censorship is strictly related to the reference to ideology. Here is an example of a Tweet trying to provide a definition of PC in these terms:

2. Il *#politicamentecorretto* è un'ideologia che ha un fondamento "culturale", una morale e una prassi. Ecco come agisce: la cultura occidentale è razzista e discriminatrice > la depenniamo dagli studi > chi si oppone è razzista e discriminatore[4].

In this Tweet, PC is described as an ideology with the sole purpose of destroying Western Culture. Interestingly, the user continues its claim in the reply section, adding that "it doesn't matter if the cultural premise is absurd and not proven. The praxis must carry out the ethics, which is based on a (fallacious) theory". Another user calls PC "the greatest threat to the Enlightenment thought since the time of Galileo", accusing this ideology to arm science as well.

Another common way to refer to PC is to consider it just a change of words that legitimate the offense:

---

3 "*#Youtube*, *#Facebook #Twitter* once kingdoms of freedom are becoming places of #censorship, distortion and manipulation of the access to the contents with #politicallycorrect filters as sensitive data, offensive or violent contents, #fakenews or alleged violations #copyright".

4 "*#politicalcorrectness* is an ideology with its 'cultural' basis, its ethics and a praxis. This is how it works: Western culture is racist and discriminatory > we cross it from education > opponents are racist and discriminatory".

3. *#PoliticallyCorrect* ovvero, se proprio vuoi offendere, usa delle eleganti perifrasi (che poi però il senso quello è)[5].

Implicit in this kind of claims is the idea that one of the main problems of PC is that it attacks just the surface, that is language use, without affecting the underlying assumptions, and therefore it is ineffective. As we will argue in the conclusion, this is actually a crucial point, that should be taken more seriously.

3.4. The topics of the debate

Other interesting directions of research emerge from a first look at the topics of the Tweets. As anticipated in the literature review, PC is invoked in many contexts, from women rights to religion and to migrants: looking at this corpus, therefore, it is possible to have a sense of what Italian users of Twitter think is the scope of PC. In the following Tweet, the idea of "a single line of reasoning" is extended to a lot of traditional topics in order to highlight, according to the author, the intrinsic incoherence of PC:

4. Il *#politicallycorrect* ci impone pensiero unico *#8marzo #lgbt #migranti #islam* dimenticando che islam donne e froci non vanno d'accordo[6].

The accusation, however, does not stop here. For example, PC is implicated in many discussions about climate, where PC supporters are accused of exploiting any cause for their own gain, as shown by the following Tweet:

5. L'apoteosi del più stucchevole *#politicallycorrect* racchiuso in una bambina, strumentalizzata da tanti adulti che hanno iniziato a strillare di clima solo dopo l'elezione di Trump *#GretaThunberg*[7].

References to Trump are not infrequent in this corpus. Needless to say, in most cases he is praised for the way in which he dealt with PC, as if ignoring PC norms is a necessary condition for actually doing politics (as opposed to the ones who just talk about it), indirectly suggesting the twisted nature and incoherence of any politically correct attitude:

---

5 *#PoliticallyCorrect* that is, if you really want to offend, use some elegant periphrasis (but the meaning does not change".

6 "*#politicalcorrect* imposes a single line of reasoning *#8march #lgbt #migrants #islam* forgetting that islam women and faggots do not get on well".

7 "The apotheosis of the most nauseating *#politicallycorrect* concentrated in a girl who has been exploited by many adults shouting about climate only after Trump's election *#GretaThunberg*".

6. Finalmente un politico che se ne frega del *#politically correct* e fa quello per cui è stato eletto. Viva *#DonaldTrump. #MakeAmericaGreatAgain*[8].

4. Discussion and conclusion

The results of this study suggest that, as for other countries, Italian speakers do not generally use the label *politicamente corretto* to refer to themselves or to positive politically correct practices. Rather, the term is mainly used to refer to a practice you want to condemn as an ideological and hypocrite imposition and, ultimately, as a challenge to the freedom of speech. Therefore, it seems that, in Italy too, Talbot's features of negativity, restriction and exaggeration are at the core of the debate around PC.

As it shown by the analysis, the hashtag community *#politicamentecorretto* seems to include mainly users which are against PC norms and, more broadly, against all the groups which, according to them, have interests in the establishment of a single perspective: in fact, common topics of conversations include not only traditional issues such as racism and sexism, but also other subjects as the climate crisis, ideology and impoliteness in general.

Obviously, this does not mean that in Italy discourses about inclusion and identity assertions are always condemned, but merely that, when encouraged, they are not defined as political correctness. Further analysis of the corpus (i.e. collocations and concordances) is needed to confirm this trend, as well as analysis of the replies and, in general, of the interactions aroused by these Tweets. Finally, direct comparisons with other languages and with other kinds of Italian corpora will be necessary to better understand how speakers use the labels related to PC in context.

References

Arcangeli, M. (2004, November 30). *La lingua imbrigliata: a margine del politicamente corretto, Italianisticaonline.it*. Retrieved September 5, 2023 from http://www.italianisticaonline.it/2004/politicamente-corretto-01

Bonnet, F., & Caillault, C. (2015). The Invader, the Enemy Within and They-Who-Must-Not-Be-Named: How Police Talk about Minorities in Italy, the Netherlands and France. *Ethnic and Racial Studies*, 38(7), 1185–1201.

8 "Finally a politician who does not give a damn about *#politicallycorrect* and who does what he has been elected for. Long live *#DonaldTrump. #MakeAmericaGreatAgain*".

Capozzi E. (2018). *Politicamente corretto. Storia di un'ideologia*. Venezia: Marsilio Editore.

Cerasa C. (2019, June 21). Gli impostori del politicamente scorretto. *Il foglio*. Retrieved September 5, 2023 from https://www.ilfoglio.it/politica/2019/06/21/news/gli-impostori-del-politicamente-scorretto-261507/.

Cuper S. (2020, February 6). Political Correctness: The UK v the US. *Financial Times*. https://www.ft.com/content/31ed22f8-47a6-11ea-aee2-9ddbdc86190d.

Fairclough, N. (2003). 'Political correctness': The Politics of Culture and Language. *Discourse and Society*, 14(1), 17–28.

Haidt, J., & Lukianoff, G. (2017). Why It's a Bad Idea to Tell Students Words Are Violence. *The Atlantic*.

Hlaváčová, L. (2006). New Approach to Frequency Dictionaries LREC. In N. Calzolari et al. (Eds.), *Proceedings of the Fifth International Conference on Language Resources and Evaluation*. Available online at https://aclanthology.org/volumes/L06-1/

Johnson, S., & Suhr, S. (2003). From 'Political Correctness to 'Politische Korrektheit': Discourses of 'PC' in the German Newspaper, Die Welt. *Discourse Society*, 14(1), 49–68.

Johnson, S., Culpeper, J., & Suhr, S. (2003). From 'politically correct councillors' to 'Blairite nonsense': Discourses of 'political correctness' in Three British Newspapers. *Discourse Society*, 14(1). 29–47.

Kilgarriff, A. et al. (2014). The Sketch Engine: Ten Years On. *Lexicography*, 1, 7–36.

Lukianoff, G., & Haidt, J. (2015). The Coddling of the American Mind. *The Atlantic*, September edition.

Mazzone, M. (2018). La performatività e I suoi vincoli: lo 'stadio ideologico' nell'animale umano. *Reti, Saperi, Linguaggi: Italian Journal of Cognitive Sciences*, 1, 191–202.

Mendoza-Denton, N. (2002). Language and Identity. In J. K. Chambers, P. Trudgill, & N. Shilling-Estes (Eds.), *The Handbook of Language Variation and Change*. Padstow (UK): Blackwell Publishing.

Suhr, S., & Johnson, S. (2003). Re-visiting 'PC': Introduction to Special Issue on 'political correctness'. *Discourse Society*, 14(1), 5–16.

Talbot, M. (2007). Political Correctness and Freedom of Speech. In M. Hellinger & A. Pauwels (Eds.), *Handbook of Language and Communication: Diversity and Change* (pp. 751–763). Berlin: De Gruyter Mouton.

Tosi, A. (2001). *Language and Society in a Changing Italy*. Cleveland – Buffalo – Toronto – Sydney: Multilingual Matters LTD.

Xiao, F., Noro, T., & Tokuda, T. (2014). Finding News-Topic Oriented Influential Twitter Users Based on Topic Related Hashtag Community Detection. *Journal of Web Engineering*, 13(5,6), 405–429.

Zaga, C. (2012). Twitter: un'analisi dell'italiano nel microblogging. *Italiano LinguaDue*, 1, 165–210.

Ester di Silvestro
University of Catania, Italy
ester.disilvestro@unict.it

Chapter 3 #primagliitaliani: A critical discourse analysis of the Italian far-right populist discourse on Twitter

Abstract: This chapter is a case study about Salvini's populist discourse on Twitter. The main aim is to highlight the strategies of inclusion and exclusion used by Salvini during two immigration crises that happened in 2018. Although the analysis focuses on Twitter, two traditional speeches were analysed to investigate the evolution of populist discourse.

Keywords: Far-right populism, social media, Matteo Salvini, immigration, Corpus Assisted Discourse Studies.

1. Introduction

This paper is a case study about Matteo Salvini's far-right populist discourse on Twitter. Specifically, the case study focuses on two immigration crises that happened in June and August 2018 since Salvini did not allow the disembarkation of immigrants on board the two NGOs Aquarius (10 June 2018) and Diciotti (22 August 2018). At the time Matteo Salvini was both Minister of the Interior and Vice Prime Minster for the new coalition government between the League and the Five Star Movement (the General Election took place on March 2018, but the new government was established the 1st June 2018). The case study aims to highlight the strategies of inclusion and exclusion used by Matteo Salvini on Twitter during the two immigration crises. Although the analysis focuses on Twitter, two traditional speeches were analysed as well in order to investigate the evolution of populist discourse.

Populism is a widespread political phenomenon, and it is particularly pervasive in Europe (Aalberg et al., 2017, p. 3) for several reasons such as the lack of ideals (Laclau, 2005, p. 88) and the current socio-economic uncertainty. Since the late 1990s in Italy there has been a significant number of populist parties with different political orientations (Bobba & Legnante, 2016); indeed, as Tarchi (2008) suggests Italy has become "*a country of many populisms*". One of the most prominent Italian populist parties is undoubtedly The League. The

Northern League was founded by Umberto Bossi in the late 1980s as a party with federalist (and even independentist) ideology (Cento Bull & Gilbert, 2001). In 2013 Salvini became the new leader; as a result, the party started to change. The ideology of the party has shifted from regionalism to nativism (Albertazzi et al., 2018). Consequently, nowadays Salvini's discourse is extremely characterised by strategies of inclusion and exclusion. From this perspective, it is interesting to investigate how these strategies proliferate on social media since Matteo Salvini uses these platforms daily to spread his populist narratives.

Nowadays social media have changed the way people interact, and how they construct individual and collective identity. Indeed, these platforms are able to change *traditional* forms of interaction but at the same time they offer new interactive dynamics (Seargeant & Tagg, 2014, p. 2). Specifically, Twitter appears to be an interesting social medium for two main reasons. Firstly, for its own structure that involves constrains and peculiarities. Secondly, Twitter seems to have a perfect synergy with populist discourse due precisely to its structure that requires simplicity (Ott, 2017).

Twitter is both a social network and a microblogging (Golbeck, 2015), and its main peculiarity is that users are able to post tweets that cannot go beyond 280 characters. This constraint does not represent a real limitation for populist discourse and its spread, since populist politicians use very often straightforward language (Kreis, 2017, p. 615). Another interesting characteristic of Twitter is that an overall analysis of tweets, posted by the same user or with the same hashtag, can reveal a new communicative structure because tweets are very similar to a coherent text (Murthy, 2013, p. 8). Twitter is employed for several purposes such as the participatory (or citizen) journalism. It is used by professional and non-professional journalists since the limitation of characters is suitable for a breaking news format (Murthy, 2013, pp. 51–52). This social network is also used by celebrities but most importantly by politicians. Indeed, Twitter and other social media are part of our everyday life (Zappavigna, 2012, p. 37); as a result, they influence the way political organisations and institutions work because political matters are represented and discussed in these platforms (Bouvier & Machin, 2018, p. 179). The United Sates have been the testing ground of the strategical employment of social media that later on has spread all over the world. Barack Obama has been the first politician to use strategically social media during the presidential electoral campaign in 2008 (Enli, 2017, p. 50). However, it is the election of President Trump that proved how crucial the strategical employment of social media is (Karpf, 2017, pp. 1–2), and how effective populist discourse is on Twitter (Galdieri et al., 2018). After the announcement of his presidential candidacy in 2015, Trump used Twitter as a primary mean of communication, and took advantage of its structure to disseminate his populist ideology (Kreis, 2017, p. 608) with a provocative and aggressive style of communication (Wodak & Krzyżanowski, 2017, p. 4). In addition to the easily dissemination of populist ideology, another reason why there is a synergy between Twitter and populist discourse is because, from a communicative perspective, Twitter can be used successfully and permanently by populist politicians as an opposition tool against the élites (Van Kessel & Castelein, 2016, p. 595). As a result, politicians with radical positions are more active than the others, and they tend to have more followers as well (Van Kessel & Castelein, 2016, p. 596). For instance, Matteo Salvini is the most active Italian politician since he has posted 41.834 tweets and he is the one with the highest number of followers (1 million) among Italian far-right politicians (the data are updated to April 2020).

The following section provides a preliminary outline of Matteo Salvini's strategical approach to Twitter and introduces his social media strategist Luca Morisi. Section 3 describes the collection of data, the corpus building, and the research questions. The results of the analysis are showed and discussed in Section 4. Section 5 discuss Salvini's approach regarding the inclusion of immigrants. The last section is dedicated to conclusions and further research.

2. @matteosalvinimi

Matteo Salvini, as almost every politician, tweets on a daily basis. His tweets are most of the times self-centred, and simultaneously coherent with his traditional speeches and his TV or radio appearances. Twitter is used to spread his populist ideology and narratives, but at the same time it is employed to create an empathetic relational bond with his electorate/followers. Consequently, in his account there are several types of tweets that aim to strategically approach some social groups, and to virtually eliminate the distance between him and his followers since he wants to present himself as a *man of the people* (Mudde & Kaltwasser, 2017). Firstly, he tries to highlight strategically his family role as father by talking about his children and posting pictures of them. Secondly, he posts tweets about religion and the Virgin Mary; for instance, the Medjugorje Virgin Mary (Bibus, 2019) in order to sympathises with Catholics and particularly with a conservative Roman Catholic wing (Renzi, 2015). Thirdly, he tweets about the Italian food that he is eating (as the majority of people on social media) to empathise even more with *common people* and to support his Eurosceptic narratives regarding Made in Italy products. In addition, another important aspect to highlight is the use of emojis that contributes to make his style of communication on Twitter very informal and even provocative in some occasions.

An overall review of Salvini's tweets reveals the repetition of specific narratives that are coherent and simultaneous with the ones that are carried out in traditional speeches; consequently, it is clear that Salvini has a communication team that supports him and takes care of his posts and tweets on social media. In this regard, it is important to mention Luca Morisi. He is the head of the communication team, but most importantly he is the man behind Salvini's success on social media. Luca Morisi has a degree in philosophy, and at the beginning of his carrier he was a local politician for the Northern League. After his political experience he became a philosophy professor at the University of Verona (Marini, 2019). Nowadays he has returned in the political field as Matteo Salvini's social media strategist.

3. Corpus building and methodological approach

The data of this case study were organised into two corpora: The Tweets Corpus and the Traditional Corpus. The Tweets Corpus counts 56 tweets that were collected on Matteo Salvini's official Twitter account @matteosalvinimi through the Google Chrome tool Data Miner. The timespan established for the selection of tweets is one week for both crises (starting from the day in which the crises began). Specifically, 30 tweets were collected during the Aquarius immigration crisis in the timespan that goes from 10 June 2018 to 17 June 2018; and 26 tweets were collected during the Diciotti immigration crisis in the timespan that goes from 22 August 2018 to 29 August 2018. The Traditional Corpus counts two traditional speeches: The Aquarius Senate Report (13 June 2018) and the Pinzolo Speech (25 August 2018). It is important to mention that the style of these two traditional speeches is different because they were delivered in two different contexts. On the one hand, the Aquarius Senate report is formal and institutional since it was delivered at the Italian Senate. On the other hand, the Pinzolo speech is informal because it was delivered during a League Party in Pinzolo (Trentino-Alto Adige). Moreover, the style of this speech is very aggressive because Salvini discovered, ten minutes earlier, that he was investigated by Agrigento public prosecutor's office for abuse of authority and for the abduction of immigrants on board the NGO Diciotti.

Both tweets and traditional speeches were analysed qualitatively using the Critical Discourse analysis approach (Machin & Mayr, 2012). CDA is particularly appropriate to investigate the strategies of inclusion and exclusion in Matteo Salvini's populist discourse. Indeed, this approach provides a set of tools useful to critically analyse language, which is perceived as a means of social construction that can reveal connections between language, power, and control (Machin & Mayr, 2012, p. 4). Specifically, the analysis focuses mainly on the representational strategies used in the description of immigrants following the approach in Van Leeuwen (1996, 2008) and van Dijk (1998). Moreover, the analysis payed attention to the semiotic choices (Machin & Mayr, 2012) and metaphors (Lakoff & Johnson, 1980) used by the then Vice Prime Minister. In addition to the qualitative approach, the quantitative approach (Baker, 2006; Partington et al., 2013) was used as well but limited to the analysis of semiotic choices. The software Sketch Engine was employed to carry out the analysis; specifically, particular attention was paid to the concordances and the collocates of some semiotic choices. The Tweets Corpus counts 1,779 words and 2,268 tokens, while the Traditional Corpus counts 9,446 words and 11,193 tokens.

This analysis aims to answer the following research questions:

1. Are there any differences between the linguistic strategies used in tweets and traditional speeches?
2. What representational strategies, metaphors and semiotic choices are used by Matteo Salvini in order to exclude (or include) immigrants?

4. Results and discussion

4.1. Representational strategies

4.1.1. Opposition us versus them

The opposition strategy provides a polarised representation of *us* and *the others;* specifically, a positive self-presentation and a negative other-presentation (Van Dijk, 1998, p. 69; Cap, 2017, pp. 3–4). As a result, this strategy is probably one of the most effective regarding the exclusion of immigrants since they are depicted as having cultures, values and traditions that are completely in contrast with *ours.* This strategy usually indicates a general opposition between the *Western World* and the *Eastern (Muslim) World.* Indeed, it is one of the most popular strategy among far-right politicians (Wodak, 2015) and Matteo Salvini is certainly one of them. In this case study, the presence of this type of opposition strategy was found just in the Traditional Corpus (specifically in the Pinzolo Speech).

1. There are these geniuses who report a Minister who does not want that in Italy arrive *people who think that homosexuality is a crime punishable with death penalty* and that *women have less rights than men.* Who thinks that the woman has less rights than man stays at home because Italy is not fit for him. [...] and *if you want cover her with carpets you do it at your home*, because

I do not want in Italy people dressed in a *Batman suit*. [italics added] (Pinzolo Speech 25 August 2018)[1]

2. I am ready to show respect to those who do the same. This means that you are welcome in my home if you are escaping from war or if you are looking for a future for your children. But if you arrive in Pinzolo, or Milan, or Turin, or Palermo and you start saying: "*I don't like the crucifix, and I don't like baby Jesus, I don't like the bells", go back to your home and do what you want, and prey the God you want, and eat what you want, and drink where you want.* Therefore, respect for respect, I do not think that I am asking too much. [italics added] (Pinzolo Speech 25 August 2018)[2]

Example 2 focuses mainly on religious opposition. Salvini depicts immigrants as capricious, disrespectful and intolerant people who want to impose their own religion. In this way, he entails the topos of threat (Wodak, 2015) and populist narratives that compares the phenomenon of immigration to an invasion (Reisigl & Wodak, 2000). Nowadays the spread of this type of narratives is particularly facilitated by social media through fake news that can even involve conspiracy theories (that clearly represent a fertile ground for populist discourse since they provide simple explanations to complex phenomena). One of the most common narratives claims that immigration is a phenomenon supported by the *élites* to erase every type of individual difference and peculiarity in order to have a homogeneous group of people easy to manipulate (Gatti, 2019). Example 1 is apparently a simple opposition of values, but it actually shows contrastive narratives. Indeed, the League as a far-right party supports a traditional idea of family, traditional gender roles, and does not support gay marriage (or any other types of same-sex couple legal recognitions). However,

---

1 Cioè ci sono questi geni che denunciano un Ministro che non vuole che arrivi gente in Italia per cui l'omosessualità è un reato punibile con la pena di morte e per cui la donna ha meno diritti dell'uomo. Chi ritiene che la donna ha meno diritti dell'uomo stia a casa sua perché l'Italia non è il paese che fa per lui […] e se vuoi coprirla con i tappeti lo fai a casa tua, perché io di gente che va vestita in giro da Batman in Italia non ne voglio.

2 Io sono pronto a dare rispetto a chi porta rispetto. Questo però significa che sei il benvenuto in casa mia se scappi dalla guerra o se cerchi un futuro per i tuoi figli. Però se arrivi a Pinzolo o arrivi a Milano o arrivi a Torino o arrivi a Palermo, e cominci a dire: "E non mi piace il crocifisso, e non mi piace Gesù bambino, non mi piacciono le campane", torna a casa tua e fai quello che vuoi e prega il Dio che vuoi, e mangia quello che vuoi, e bevi dove vuoi. Quindi rispetto in cambio di rispetto, non penso di chiedere troppo.

in this example the leader of the League depicts positively these topics as representatives of western societies. In this way, he manages to make appear himself as a tolerant and respectful man that defend "liberal values", but at the same time he compares in a derogatory way the Burqa to a Batman suit.

In the Traditional Corpus was found another interesting example of opposition strategy that compares the current immigration to Italian immigration.

3. [...] *Workers from Trentino have brought their labor and effort, but no one payed to them breakfast, lunch, and dinner at the hotel with 35 euros per day. And these workers brought effort, sweat and tears, and wealth.* Therefore, I am willing to accept in Italy good, legal, and skilled immigrants, who can contribute to the growth of our country, as in Canada or Australia [...]. [italics added] (Pinzolo Speech 25 August 2018)[3]

On the one hand, Salvini describes Italian immigrants as good workers that contributed to the growth of other nations. On the other hand, he represents the other immigrants as a privileged group. Indeed, he uses the populist narrative (based on fake news) regarding their accommodation in hotels (Barlassina & Siviero, 2016) and the pocket money provided by the government.

The analysis shows that Salvini uses the opposition strategy in another way as well. He does not oppose generally and homogenously Italians to immigrants, he rather opposes two groups of social actors who are suffering. As shown in examples 4 and 5, this strategy is present in both tweets and traditional speeches.

4. There is *a million of children in Italy*, in our Italy. Sons of Italians, grandsons of Italians who cannot have lunch and dinner. They have found a Government and a Minister who thinks to *Italians first* and then to *the rest of the world*, who thinks to *Italian disabled people, separate parents, unemployed* and *precarious people* first and then to *those who disembark tomorrow*. [italics added] (Pinzolo Speech 25 August 2018)[4]

---

3 [...] Dei lavoratori trentini hanno portato il loro lavoro e la loro fatica ma nessuno gli pagava colazione, pranzo e cena in albergo con 35 euro al giorno. E questi lavoratori portavano fatica, sudore, e ricchezza, quindi io son disposto ad accogliere in Italia immigrati perbene, regolari e qualificati che portino crescita al nostro paese, come in Canada o come in Australia [...].

4 Ci sono un milione di bambini in Italia, nella nostra Italia. Figli di italiani, nipoti di italiani che non riescono a mettere insieme il pranzo con la cena, hanno trovato un Governo e un Ministro che pensa prima agli italiani e poi al resto del mondo, che pensa prima ai disabili italiani, ai genitori separati, ai disoccupati, ai precari e poi a chi sbarca domani mattina.

5. *#Diciotti immigrants on hunger-strike?* Do as they please. *In Italy 5 million of people* live in absolute POVERTY (1.2 million of *CHILDREN*), who *go on hunger-strike every day*, in the silence of do-gooders, journalists and various comrades. *#Italiansfirst* [italics added] (Tweet 24 August 2018)[5]

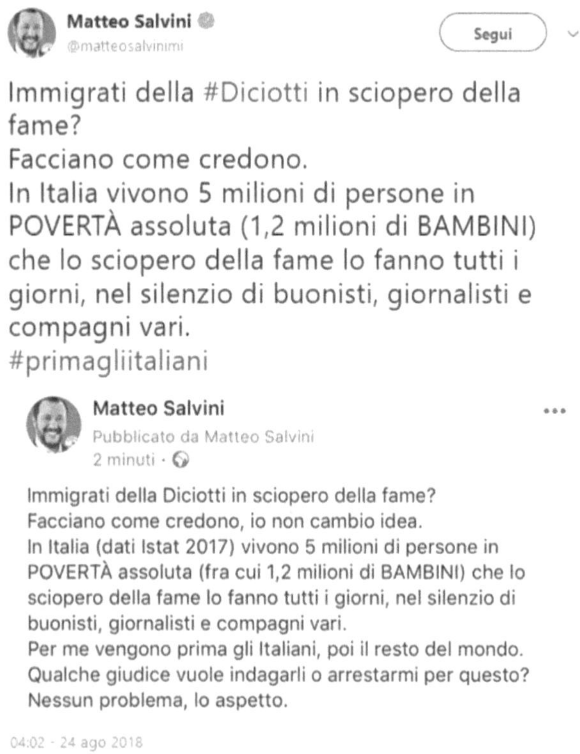

Figure 3.1. Tweet 24 August 2018. Opposition strategy regarding the Diciotti case

5 Immigrati della #Diciotti in sciopero della fame? Facciano come credono. In Italia vivono 5 milioni di persone in POVERTÀ assoluta (1,2 milioni di BAMBINI) che lo sciopero della fame lo fanno tutti i giorni, nel silenzio di buonisti, giornalisti e compagni vari. #primagliitaliani.

Examples 4 and 5 show how Salvini opposes immigrants to Italian suffering people such as poor Italians, poor children, disabled people, separate parents, unemployed and precarious people. In this way, Salvini tries to trigger Italians' emotions, and implies that Italians should feel more empathetic towards other Italians (since they are physically and culturally closer) rather than towards immigrants. This approach is connected to the strategy of victim/perpetrator reversal that is an exclusionary discursive strategy often used by right-wing populist politicians (Wodak, 2015). Moreover, it can be linked to a type of reverse racism (Renzi, 2015) since immigrants are depicted as a privileged group that has a priority over the group of Italians. Italians are described as the real victims because they are neglected by the élite (in example 4 Salvini talks about the previous governments, while in example 5 he refers to the media and left-wing do-gooders). The main aim of this type of opposition strategy is to present a point of view that can be shared easily by everyone despite political orientations.

4.1.2. Aggregation

The aggregation strategy is very useful when it comes to exclude immigrants since it completely dehumanises this category of social actors. Indeed, immigrants are presented as numbers, percentages, and statistics (Machin & Mayr, 2012). The aim of this strategy is to reduce and eliminate the feeling of empathy. As a result, it will be easier to exclude people who are not perceived as human beings at all.

6. I am not mad at anyone, but in the last years more than *700.000* have disembarked and most of these *700.000* were not escaping from war. Instead, they have brought war in our home. […] Last year *37.000* have disembarked, this year less than *6.000*. Where there is a will, there is a way. [italics added] (Pinzolo Speech 25 August 2018)[6]

As example 6 shows, Salvini completely dehumanises immigrants talking about them just in terms of numbers. It is also important to mention that the aggregation strategy is present in both corpora, but it is more common in the Traditional Corpus.

---

6 Io non ce l'ho con nessuno, però negli ultimi anni ne sono sbarcati più di 700.000 e di questi 700.000 la gran maggioranza non scappava da nessuna guerra, ma la guerra ce l'ha portate in casa nostra […]. L'anno scorso ne erano sbarcati 37.000, quest'anno ne sono sbarcati meno di 6.000. Volere è potere. Volere è potere.

4.1.3. *Crime, terrorism and fear*

Another strategy that Matteo Salvini uses in both traditional speeches and tweets is the connection between the immigration phenomenon, crime, and terrorism. This type of connection is quite stereotypical. Specifically, the one between immigration and terrorism has increased after 9/11 (Renzi, 2015) since immigrants (especially the ones who follow the Muslim faith) are commonly recognised as potential terrorists.

7. [...] I wait for a prosecutor who investigates human traffickers and those who favor illegal immigration, instead of investigating a Minister. Because I remind to this prosecutor [...] that *the traffickers buy weapons and drug with the thousands of dollars that the immigrants give to them. Weapons and drug*, and probably *this drug is pushed in Dante square in Trento or outside our children's schools* and I am sick and tired of financing the pushers of death and weapons. [italics added] (Pinzolo Speech 25 August 2018)[7]
8. This night *Mohamed Gueye, illegal Senegalese immigrant, accused to have RAPED* a 15 y.o. girl in Jesolo, *has been arrested* by Mestre Police. SHEER MADNESS! With #SecurityDecree if a clandestine rapes, steals, kills or pushes, he goes back home immediately. [italics added] (Tweet 25 August 2018)[8]
9. A couple of months ago the prosecutor of Agrigento (the one who is investigating me) said: "*there is a high risk of terrorists' presence on board of immigrants' boats*". Has he changed his mind? For me the problem is the same even TODAY. [italics added] (Tweet 26 August 2018)[9]

---

7 [...] io aspetto un procuratore che invece di indagare un Ministro, indaghi i trafficanti di essere umani e chi favoreggia l'immigrazione clandestina. Perché io ricordo a questo procuratore [...] che gli scafisti con le migliaia di dollari che portano a casa dagli immigrati comprano armi e droga. Armi e droga, che poi magari viene spacciata in piazza Dante a Trento o fuori dalle scuole dei nostri figli e io sono stufo di finanziare gli spacciatori di morte e di armi.

8 Arrestato questa notte dalla Polizia di Mestre Mohamed Gueye, immigrato senegalese irregolare, accusato di avere STUPRATO a Jesolo una ragazza di 15 ANNI. ROBA DA MATTI! Con il #DecretoSicurezza, se un clandestino stupra, ruba, uccide o spaccia, se ne torna a casa subito.

9 Qualche mese fa il procuratore di Agrigento (quello che mi sta indagando) diceva: "Il rischio di terroristi a bordo dei barconi è alto". Ha cambiato idea? Per me il problema rimane lo stesso anche OGGI.

10. *A Nigerian asylum seeker has been arrested for heroine dealing* for the third time in the same month, Sheer madness! In the #SecurityDecree that I am preparing it is expected the annulment of the asylum application and the expulsion for those who commit a crime: TO HOME!!! [italics added] (Tweet 26 August 2018)[10]

Example 9 shows how Salvini connects immigration to terrorism. Moreover, the tweet has also the aim of delegitimising the prosecutor who was investigating him for the abduction of immigrants on board the NGO Diciotti. An implicit connection between immigration and organised crime is shown in example 7. Indeed, Salvini blames human traffickers, but at the same time he depicts immigrants as the ones who finance organised crime. Immigrants are implicitly the reason why drug is pushed outside children's schools. On the other hand, examples 8 and 10 present two explicit connection between immigrants and crime. In example 8 Salvini talks about an *illegal Senegalese immigrant* who was accused to have raped a teenager (this example is present also in the Pinzolo Speech but in this occasion Salvini was able to discuss and deepen more this story). In example 10 he talks about a *Nigerian asylum seeker* who was arrested for heroine dealing. Firstly, it is important to notice that in both examples Salvini highlights their nationality in order to reinforce stereotypes linked to some ethnicities. Secondly, the explicit connection between crime and immigration allows him to present immigrants and asylum seekers as a real threat.

10 Richiedente asilo nigeriano è stato arrestato per la TERZA volta in un mese, sempre per spaccio di eroina. Roba da matti! Nel #DecretoSicurezza che sto preparando è previsto l'annullamento della domanda di asilo e l'espulsione per chi delinque: A CASA!!!

Figure 3.2. Tweet 25 August 2018 and Tweet 26 August 2018. Association between immigration and crime

Figure 3.3. Tweet 26 August 2018. Association between immigration and terrorism

The implicit and explicit connection between immigration, crime, and terrorism leads to the legitimisation of Salvini's narratives concerning the need to protect national borders; but most importantly this strategy legitimises his actions and governmental measures.

11. This is my speech at Gruber' s program on La7 tonight. *Hard line? Just COMMON SENSE, my duty is to guarantee the security* to 60 million of Italians. Share it too! [italics added] (Tweet 12 June 2018)[11]
12. Live from Senate, my first speech as Minister of the Interior about the first actions of the government in order *to defend the borders and to stop the business of illegal immigration*. Follow me. [italics added] (Tweet 13 June 2018)[12]
13. Honour to our men and our women, who *DEFEND* our *sea, land*, and *air borders*. #Italiansfirst [italics added] (Tweet 23 August 2018)[13]

---

11 Ecco il mio intervento di questa sera dalla Gruber su La7. Linea dura? Solo BUONSENSO. Il mio dovere è garantire la sicurezza a 60 milioni di italiani. Condividete anche voi!

12 In diretta dal Senato, il mio primo intervento da ministro dell'Interno sulle prime azioni del governo per la difesa dei confini e il blocco del business dell'immigrazione clandestina. Seguitemi.

13 Onore ai nostri uomini e alle nostre donne che DIFENDONO il nostro Paese e i nostri confini di mare, di terra e di cielo. #primagliItaliani.

In example 11 Salvini describes his governmental measures regarding immigration (specifically concerning the prohibition for the NGO Aquarius to dock in any Italian harbour) as *common sense*, since he was elected by Italians to guarantee their security. As a result, Italians' security is the reason why he can jeopardise immigrants' lives. From a linguistic perspective, he is legitimised in doing this by his own populist narrative that connects immigrants to crime and terrorism, and depicts them as dangerous. Examples 12 and 13 focuses on the defense of the borders and consequently on the physical exclusion of immigrants from the national soil. Specifically, in the tweet showed in example 12, Salvini announces his first speech as Minister of the Interior (the Aquarius Senate Report). He underlines the need to stop illegal immigration and defines it as a *business*. In example 13 he highlights once again the need of defending every type of border.

4.2. Metaphors

Conceptual metaphors are powerful means of communication deeply embedded in our everyday language; indeed, according to Lakoff and Johnson (1980) metaphors help human beings to organise their experiences.

When it comes to (populist) right-wing discourse about immigration, immigrants are often associated with dehumanising and toxic metaphors; for instance, they can be represented as diseases or parasitic insects (Musolff, 2015). In this case study was found another type of dehumanising metaphor that represents immigrants simply as objects.

14. Today the ship Sea Watch 3, a German NGO flying the flag of Holland, is off the coast of Libya too, waiting to carry out the umpteenth *load of immigrants* to bring to Italy. Italy has stopped to bend the head and to obey, this time THERE IS SOMEONE WHO SAYS NO. #closetheharbours [italics added] (Tweet 11 June 2018)[14]
15. This man is part of the German NGO ship crew and while he is waiting *to load immigrants* he says that I am "fascist" … reassuring I would say! [italics added] (Tweet 16 June 2018)[15]

---

14 Oggi anche la nave Sea Watch 3, di Ong tedesca e battente bandiera olandese, è al largo delle coste libiche in attesa di effettuare l'ennesimo carico di immigrati, da portare in Italia. L'Italia ha smesso di chinare il capo e di ubbidire, stavolta C'È CHI DICE NO.#chiudiamoiporti.

15 Questo signore è nell'equipaggio della nave della Ong tedesca che, in attesa di caricare immigrati, mi dà del "fascista" ... Rassicurante direi!

In examples 14 and 15 immigrants are compared to merchandise that the NGO loads in the Mediterranean Sea and unloads in Italy. In this case Salvini dehumanises immigrants comparing these social actors to inanimate objects; as a result, he tries to background and suppress all the suffering that surround the phenomenon of immigration.

Moreover, in example 15 Salvini tries to delegitimise the NGO crew referring to the appearance of one of them (see Figure 3.4) who according to him is not reassuring.

Metaphors connected to exclusion of immigrants were found just in the Tweets Corpus. The reason why is probably because metaphors are able to convey immediately powerful messages; as a result, they are more useful in tweets since there is a limitation of characters.

Figure 3.4. Tweet 11 June 2018 and Tweet 16 June 2018. Dehumanizing metaphors

4.3. Semiotic choices

4.3.1. Immigration

In addition to the connection between immigration, terrorism and crime, Salvini represents immigrants and legitimises his action through specific semiotic choices. Indeed, when it comes to talk about immigration he often associates this word to other words with a negative connotation such as *illegal* and *business* (see Example 12).

Table 3.1. Occurrences of the word *immigration* in the Tweets Corpus and co-occurrences of this word with the words *illegal* and *business*

Immigration	Illegal	Business
10	5	5

Table 3.1 shows that in the Tweets Corpus the word *immigration* co-occurs 5 times with the words *illegal* and *business*, while Figure 3.5 shows that the word *immigration* co-occurs 4 times with the words *illegal (clandestina)* and *business* simultaneously. As a result, the quantitative approach suggests that this is a cluster of words that Salvini usually employs in his populist discourse on Twitter.

Figure 3.5. Collocates of the word *immigration*

Figure 3.6. Concordances of the word *immigration*

Figure 3.6 shows all the concordances of the word *immigration* in the Tweets Corpus. It is important to notice other cluster of words such as *dictatorship of finance and immigration/dittatura di finanza e immigrazione* (line 8) and *limitless immigration/immigrazione senza limiti* (line 9), since they are useful in order to understand better how Salvini frames immigration and how represents immigrants through these semiotic choices. Specifically, they remind once again the idea of invasion, the topos of threat, and they are both linked to Eurosceptic narratives.

Table 3.2 shows that in the Traditional Corpus the word *immigration* occurs 17 times. Moreover, it co-occurs 7 times with the word *illegal* and 0 times with the word *business*.

Table 3.2. Occurrences of the word *immigration* in the Traditional Corpus and co-occurrences of this word with the words *illegal* and *business*

Immigration	**Illegal**	**Business**
17	7	0

Even though the word *business* does not co-occur with the word *immigration*, these two words are implicitly linked. Indeed, the concordances of *business* show that this word is present in other cluster of words such as *business of human trafficking*.

4.3.2. *Human beings and Passengers*

It is important to mention that Matteo Salvini uses some semiotic choices in order to humanises immigrants. This strategy is not employed to include immigrants; on the contrary, it is used by the then Minister of the Interior for other purposes.

16. I want to give the numbers to this Senate and to those who are following us. From 1 January to 31 May 2018 the pushbacks at the border between Italy and France have caused the comeback of 10.249 *human beings* to our home, included *women*, *children* and *disabled people*. According to the reallocation agreements of 2015, France has committed to receive 9.816 *immigrants*. In three years, France accepted 640 *immigrants*, instead of 9.816. [italics added] (Aquarius Speech 13 June 2018)[16]

16 Ci tengo a dare a questo Senato e a chi ci segue i numeri. Dal 1° gennaio di quest'anno al 31 maggio i respingimenti alla frontiera Italia e Francia hanno visto rispedire a casa nostra 10.249 esseri umani, compresi donne, bambini e disabili. E sulla base degli accordi sui ricollocamenti del 2015, la Francia si era impegnata ad accogliere 9.816 immigrati. In tre anni, invece di 9.816 immigrati, ne ha accolti 640.

Example 16 shows that Salvini strategically humanises this category of social actors. His aim is to discredit and delegitimise the French government since they have stopped immigrants at the border between Italy and France. Specifically, Salvini talks about them in terms of numbers but this time the numbers are linked to the words *immigrants*, *human beings*, *women*, *children*, and *disabled people*.

Another semiotic choice associated with immigrants is *passengers*. In this case study this semiotic choice was found just once in the Tweets Corpus, but it is worth to pay attention at its use because it involves interesting implications.

17. Boldrini is shocked because *Diciotti passengers* "have not accepted food". This woman lives in another planet…My thought goes to the millions of Italians who live in poverty. They would have accepted that food gladly. [italics added] (Tweet 25 August 2018)[17]

The word *passengers* could even appear as a neutral semiotic choice in this tweet, but it frames the NGO Diciotti as a simple means of transport. In this way, Salvini completely omits that NGOs rescue people, and he describes immigrants as ungrateful people who even dare to refuse food. This kind of representation is particularly useful to Salvini in order to present once again to his followers the *opposition (strategy)* between (poor) Italians and immigrants. Moreover, the tweet involves a socio-political of Laura Boldrini (deputy of the party Liberi e Uguali at the time of the events) and the government opposition.

4.3.3. Hashtags

The hashtags are definitely one of the main peculiarities of Twitter and they can be compared to keywords. Their function is to link conversations of people who do not know each other (Murthy, 2013, p. 3) and who do not necessarily share the same values (Seargeant & Tagg, 2014, p. 142). Hashtags are very useful because of their potential virality that facilitates the spread of populist narratives and political ideologies. These narratives and ideologies are synthesised in the hashtags and they can reach very easily the electorate and possible new supporters. Another advantage of hashtags is that they can also legitimise the narratives and consequently the governmental actions. Indeed, according to Pond and Lewis (2017) hashtags are "symbols of personalised action frames".

---

17 La Boldrini è rimasta scioccata perché i passeggeri della Diciotti "non hanno accettato il cibo". Questa vive su un altro pianeta...Un pensiero ai milioni di italiani in condizione di povertà che quel cibo lo avrebbero accettato volentieri.

There are two hashtags (see Figures 3.1 and 3.4) that Matteo Salvini uses to exclude immigrants: #primagliitaliani (#Italiansfirst) and #chiudiamoiporti (#closetheharbours). Both of these hashtags frame implicitly and explicitly the exclusion of immigrants.

18. #Diciotti immigrants on hunger-strike? Do as they please. In Italy 5 million of people live in absolute POVERTY (1.2 million of CHILDREN), who go on hunger-strike every day, in the silence of do-gooders, journalists and various comrades. *#Italiansfirst* [italics added] (Tweet 24 August 2018)[18]
19. Today the ship Sea Watch 3, a German NGO flying the flag of Holland, is off the coast of Libya too, waiting to carry out the umpteenth load of immigrants to bring to Italy. Italy has stopped to bend the head and to obey, this time THERE IS SOMEONE WHO SAYS NO. *#closetheharbours* [italics added] (Tweet 11 June 2018)[19]

Differently from other hashtags such as #SecurityDecree (see Figure 3.2, and examples 8 and 10) that appears in the middle of the tweets bodies, both the hashtags #Italiansfirst and #closetheharbours appear at the end of the tweets. Indeed, they perfectly summarise and reinforce the messages embedded in the tweets. The hashtag #Italiansfirst implicitly excludes immigrants and implies that for Salvini Italians always come first, especially the ones in need. In example 19 the hashtag #closetheharbours excludes immigrants explicitly and in a physically way since he is talking about blocking the disembarkations.

4.3.4. Overlexicalisation

The strategy of overlexicalisation (Machin & Mayr, 2012) is used by Matteo Salvini in order to include a specific group of social actors: Italians. The inclusion of Italians is worth to mention because, in this way, Salvini excludes implicitly immigrants that are the opposite social group. Table 3.3 shows the occurrences of the words *Italy*, *Italian* and *Italians* in both corpora, and it highlights that especially in the Traditional Corpus there is a considerable repetition of the word *Italian(s)*.

18 For the Italian text see footnote 5.
19 For the Italian text see footnote 14.

Table 3.3. Occurrences of the words *Italy*, *Italian* and *Italians* in both corpora

Corpus	*Italy*	*Italian/s*
Tweets	14	9
Traditional	23	46

20. This is my speech at Gruber' s program on La7 tonight. Hard line? Just COMMON SENSE, my duty is to guarantee the security to *60 million of Italians*. Share it too! [italics added] (Tweet 12 June 2018)[20]
21. We have received 700.000, we have supported 700.000, enough! Enough! We have done everything we could and must, enough. [...] There are these left-wing geniuses -absent at Genoa funerals and present on board of immigrants' boat- I remind to them whispering that there are more than *5 million of Italians* who live in absolute poverty, who have not gone on vacation, who cannot buy the backpack to their children [...]. [italics added] (Pinzolo Speech 25 August 2018)[21]
22. There is a million of children in *Italy*, in *our Italy*. *Sons of Italians*, *grandsons of Italians* who cannot have lunch and dinner. They have found a Government and a Minister who thinks to *Italians first* and then to the rest of the world, who thinks to *Italian disabled people*, separate parents, unemployed and precarious people first and then to those who disembark tomorrow. [italics added] (Pinzolo Speech 25 August 2018)[22]

Examples 20 and 21 show that Salvini represents Italians in terms of numbers. Although this strategy could resemble the *aggregation* strategy used to represent immigrants, Salvini talks about *millions of Italians* to highlight the seriousness of some situations (this strategy is used in example 16 for immigrants as well). Specifically, in example 19 he talks about *60 million of Italians* to underline that he represents all the Italian people and he intends to protect all of them. In example 21 he says that in Italy there are 5 million of people that live in absolutely poverty. He highlights that these people are Italians because his intent is to compare the suffering of his compatriots to immigrants' suffering. He uses

20 For the Italian text see footnote 11.

21 Ne abbiamo accolti 700.000, ne abbiamo mantenuti 700.000, basta, basta. Abbiamo fatto tutto quello che potevamo e dovevamo, basta [...] Ci sono, a questi fenomeni di sinistra, assenti ai funerali di Genova e presenti sulla nave degli immigrati, io ricordo sottovoce, ricordo sottovoce che ci sono più di 5 milioni di italiani che vivono in condizione di povertà assoluta, che non si sono fatti neanche un giorno di vacanza, che hanno il problema di comprare lo zainetto ai loro bimbi [...].

22 For the Italian text see footnote 4.

the same strategy in example 22, but here he specifies all the (Italian) social categories that have difficulties such as children and precarious people.

5. The possibility of inclusion

In addition to Italians, Salvini opens up to the possibility of some immigrants' inclusion but with one fundamental condition: the respect of Italian culture, tradition, and religion. It is important to highlight that in this case study Matteo Salvini talks about the possibility of immigrants' inclusion just in the traditional speeches.

23. […] «Love your neighbour as yourself». Right. My neighbours are therefore *women and children who are escaping from war and who are the first victims of the confusion we are living. Because those few boys, women, and children, who escape from war, must find their home in ours and they cannot be mixed with illegal immigration* that simply causes social conflict. However, «Love your neighbour as yourself» means also to love the millions of Italians who have lost in silence home, job and hope. [italics added] (Aquarius Senate Report 13 June 2018)[23]
24. […] I will do whatever is humanly possible to give voice to these *true refugees, good and legal immigrants who come here to build a future for themselves and their children, respecting our history, our culture and our traditions*, and most of all I will do everything for the Italians who have lost hope […]. [italics added] (Aquarius Senate Report 13 June 2018)[24]
25. I am ready to show respect to those who do the same. This means that *you are welcome in my home if you are escaping from war or if you are looking for a future for your children*. But if you arrive in Pinzolo, or Milan, or Turin, or Palermo and you start saying: "I don't like the crucifix, and I don't like baby

---

23 […] «Ama il prossimo tuo come te stesso». Giusto. Il mio prossimo, quindi, sono donne e bambini che fuggono della guerra e che sono le prime vittime della confusione che stiamo vivendo. Perché quei pochi ragazzi, donne e bambini che scappano dalla guerra devono avere in casa nostra casa loro e non possono essere mischiate a una immigrazione clandestina che porta semplicemente allo scontro sociale. Però «ama il prossimo tuo come te stesso» significa anche amare i milioni di italiani che in silenzio hanno perso casa, lavoro e speranza. Che hanno perso casa, lavoro e speranza.

24 […] farò tutto quello che è umanamente possibile per dare voce a questi rifugiati veri, agli immigrati regolari e perbene che vengono qua per costruire per sé stessi e per i loro figli un futuro, rispettando la nostra storia, la nostra cultura e le nostre tradizioni, e farò soprattutto di tutto perché a questi italiani che hanno perso la speranza […].

> Jesus, I don't like the bells", go back to your home and do what you want, and prey the God you want, and eat what you want, and drink where you want. Therefore, respect for respect, I do not think that I am asking too much. [italics added] (Pinzolo Speech 25 August 2018)[25]

As all the example above show, Salvini is willing to include just *true refugees* (specifically *children, women,* and *few boys*) and *legal immigrants* who respect Italian history, culture, tradition, and religion. Moreover, it is interesting to notice that Salvini just talks about children and women but never about (grown-up) men. He just mentions *boys* in example 23; specifically, he talks about *few* boys surely to underline the fact that according to some common beliefs the majority of immigrants are young men. This supports the connection between immigration and crime; and legitimises Salvini's narratives and actions. Salvini presents foreign men as a threat; indeed, in examples 10 there is a stereotypical connection between male immigrants and drug dealing, but most importantly example 8 shows a stereotypical representation of male immigrants as sexual predators. Another possible reason why he does not mention grown-up men is because, according to a stereotypical vision of gender roles (particularly supported by far-right parties), men do not need to be protected since they are usually the ones who protect women and children.

It is also important to highlight that in all the example even though he is talking about the possible inclusion of immigrants, he always mentions Italians. In this way, he assures his electorate that Italians will always come first. It is clear then that the possibility of a real inclusion for immigrants is very limited and strict.

6. Conclusion

The main aim of this research was to analyse the strategies used by Matteo Salvini in order excludes or even includes immigrants. Specifically, the analysis aimed to answer to the two research questions presented in the third section.

The first research question examines if there are any differences in the way Salvini uses the linguistic strategies in tweets and traditional speeches. The communication style is basically the same in both corpora. The only exception is the Aquarius Senate Report that is more formal since it was delivered in Senate. The differences between tweets and traditional speeches are mainly due to Twitter constraints; specifically, regarding the limitation of characters. Indeed,

25 For the Italian text see footnote 2.

it is possible to notice that in the Tweets Corpus there are strategies that have strong and immediate impact. First of all, dehumanising metaphors (they are present just in the Tweets Corpus) that can convey immediately powerful images. Secondly, the opposition between immigrants and suffering Italian people is the only type of opposition strategy present in the Tweets Corpus since it does not need further and longer argumentations. Indeed, the opposition strategy that involves culture and religion was found just in the Traditional Corpus. On the one hand, the religious and cultural opposition could be ineffective and appear too simplistic without a proper reasoning (that is impossible to give because of Twitter constraints). On the other hand, Salvini clearly prefers to use the opposition strategy between suffering group of people in order to frame a reverse racism. Although the connection between immigration, crime, and terrorism is very similar to the cultural and religious opposition in terms of the need of proper reasoning, this strategy is present in both corpora. This connection can be perceived differently on Twitter because it is presented by Salvini as breaking news. As a result, the strategy allows Salvini to reinforce stereotypes (especially the ones connected to specific ethnicities) and to instigate fears. Thirdly, the hashtags are obviously present just in the Tweets Corpus since they are part of Twitter structure. Hashtags can have an immediate impact if they are used strategically and accurately; consequently, they contribute to frame and spread populist narratives and ideologies.

The second research question investigates what representational strategies, metaphors and semiotic choices are used by Salvini in order to include or exclude immigrants. The analysis showed that the then Minister of the Interior uses some representational strategies such as aggregation, opposition us versus them and the connection between immigration, crime and terrorism. In addition, he employs dehumanising metaphors and specific semiotic choices to exclude immigrants. Indeed, all these strategies are used just to exclude the social group of immigrants. Even if Salvini talks about a possible inclusion of immigrants, he does not use any linguistic strategy that makes this possibility true and real. On the contrary, he opposes *true refugees* and *legal and skilled immigrants* to *illegal immigrants*. Among *true refugees* just women, children, and *few* boys are worthy to be included if they respect Italians and their customs. This underlines how important the *opposition us versus them* strategy is. The results showed that Salvini focuses on cultural and religious opposition in order to highlight his point of view regarding the complex and unrealistic integration of immigrants. The use of the opposition strategy is not very surprising, since Salvini is a far-right politician and wants to represent immigrants as a social, cultural, and religious threat. However, the results showed that this strategy is used by Salvini in another interesting way. The then Vice Prime Minister opposes very often immigrants just to a specific group of Italians: the suffering ones. Coherently with his populist rhetoric, Salvini aims to trigger people's emotions. The connection between immigration, crime and terrorism clearly aims to trigger fear, while the opposition between immigrants and suffering Italian people aims to trigger Italians' empathy. Specifically, Salvini tries to shift Italians' empathy towards suffering Italians since they are compatriots.

This case study has aimed to be a contribution to the larger field of discourse studies concerning populism. Further research will involve an additional integration of the quantitative approach and investigations regarding other populist narratives (such as Euroscepticism), and other strategies (e.g., self-legitimisation and other-delegitimation) embedded in the tweets regarding immigration.

References

Aalberg, T., Esser, F., Reinemann, C., Stromback J., & De Vreese, C. (Eds.). (2016). *Populist Political Communication in Europe*. New York: Routledge.

Albertazzi, D., Giovannini, A., & Seddone, A. (2018). 'No regionalism please, we are Leghisti!' The Transformation of the Italian Lega Nord under the Leadership of Matteo Salvini. *Regional & Federal Studies*, 28(5), 645–671.

Baker, P. (2006). *Using Corpora in Discourse Analysis*. London: Continuum.

Barlassina, G., & Siviero, G. (2016, September 8). I posti dove ospitiamo i migranti. *Il Post*. Retrieved September 5, 2023 from https://www.ilpost.it/2016/09/08/migranti-alberghi-salvini/

Bibus, O. (2019, December 5). Cosa c'entra la Madonna con il Mes e perché Salvini ha usato Medjugorje per attaccare Conte. *Open*. Available at https://www.open.online/2019/12/05/cosa-c-entra-la-madonna-con-il-mes-e-perche-salvini-ha-usato-medjugorje-per-attaccare-conte/

Bobba, G., & Legnante, G. (2016). Italy. A Breeding Ground for Populist Political Communication. In T. Aalberg, F. Esser, C. Reinemann, J. Stromback, & C. De Vreese (Eds.), *Populist Political Communication in Europe* (pp. 231–244). New York: Routledge.

Bouvier, G., & Machin, D. (2018). Critical Discourse Analysis and the Challenges and Opportunities of Social Media, *Review of Communication*, 18(3), 178–192.

Cap, P. (2017). *The Language of Fear. Communicating Threat in Public Discourse*. London: Palgrave Macmillan.

Cento Bull, A., & Gilbert, M. (2001). *The Lega Nord and the Northern Question in Italian Politics*. London: Palgrave Macmillan.

Enli, G. (2017). Twitter as an Arena of the Authentic Outsider: Exploring the Social Media Campaign of Trump and Clinton in the 2016 US Presidential Election. *European Journal of Communication*, 32(1), 50–61.

Galdieri, C. J., Lucas J. C., Sisco, T. S. (Eds.). (2018). *The Role of Twitter in the 2016 US Election*. London: Palgrave Macmillan.

Gatti, C. (2019). *I demoni di Salvini. I postnazisti e la Lega*. Milano: Chiarelettere.

Golbeck, J. (2015). *Introduction to Social Media Investigation*. Rockland: Syngress.

Karpf, D. (2017). Digital Politics after Trump. *Annals of the International Communication association*, 41, 198–207.

Kreis, R. (2017). The "Tweet Politics" of President Trump. *Journal of Language and Politics*, 16(4), 607–618.

Laclau, E. (2005). *On Populist Reason*. London-New York: Verso.

Lakoff, G., & Johnson, M. (1980). *Metaphors We Live By*. Chicago: University of Chicago Press.

Machin, D., & Mayr, A. (2012). *How to Do a Critical Discourse Analysis. A Multimodal Introduction*. London: SAGE.

Marini, A. (2019, April 22). Chi è Luca Morisi, il guru del web che ha postato la foto di Salvini col mitra, *Il sole 24 ore*. Retrieved September 5, 2023 from https://www.ilsole24ore.com/art/chi-e-luca-morisi-guru-web-che-ha-postato-foto-salvini-col-mitra-ABQLG7qB

Mudde, C., & Kaltwasser, R. C. (2017). *Populism: A Very Short Introduction*. Oxford: Oxford University Press.

Murthy, D. (2013). *Twitter. Social Communication in the Twitter Age*. Cambridge: Polity Press.

Musolff, A. (2015). Dehumanizing Metaphors in UK Immigrant Debates in Press and Online Media. *Journal of Language Aggression and Conflict*, 3(1), 41–56.

Ott, B. L. (2017). The Age of Twitter: Donald J. Trump and the Politics of Debasement. *Critical Studies in Media Communication*, 34(1), 59–68.

Partington A., Duguid A., & Taylor C. (2013). *Patterns and Meanings in Discourse: Theory and Practice in Corpus-Assisted Discourse Studies (CADS)*. Amsterdam: John Benjamins.

Pond, P., & Lewis, J. (2017): Riots and Twitter: Connective politics, Social Media and Framing Discourses in the Digital Public Sphere. *Information, Communication & Society*, 22(2), 213–231.

Reisigl, M., & Wodak, R. (2000). *Discourse and Discrimination: Rhetorics of Racism and Antisemitism*. London-New York: Routlegde.

Renzi, V. (2015). *La politica della ruspa. La Lega di Salvini e le nuove destre europee*. Roma: Edizioni Alegre.

Seargeant, P., & Tagg, C. (Eds.). (2014). *The Language of Social Media. Identity and Community of the Internet.* London: Palgrave Macmillan.

Tarchi, M. (2008). Italy: A Country of Many Populisms. In D. Albertazzi & D. McDonnell (Eds.), *Twenty-First Century Populism the Spectre of Western European Democracy* (pp. 84–99). London: Palgrave Macmillan.

Van Dijk, T. A. (1998). *Ideology*. London: SAGE.

Van Kessel, S., & Castelein, R. (2016). Shifting the Blame. Populist Politicians' Use of Twitter as a Tool of Opposition. *Journal of Contemporary European Research*, 12(2), 594–614.

Van Leeuwen, T. (1996). The Representation of Social Actors. In C. R. Caldas-Coulthard, & M. Coulthard (Eds.), *Texts and Practices: Readings in Critical Discourse Analysis* (pp. 32–70). London: Routledge.

Van Leeuwen, T. (2008). *Discourse and Practice. New Tools for Critical Discourse Analysis*. Oxford: Oxford University Press.

Wodak, R. (2015). *The Politics of Fear. What Right-Wing Populist Discourses Mean*. London: SAGE.

Wodak, R., & Krzyżanowski, M. (2017). Right-Wing Populism in Europe & USA Contesting Politics & Discourse beyond 'Orbanism' and 'Trumpism'. *Journal of Language and Politics*, 471–484.

Zappavigna, M. (2012). *Discourse of Twitter and Social Media: How We Use Language to Create Affiliation on the Web*. London: Bloomsbury.

Davide Bennato

University of Catania, Italy

davide.bennato@unict.it

Chapter 4 Self-exclusion towards technology. The neo-Luddite culture: Dimensions, ideology, case studies

Abstract: The paper discusses two opposite views towards technology: transhumanism, an optimistic one, and neo-Luddism, a pessimistic ideology claiming that technology will lead to undesirable outcomes. Some case studies are provided to show how neo-Luddists will be unavoidably excluded from a technologically mediated community.

Keywords: Technology, Technopoly, transhumanism, neo-luddism, exclusion.

1. Introduction

Contemporary society is characterised by the seamless integration between culture and digital technologies. This new kind of complex ecosystem is based on digital technologies and emerging social behaviour. As a result, the current complex technological environment – in which the social and the technological spheres are inextricably interwoven – is deeply influenced by several phenomena such as the global expansion of social media platforms, the growing importance of technologies (e.g., artificial intelligence and robotics), the ubiquity of the algorithms and data-based processes, the emergence of digital lifestyles (e.g., the quantified-self movement) and the digital nomadism.

Nowadays, from a cultural point of view, we witness the establishment of an optimistic ideology that considers digital technologies as a useful means to achieve and overcome both individual and social limitations (Harari, 2016). "Transhumanism", the term that is usually used to describe this emerging cultural paradigm, indicates the possibility to let humanity move a step forward in the direction of a new evolutionary leap in which technology is embedded in human beings and social systems (Bostrom, 2005).

On the other hand, the neo-Luddite paradigm maintains a critical approach concerning the deep integration between humanity and technology. This cultural movement claims that there is an important difference between technological development and technological progress since the former does not necessarily imply the latter. Indeed, according to a pessimistic point of view, the integration of humanity with technology could lead to serious problems. Consequently, we should reconsider our relationship with technology, especially the digital one. The neo-Luddite culture has a long tradition; more precisely, it is based upon the Luddite movement, a kind of trade union of the early XIX century that was born as a reaction to the technological unemployment caused by the introduction of the power loom (Landes, 1969). This was the first movement that reacted violently against mechanisation. The criticism towards technology and mechanisation was renewed in the 80ties with critical reflections against the computer culture (Roszak, 1986) and in the 90ties with criticism concerning the internet culture (Postman, 1992).

In this essay I argue that there is an emerging culture based on neo-Luddism; specifically, this emerging culture – that has a highly critical attitude towards digital technology – aims to create self-exclusion towards technologically mediated communities through a particular set of values.

2. From Luddites to neo-Luddites

The term Luddism comes from the mythical character Ned Ludd or King Ludd, who was the leader of a series of riots against the mechanisation of labour in England during the industrial revolution of the XVIII century. These riots were caused primarily by the introduction of the power looms – that substituted skilled textile workers – that led to negative social and political consequences; indeed, this is traditionally remembered as the very first example of technological unemployment in history (Landes, 1969). In a more extensive view, the term "Luddism" stands for a generic anti-technological stance; however, this concept does not belong to the classical scientific approach of the economy or the industrial relation history but rather to mass media research. Media studies have a long tradition concerning the study of the negative reactions against the electronic media in comparison to the analogical one (e.g., television vs. printing press). The classical argument involves the myth of the birth of writing exposed in Plato's Phaedrus and part of the analysis of the Media Ecology School (Ong, 1982; Postman, 1992). In this myth, Plato recounts – through Socrates' narrating voice – the history of the ancient Egyptian King Thamus who receives the gift of writing from the god Toth (the Egyptian version of the Greek god Prometheus). Thamus perceives this gift as unpleasant because he is afraid that writing will atrophy people's memory. This is hardly a symbolic myth. In fact, the writing is usually used as an argument against new electronic technologies, but in Thamus' case, it is writing to be a technical innovation leading to some concerns. As a result, this platonic myth can be considered as the first cultural anti-technological stance that expresses a Luddite vision of writing as innovation (Postman, 1992).

There are many types of technological resistance or overreactions against innovations, some of which are analysed in social studies of science (Bennato, 2010). Here I will define the intellectual framework connected to this point of view. For this purpose, I will distinguish four different building blocks of the contemporary Luddism: the philosophical, the political and the social dimensions and the technological resistance.

In order to understand the philosophical dimension of contemporary Luddism, we have to focus our attention on the masters of suspicion and the postmodern condition.

Arguments against technology usually have the same defined structure; specifically, these arguments claim that the introduction of technology in society will lead to social (cultural, political, and economical) unexpected consequences (Beck, 1992; Feenberg, 1999). From this point of view, it is possible to intertwine the different attitudes against technology with the philosophical position of the masters of suspicion (Ricoeur, 1965). According to this position, there is a philosophical tradition that wants to unveil the structure of the shared reality that is obfuscated by political power or other social forces. The main thinkers of this tradition are Karl Marx, Friedrich Nietzsche, and Sigmund Freud. Marx criticises the oppressive use of religion perpetrated by the political power (his classic quote is "*religion is the opium of the people*").

Nietzsche blames Christian morality – though the employment of the concept "the death of god" – for its defence of the weak against the strong.

Freud reveals that our rationality is just an ex-post justification of our deep desires and impulses. This philosophical tradition is represented by the radicalisation of Rene Descartes' methodical doubting strategy, but from a rationalist approach, it comes to a hermeneutic one.

The philosophy of the masters of suspicion is also a good framework to understand conspiracy theories' arguments and discourse strategies that are employed by the followers of these theories. For this reason, conspiracy theories can be also found in the Luddite and neo-Luddite social criticism. The hermeneutics of suspicion is useful to describe the philosophical horizon but, at the same time, it is not sufficient to socially legitimise it. In this regard, it is possible to combine the social and cultural analyses of contemporaneity with the concept of postmodern condition (Lyotard, 1979). According to this approach, the starting point of the contemporaneity is the condition of knowledge in the developed society that is characterised by the computerisation of society and the legitimation crisis of the social institutions. The great metanarratives of modernity – science, politics, religion – have failed in legitimising themselves and the surrounding social world. The postmodern condition is based on the incredulity towards metanarratives; consequently, this condition provides a space for an alternative interpretation of the social reality. Technology is not only seen as a source of progress, but it is also seen as a source of social problems. In addition, technology is seen as a mean that people in power could exploit in order to legitimise themselves and to create a technocratic society. As a result, the postmodern condition is a concept useful to reinforce the idea that technology is not the solution, but it is actually the problem.

The neo-Luddism traces a path to technological resistance through political dimension. The political dimension of contemporary Luddism is part of the classic Luddite ideas. Specifically, the original Luddite ideology is defined by two characteristics (Salvatori & Villi, 1987; Fox, 2002; Jones, 2006). The first characteristic is the ideology of the replacement of human beings. According to this ideology, technology can replace the workforce and – in recent times – cognitive labour. From this point of view, human beings are represented only as part of the industrial system and as the ones who give just fragmented contributions in the building of other technologies. In this regard, they lose their humanity and became a functional element in the technocratic ensemble. It is possible to find this argument in a great number of social critics about technology; for example, in Mumford (1934) and in the Frankfurt School (Adorno & Horkheimer, 1947; Ellul, 1950). The main claim of this ideology is that humankind has not a central role in society since it is relevant only for its role in the technological evolution. The second characteristic – that defines the original Luddite ideology – is the ideology of society replacement. This ideology claims that technology can substitute society through the embedding of social rules in the machine. This topic points out that society can express itself using technology, since technology is a social product and can be subjected to the same rules that regulate society. This topic is supported by the panopticon argument (Foucault, 1975). The panopticon is the prison invented by the philosopher Jeremy Bentham in the XVIII century, whose idea was to monitor the maximum number of prisoners employing the minimum number of guards. The prison has a ring shape; and its cells are monitored by a surveillance tower positioned in the centre. In this way, the prisoners know that they are under control, but they do not know when. As a result, they behave in a respectful way because they internalise the rules of the prison. From a sociological point of view, the panopticon embodies a social institution since the prison's rules are guaranteed by a social control embedded into the architecture of the prison. The panopticon is an interesting argument because it provides a metaphorical representation of the elements of the surveillance society and, in recent times, of the exploitation of data in digital platforms – following the rules of capitalistic modes of production – to control people (surveillance capitalism: Zuboff, 2019).

The social dimension of the contemporary Luddism emphasises the contrast between humanity and technology. The ideas that support this dimension are perceived as commonsense concepts and they are well rooted in public discourse. However, it is important to specify that technology is part of human creativity because the identity of humankind descends from *Homo Faber*. As a result, there is no opposition between humanity and technology because technology is part of humanity and vice versa.

This point of view is supported by several contributions of technology such as the importance of technology in the anthropological evolution of humans (Diamond, 1997), the role of technological innovation in the Renaissance (Rossi, 1962), and the existence of technology as a cultural and symbolic innovation even beyond its physical existence as an artifact (Pacey, 1983). Nevertheless, it is hard to eradicate the idea that technology is the opposite of humanity or – in extreme cases – anti-human. Indeed, the mistrust towards technology is based on a different set of values that are deeply interwoven with each other. For the sake of simplicity, it is possible to identify three different worldviews connected to these values. The first worldview is represented by the radical ecology argument that supports the contrast between nature and technology since nature is seen as the value that has to prevail over technology This worldview has an ideological position because there is no real opposition between nature and technology. More precisely, nature has been shaped during the centuries – and especially after the industrial revolution – in order to adapt itself to the presence of humans. For instance, agriculture represents one of the biggest changes produced by humans. This point of view can be sustained by the environmentalism argument; however, environmentalism does not oppose to the fair use of technology. For instance, in the early 70ties, global environmentalism used to support nuclear power rather than carbon power because the latter was considered more polluting than the former. This attitude changed dramatically when people became aware of nuclear waste; notwithstanding, nowadays this position has been reconsidered because of Global Warming (Lynas, 2007).

The second worldview concerns the argument of radical humanism that is based on human pureness. According to this perspective, technology is a path that leads to dehumanisation; as a result, it is necessary to reject technology in order to save human pureness. In this case, humanity – as nature in the radical ecology argument – has to be defended against technology. This is an ideological position as well since human beings express themselves through artifacts and other technologies. Therefore, human pureness does not exist. Humanity exists only in societies where people define it as a concept. If we look at the evolution of humans in prehistory, we can see that it is followed step by step by the evolution of technological manipulation (e.g., stone age, bronze age, iron age). Consequently, being human does not contrast with the use of technology.

The third worldview involves the cyborg argument. This worldview claims that there is a continuity between the natural and the artificial, and that this continuity affects the original biological identity. This argument is different from the previous one because there is not a rejection of technology, which is actually considered a way to overcome the biological limitations of the subject. Indeed, contemporary feminism contributed to the spread of this argument since the cyborg subject could represent a new kind of non-binary identity that overcomes the cultural and physical limitation of the ordinary subjects (Haraway, 1985).

This argument is also part of the Luddite ideology because it can be used to legitimise the rejection of technology. For instance, if social forces allow to people to become partly human and partly technological, it is necessary to prevent this possibility. The cyborg argument is deeply different from the other ones because it is typical of the current neo-Luddism ideology.

Starting from these premises, it is possible to outline the neo-Luddite ideology. The three crucial elements that distinguish the Luddite and the neo-Luddite ideologies are "the digitalization as a target", "the resistance as an everyday act", and "the paradox of technology".

At first, in the Luddite movement the target was mechanisation during the industrial revolution (Landes, 1969), and automation during postwar industrialism (Pollock, 1956), while in the neo-Luddite movement the target is digitalisation (e.g., computers, internet, smartphones).

It is important to highlight this difference because mechanisation and automation are technologies that have a space in factories and afflict the workforce. Instead, digitalisation does not exist in a particular social space, since it could be everywhere, and represents an ecosystem in which people are immersed.

The second element is "the resistance as an everyday act". On the one hand, in the Luddite movement the resistance (concerning workers' reaction against power loom) takes place in a particular space (the factory) and in a particular moment (the working time). On the other hand, in the neo-Luddite movement digital technology needs a continuous act of resistance because it is not used in a specific space nor in a particular time.

Third, for what concerns "the paradox of technology", the Luddites smashed the power looms using the tools of the rural tradition (such as axes, hoes and mattocks). The neo-Luddites have to use digital technologies to act against digital technologies. For instance, they have to use an internet connection to criticise social media, smartphones to comment against the technological dependence, and computers to express concerns against computers.

Finally, it is possible to summarise the differences between these two movements saying that the Luddite movement was a social reaction against the political use of the means of production in the factory life, while the neo-Luddite movement is a cultural resistance against a particular use of digital communication technologies in everyday life.

3. The neo-Luddism nowadays

It is not easy to define neo-Luddism because nowadays it is ubiquitous, and it is part of the internet contemporary digital culture. However, it is possible to describe a path moving from classical Luddite culture to neo-Luddism. In this regard, I argue that there is a growing neo-Luddite culture that is part of the daily life of the digital society and that this culture expresses itself in the popular discourse through digital media but it is not able to normalise the problem.

First, it is necessary to specify who the scholars that contributed to the spreading of the building blocks of the Luddite dimension are. This will not be a systematic review since I've selected those scholars whom I believe to be more interesting specifically because they question technology using a culture-based gaze.

The first scholar who combines computer culture and neo-Luddism is Theodor Roszak (professor of History at California State University, East Bay). He has begun to analyse the society's infatuation for computers using the lens of technology criticism in his seminal book *The cult of information* (Roszak, 1994). His criticism of technology involves two main concepts: information and the social legitimation of information. Information is a polysemic word that was coined to describe the founding element of the computer. Later, this word spread in popular culture – through different intellectual traditions such as cybernetic and artificial intelligence – to describe a new way of thinking about people and society. Information is the element of computer software, information is the characteristic of mass media, information is the raw material of economy and finance, information is what schools and universities have to teach to young generations. The overuse of this word has created a computer ideology that seems to have the structure of a new secular cult. In this cult the celebrants are the data merchants – who are the ideologists of this new religion that come from different institutions such as industry, finance, army, university, and research – who want to exploit the importance of information and computers in order to increase their power. Roszak points out clearly that he is not technophobic; instead, he addresses the importance of a "naked mind", a mind that is able to think without a computer as an intellectual or cultural model. The book is a seminal work in computer critics' literature – the first edition dates back to 1986 –because of its references such as the commercial war between Microsoft and Apple, the research on expert systems and artificial intelligence and the introduction of computers in schools and universities. For this reason, *The cult of information* is also an important piece of evidence of the early years of computer society that exposes the ethical problem of digital technology in society.

Neil Postman is another important scholar who investigated the social and ethical consequences of technology. He was a media theorist and a cultural critic who wrote on this subject twenty books and several papers. In *Technopoly: the surrender of culture to technology* (Postman, 1992), he expresses his vision on cultural criticism of technology. More precisely he claims that contemporary culture depends on technology not only as an artifact, but also as an ethical and symbolic horizon. According to Postman (1992, p. 20):

> New technologies alter the structure of our interests: the things we think about. They alter the character of our symbols: the things we think with. And they alter the nature of community: the arena in which thoughts develop.

In order to outline his point of view; Postman argues that the history of the relationship between technology and culture is characterised by three moments. The first one is represented by the "tool using culture": technology is invented to solve urgent problems of physical life or to serve the symbolic world of art, politics, religion. Furthermore, this kind of technology did not undermine culture's dignity. The second one is technocracy; during this second moment technological tools are not integrated with culture because they aim to become part of it. The technological and symbolical consequences of the invention of some tools such as the clock, the printing press, and the telescope are a typical example of technocracy. For instance, the telescope employed by Galileo represented a dangerous threat for Catholicism because it attacked and questioned an important dogma and the political role of the Church. The third moment is "Technopoly", that is a totalitarian version of technocracy. In Technopoly, the access to information is central but, at the same time, it is difficult to handle. For this reason, culture must use technology in order to overcome information generated by technology itself.

Nor only does Postman consider technology as the "hard" type of equipment (e.g., the computer) but also as the "soft" equipment, such as opinion polls, IQ tests, standardised forms, which he calls invisible technologies, or every technology that can easily apply the bureaucracy methodology to every aspect of culture.

In the final pages of the book, he encourages a resistance attitude against Technopoly even through school and university practices training for cultural criticism. Postman does not refer explicitly to Luddites or Luddism; however, his description of the clash between technology and culture is essential for conscious critics of the computer society.

While the previous authors can be categorised as scholars, the third thinker that I introduce, Kirkpatrick Sale, is an activist whose ideas on technology resistance were very popular in the '90s. In his book *Rebels against the future* (Sale, 1995), he outlines a history of the Luddite movement. In the final chapters, he tries to describe what the neo-Luddite movement can learn from political and cultural resistance concerning the invasion of technology.

Sale is the true spokesperson of the technological resistance since his ideas are rooted in environmentalism, decentralism, and anti-globalisation movements. His book is a political reconstruction of the Luddite movement in the first and the second industrial revolution. Specifically, he argues that the Luddite movement was not against technology. According to him, it was a movement that fought against the ideology of progress and its values – such as of mechanisation, consumption, exploitation, growth, competition, and novelty – that aimed to impose a form of anti-human capitalism.

He points out that the political ideas of the neo-Luddites are essentially the consequences of the unaware use of industrial technologies disregarding people and the environment (a position also shared by the green movement).

Concerning the neo-Luddite movement of the '90s, he mentions some ideologists who criticise technology: Langdon Winner, David Noble, Theodore Roszak, Jerry Mander, Jeremy Rifkin, John Zerzan, Fritjof Capra, Vandana Shiva. The book has the same structure of a political *pamphlet*, therefore there is no deep analysis of the movement; however, the book is important for two reasons. First, because it provides an introduction of the political anti-technological ideas in the public sphere of the late '90s. Second, the peculiar book launch struck the imagination of the audience. Indeed, Sale usually began the launches by smashing a computer. This act was typical of the critics of technology who wanted to capture attention. In Italy, the comedian Beppe Grillo smashed computers during his shows before he began to be a technophile and became the founding father of the Five Stars Movement and its techno-libertarian ideology (Tiso, 2013).

The '90s are crucial years for neo-Luddism. In addition to the growing academic and political literature that points out the existence of a set of very critical values towards technology (namely computer technology), there is also an important event that makes the United States aware of a rising political anti-technological attitude: the terrorist Unabomber was captured by the FBI. Unabomber is the nickname that the U.S. press gave to Theodore Kaczynski. He was responsible of sixteen bombings between 1978 and 1995 that targeted university professors and airline companies (Unabomber: University and Airline bomber). The ideology behind his attacks is extremely connected to the neo-Luddite attitude; more precisely, he believes that the origin of contemporary discomfort lays in the radicalisation of the industrial society. According to Kaczynski, the destruction of this social organization is the only solution to the problem of radicalisation.

His ideology is described in the political pamphlet "Industrial society and its future" – that is also known as the Unabomber's Manifesto – published by *The New York Times* and *The Washington Post* upon Kaczynski' s request. The manifesto has 232 paragraphs including Kaczynski's critique to the contemporary left, an analysis of the system of scientific research and development, and the resistance towards the ubiquity of technology. The manifesto is well-argued thanks to Kaczynski's experience in academic writing acquired during his years as a university researcher. Kaczynski claims that the contemporary left has a failed ideology that hides its desire for power through apparent moral norms which, in reality, are only functional to people who want to achieve power. The scientific system – represented by the apparatus of researchers – is not interested in constructing knowledge, but it just wants to achieve the interests of scientists and those who finance their research and studies. Technology is a potentially dehumanising project; for this reason, it is necessary to act to prevent its spread, and to develop an ideology that opposes it. According to Kaczynski' s vision, ecological struggles fail to affect the industrial system that must be brought down by acting on its vital points: telecommunications, the electricity network, technical-scientific education, and the system of global connections. Different analysts state that the ideas expressed in the manifesto have different sources of inspiration such as Jacques Ellul (the criticism to industrialism), Herbert Marcuse (the cultural characteristics of the left), John Zerzan (the importance of anarchism and primitivism) and Aldous Huxley (the dystopian view of the future). Thanks to his anti-technological vision of the world, the character of Unabomber rapidly became part of the contemporary imagery. He is cited in some movies, *Good Will Hunting* (1997, Gus van Sant, USA), *Fun with Dick and Jane* (2005, Ted Kotcheff, USA), and different Tv series, *Dexter* (2008, *The damage a man can do*, S3E8, Showtime, Marcos Siega), *Lie to Me* (2011, *Saved*, S3E11, Fox, Michael Offer), *House M. D.* (2011, *The Dig*, S7E18, Fox, Matt Shakman); moreover, in 2017 Netflix produced a mini-series based on the story of his capture (*Manhunt: Unabomber*).

The inclusion of Unabomber as a character of pop culture is not surprising; as a serial killer he was an anti-hero dominating the narrations of the media (e.g., the role of the press in his capture). On the other hand, he embodied the anti-technological attitude that was growing in technological societies. The idea of technology resistance is well-rooted in pop culture since the '80s. It is also interesting to notice that in the '80s technology resistance was part of the science fiction narration, while in the following years it became part of a kind of hyperrealist storytelling. Hollywood is a good example of this imaginary shift. In *Contact* (1997, Robert Zemeckis, USA) – a movie based on a fiction book by Carl Sagan – the spatial mission is slowed down because of a religion-inspired terroristic attack. *Antitrust* (2001, Peter Howitt, USA) is the story of a group of idealistic programmers guided by Milo Hoffman (Ryan Philippe) who are hired by the NURV – a global communication enterprise – to improve Synapse that is a communication satellite-based system. Hoffman discovers that the real goal of the CEO – a dark version of Bill Gates played by Tim Robbins – is a worldwide surveillance system; consequently, he will destroy it. In *Her* (2013, Spike Jonze, USA) Theodore Twombly (Joaquin Phoenix) falls in love with a computer operating system – that has the voice of Scarlett Johansson, with dramatic consequences. *Kingsman the secret service* (2014, Matthew Vaughn, USA) is the story of a very secret organization that must stop the plan of the multimillionaire Richmond Valentine (Samuel L. Jackson) who wants to kill common people through a smartphone-based technology that makes them go crazy. *The Circle* (2017, James Ponsholdt, USA) is the name of a tech and social media company whose mission is to sell their technology all over the world in order to control people. Their new intern Mae Holland (Emma Thompson) will understand that life sharing is very dangerous for humans' identity and privacy and will stop the plan of Eamon Bailey (Tom Hanks), a kind of unscrupulous Steve Jobs.

It is also possible to find a neo-Luddite attitude in tv series. *Mr. Robot* (2015–2019, Sam Esmail, NBC) is the story of Elliot Anderson (Rami Malek) – a cybersecurity programmer and hacker – who is recruited by the anarchist Mr. Robot (Christian Slater) to join fsociety that is formed by a group of hacktivists who wants to destroy the database debt of the eCorp. *Black Mirror* (2011–2019, Charlie Brooker and Annabel Jones, Channel 4 and Netflix) is a dystopian science fiction anthology tv series whose standalone episodes expose the dark consequences of the use of new technologies.

The imaginary of the recent years is actually a good battlefield to observe the dichotomy between the acceptance and rejection of technology – together with the technophile and technophobic attitude –, and it is also a good starting point to understand how society is reflecting about its technological dependency and the resulting social consequences.

4. The widespread neo-Luddism: Some case studies

How does the neo-Luddite culture express itself in contemporary society? Nowadays, neo-Luddism can be identified in many ways because the ubiquity of digital technology can trigger a rejection in anyone. I will present three case studies – that have different contests and public perceptions – that can show the neo-Luddism's attitude concerning the digitalisation as a target, the resistance as an everyday act and the paradox of technology.

The first case study is Chiara Ferragni's digital detoxing. On September 14, 2018, Chiara Ferragni – a famous Italian fashion blogger and influencer– - announced on Instagram that she would disconnect from the social media platform throughout the day. When she came back on the platform, she thanked her followers in this way:

> Guys thank you for all the sweet messages and for asking me what happened yesterday. I wanted to get some time off social media to rest and to treat my skin with the new @EsteeLauder Advanced Night Repair Eye crème, I can already see the results and I want to do this more often! #AreYouSeeingBlue #AdvancedNightRepair #sponsoredbyEstéeLauder
> https://www.instagram.com/p/BnvRBQ5HfIE/

The caption of the post and the use of the hashtags reveal that Ferragni's detox was actually part of the marketing campaign of Estee Lauder (organised by the social media agency OMD). This Instagram post is very interesting because of her followers' reaction. Ferragni wanted to thank her followers for the great number of messages she received during the day off; moreover, during 14 September 2018 in the Italian Twittersphere the hashtag *#chiaradovesei* (Chiara where are you: https://twitter.com/hashtag/chiaradovesei) was one of the most used of that day. This case study is very interesting from a neo-Luddite perspective. The target of the event is Instagram. The digital platform is very important for Chiara Ferragni since it contributes to her success as a fashion influencer; as a result, the day away from the platform is a symbolic message for her followers. Indeed, the idea of a digital detox is a particular and interesting resistance strategy. Detoxing is a concept that is part of the wellness culture. According to this culture, it is necessary to deprive the body of toxins during the day to have stronger health and beauty effects. The analogy is fascinating. In the same way, the digital detox deprives the mind from toxins that are represented by social media (and smartphones) in order to have a less stressful social life. Many scholars consider the concept of digital detox as a new narrative of the idea of technology disconnection (Jorge 2019; Syvertsen & Enli, 2019). The paradox of technology is clear. An important Italian influencer, well known for her ubiquitous social media presence, uses her temporary drop out of Instagram for a social media marketing strategy that reinforces her comeback on the platform. From the neo-Luddite perspective, the frame of signification is essential to define the behaviour. In this way, an apparent rejection strategy can be decoded as a confirmative belonging to the digital platform.

The second case study is the Nasim Aghdam's attack on YouTube. On April 3 2018, Nasim Najafi Aghdam – a blogger and a YouTuber of San Bruno in California – opened the fire against YouTube headquarter, wounding three people and then committing suicide. Aghdam was an activist for animal rights, vegan, and a bodybuilder with a very active digital life. She had profiles on YouTube, Facebook, Instagram, Telegram, a personal website, and she posted in English, Farsi, and Turkish. The contents of her videos and posts were about animal rights, vegetarian recipes, and domestic workouts. She was angry because she claimed that YouTube was censoring and filtering her videos; consequently, she had fewer views and therefore less revenue. The demonetisation of her videos – caused by a change in the revenue algorithm of YouTube – represented the point of no return. The apocalypse (advertising apocalypse) is the ironic name given by the worldwide YouTubers community to the big investors' reactions to the presence of very controversial content in the video-sharing platform (Kumar, 2019). The investors' threat was to dramatically reduce advertising investments on YouTube; as a result, the company decided to filter out controversial contents and to demonetise all videos that were not compliant with the new rules. The global community of YouTubers saw an important reduction in the advertising revenue, and they called the new situation "adpocalypse". According to different analysts, one of the most important triggers of Nasim Aghdam's YouTube attack was precisely the adpocalypse. In this case, it is possible to observe how the neo-Luddite culture turns in a social threat. Is it clear that digitalisation is the real target. YouTube is the cultural and economic framework of Nasim Aghdam's social life; consequently, when YouTube changed the platform's terms of service, Aghdam's world was destroyed just as her identity as YouTuber and blogger. It should be highlighted that YouTube is not just a platform used by Aghdam to earn money, but it is also a social space that Aghdam – as a public figure – used for several months to construct her audience and her (online) identity. Moreover, in this case the resistance is an everyday act. The main trigger of her resistance was the adpocalypse. Aghdam began to feel discriminated by YouTube and became resentful. She perpetrated different acts of resistance against the social media company without success. Her violent act was probably a way to express her grudge against YouTube. Furthermore, in this case it is possible to notice the paradox of technology underway. A person – who owes her success as a public figure and microcelebrity (Senft, 2008) to YouTube – turned in a YouTube opponent once the platform social trust was turned off.

The third case study is the A-level grading fiasco. On August 14, 2020, hundreds of students protested in front of The Department of Education in England asking to change the results of the A-level exam grades. The English Government decided to mark students' A-grades with an algorithm rather than with the scoring system because of the pandemic. The A-grades are important because students with a high score can have a good academic career, since this exam is an important element of UK academic institutions' admission procedure. The Ofqual (Office of Qualifications and Examinations Regulation) and the Department of Education decided to attribute the A-level grade with an algorithm. This algorithm used three different data sources: "1. The historical grade distribution of schools from the three previous years (2017–2019); 2. The rank of each student within his/her school for a particular subject, based on a teacher's evaluation of their average grade had the A-levels gone forward as planned (called the "Centre Assessed Grade" or CAG for short); 3. The previous exam results for a student per subject" (Kolkman, 2020). As a result, the algorithm attributed grades with a great number of biases. For example, the latent bias of the algorithm implicates that the results of the grade were deeply influenced by the schools' history. Another bias was 'smaller schools, worse grades. Students from smaller schools obtained very low grades compared to students from larger (and richer) schools. As an overall result, the algorithm gave low evaluation to students from the lower socio-economic background. For this reason, many students protested against the Department of Education. Moreover, many schools have threatened legal actions concerning the results. At the time of writing, the English Government was trying to resolve the situation in order to avoid more protests and legal actions. This neo-Luddite case is very interesting because of the social consequences of political decisions connected to the algorithm. It is possible to analyse this case applying neo-Luddite elements. First, the digitalisation is the target. The 2020 pandemic has created many problems and some of them can be dealt with using ad hoc technologies; however, the misguided use of technology can cause more negative consequences than solutions. Evgeny Morozov called this attitude solutionism (Morozov, 2013). Second, the resistance as an everyday act. The social consequences of the algorithm biases caused a rapid reaction of students and schools. This is an important step because the unfair or dangerous effects of black-boxed technologies must be stopped in order to create a critical audience (Kolkman, 2020) that is able to deal with technology and its hidden political decisions. Third, the paradox of technology. A technology – that is employed to solve a problem – creates more problems than it solves. Furthermore, this controversy will probably cease – through a technological decision such as an increase of the public accountability of the same algorithm.

Although these case studies are different from many points of view (e.g., the fashion discourse, the terroristic attack, the political solutionism), they have the same root: a growing attitude to technology rejection embedded in cultural and social institutions.

Table 4.1. Neo-Luddism case studies and neo-Luddism elements

Neo-Luddism case studies	*Neo-Luddism elements*			
		The digitalization as a target	*The resistance as an everyday act*	*The paradox of technology*
	Digital detoxing of Chiara Ferragni	*Shutting off Instagram for a day*	*Digital detox for the wellness of the mind*	*Dropping out from Instagram to confirm the importance of Instagram*
	The attack on YouTube by Nasim Aghdam	*YouTube as a social and economic framework*	*Fighting against YouTube "discrimination"*	*YouTube attacks from a YouTuber*
	The A-level grading fiasco	*The algorithm as a solution to the pandemic situation of the schools*	*The formation of a critical audience*	*Solving the technology problems improving technology accountability*

5. Conclusion

Nowadays, the rise of a neo-Luddite culture is not surprising as the contemporary digital society is embedded in a social environment where it is possible to find a great number of technologies that are digital but also biotechnological (Castells, 1996). However, the reason why this culture is rising is much more difficult to understand. Technology and innovations improved our life. For instance, it is very hard to imagine facing the coronavirus pandemic without digital social connection technologies (such as social media and streaming platforms) global logistic companies (e.g., online markets), and without global scientific institutions and research communities (World Health Organization). Despite the technological improvements, the rising of a technological attitude against technology is symptomatic of the existential distress of people who hardly adapt to a fast-growing technology. Even in this case, this is a political problem. During the industrial revolution Luddite had to fight against technological unemployment, while in digital society the neo-Luddite have to fight against the obsolescence of humanity.

Is it possible to create a balance between technology and society? Yes, but politics should not allow for an uncontrolled technology expansion and should not use social legitimisation discourses (e.g., the importance of innovation as a value in itself, or the idea that of all contemporary problems can be solved with the technological progress). There are many signals of a widespread controversial neo-Luddite culture such as anti-vaccination movements, 5G resistance groups and anti-mask movements. All these post-global movements share the same worldview that involves irrational technology rejection, community-building based on social media, a skeptical attitude towards reality based on fake news, and conspiracy theories. In the next years, these problems will grow if we do not witness a global political response. Otherwise, it is not hard to imagine the rising of a violent reaction against technology (e.g., the Nasim Aghdam case study). Neo-Luddism can be currently defined as a self-exclusion attitude towards a shared optimistic vision of technology; but in the future it is possible to imagine the rising of anti-modernity parties that will take to the extremes the same worldview of the first ecology political party of the '70s. This anti-technology culture will have different forms such as technology critical attitudes, technology rejection, technophobia and neo-Luddism. However, since technology will have a growing and important role in the structure of the forthcoming society, it is impossible to think that we will not face these problems in the near future.

References

Adorno, Th. W., & Horkheimer, M. (1947). *Dialectic of Enlightenment*. Stanford: Stanford University Press.

Beck, U. (1992). *Risk Society*. London: SAGE.

Bennato, D. (2010). La circolazione delle tecnologie. In *XXI Secolo, volume: L'Universo Fisico* (pp. 577–586). Roma: Istituto dell'Enciclopedia Italiana Giovanni Treccani.

Bostrom, N. (2005). A History of Transhumanist Thought. *Journal of Evolution and Technology*, 14(1), 1–25.

Castells, M. (1996). *The Rise of the Network Society*. New York: John Wiley and Sons.

Diamond, J. (1997). *Guns, Germs, and Steel. The Fates of Human Societies*. New York: W. W. Norton.

Ellul, J. (1950). *The Technological Society*. New York: Knopf.

Feenberg, A. (1999). *Questioning Technology*. London: Routledge.

Foucault, M. (1975). *Discipline and Punish: The Birth of the Prison*. New York: Vintage.

Fox, N. (2002). *Against the Machine. The Hidden Luddite Tradition in Literature, Art, and Individual Life*. Washington: Island Press.

Frobish, T. (2002). Neo-Luddites and Their Rhetorical Paradox. *Peace Review*, 14, 207–15.

Harari, Y. N. (2016). *Homo Deus: A Brief History of Tomorrow*. New York: Random House.

Haraway, D. (1985). A Manifesto for Cyborgs. Science, Technology and Socialist Feminism in the 1980's, *Socialist Review*, 15(80), 65–107.

Jones, S. E. (2006). *Against Technology. From the Luddites to Neo Luddism*. Routledge: New York.

Jorge, A. (2019). Social Media, Interrupted: Users Recounting Temporary Disconnection on Instagram. *Social Media+ Society*, 5(4), 1–19.

Kolkman, D. (2020, August, 26). 'F**k the algorithm'?: What the World Can Learn from the UK's A-Level Grading Fiasco. *Impact of Social Sciences*. Retrieved September 5, 2023 from https://blogs.lse.ac.uk/impactofsocialsciences/2020/08/26/fk-the-algorithm-what-the-world-can-learn-from-the-uks-a-level-grading-fiasco/

Kumar, S. (2019). The Algorithmic Dance: YouTube's Adpocalypse and the Gatekeeping of Cultural Content on Digital Platforms. *Internet Policy Review*, 8(2), 1–21.

Landes, D. S. (1969). *The Unbound Prometheus: Technological Change and Development in Western Europe from 1750 to the Present*. Cambridge: Cambridge University Press.

Lynas. M. (2007). *Six Degrees: Our Future on a Hotter Planet*. New York: Harper & Collins.

Lyotard, J. F. (1979). *The Postmodern Condition: A Report on Knowledge*. Minneapolis: University of Minnesota Press.

Morozov, E. (2013). *To Save Everything, Click Here: Technology, Solutionism, and the Urge to Fix Problems That Don't Exist*. London: Penguin.

Mumford, L. (1934). *Technics and Civilizations*. London: Harcourt Brace & Company.

Ong, W. J. (1982). *Orality and Literacy: The Technologizing of the Word*. London: Routledge.

Pacey, A. (1983). *The Culture of Technology*. Cambridge: MIT Press.

Pollock, F. (1956). *Automation: A Study of Its Economic and Social Consequences*. New York: Frederick A. Praeger.

Postman, N. (1992). *Technopoly: The Surrender of Culture to Technology*. New York: Vintage.

Ricoeur, P. (1965). *Freud and Philosophy: An Essay on Interpretation*. New Haven: Yale University Press.

Rossi, P. (1962). *Philosophy, Technology, and the Arts in the Early Modern Era*. New York: Harper & Row.

Roszak, T. (1986). *The Cult of Information: A Neo-Luddite Treatise on High Tech, Artificial Intelligence, and the True Art of Thinking*. Berkeley: University of California Press.

Roszak, Th. (1994). *The Cult of Information. A Neo-Luddite Treatise on High-Tech, Artificial Intelligence, and the True Art of Thinking* (2nd ed.). Berkeley: California University Press.

Sale, K. (1995). *Rebels Against the Future. The Luddites and Their War on the Industrial Revolution: Lessons for the Computer Age*. Reading: Addison-Wesley.

Salvatori, L., & Villi, C. (1987). *Il Luddismo. L'enigma di una rivolta*. Roma: Editori Riuniti.

Senft, T. M. (2008). *Camgirls: Celebrity & Community in the Age of Social Networks*. New York: Peter Lang.

Syvertsen, T., & Enli, G. (2019). Digital Detox: Media Resistance and the Promise of Authenticity. *Convergence*, 26(5–6), 1269–1283.

Tiso, G. (2013). 'The net will save us': Political Solutionism and the Five Star Movement. *Overland*, 211, 55–60.

Zuboff, S. (2019). *The Age of Surveillance Capitalism*. New York: Public Affairs.

Alessandra Micalizzi

SAE Institute; Universita telematica Pegaso, Italy

alessandra.micalizzi@unipegaso.it

Chapter 5 Veg-eaters: Lexical labels and inclusion/exclusion perspective in Italy

Abstract: Chapter 5 provides evidence that nowadays personal and social identity is increasingly defined by dietary choices ("we are what we don't eat"). The paper analyses a corpus of narratives coming from vegetarian and vegan Italians, together with some online conversations collected in some famous Italian food-blogs. The results show that especially junior vegs underline the presence of social barriers in maintaining their diet, suggesting interesting dynamics of inclusion/exclusion among veg-people with a neat difference (in perception, practices and languages) between vegetarians and vegans.

Keywords: Food blogs, narratives, vegetarian, vegan, identity

1. Culture, food and languages

When we think about the forms in which a culture finds its expression, we have to consider the dietary choices, too, and the way in which they are transmitted, communicated and labelled. As De Backer and Fisher (2019, p. 2) suggested in their recent work:

> The decision of whether to eat or not to eat meat is never an individual process. The decision may be very personal but the consequences will filter through different layers of social processes. What we eat is inherently connected to our personal identity, as well as our group identity.

This chapter will focus on the veggie world in Italian culture. Our aim is to identify how and if the digital discourse about vegetarian and vegan food, and their communities, has been affecting the social representation of veggie-eaters in their own perception, in order to identify linguistic and cultural borders among the communities of vegetarians, vegans and omnivores.

In the following pages we shall present a sociocultural overview of the veggie world and a description of the role of digital platforms as online sociocultural contexts where people can share and co-construct social representations (Boccia Artieri, 2013; boyd, 2008, 2013). After this premise, we shall focus our attention on presenting the methodological design of the research and its main results, which demonstrate the presence of two opposing trends: on the one hand, the so-called *echo chamber* (advocated by, among others, Del Vicario et. al., 2016) contributes to structure and reinforces the distance and the borders among supporters of opposing positions; on the other hand, a positive use of digital spaces helps to spread information and tolerance of other visions of the world that can then contribute to reducing the distance and weakening both linguistic and behavioural boundaries (Konrad et.al., 2018) among users (boyd, 2008).

Before focusing on the main results of our research, we would like to give an overview of the sociocultural and sociolinguistic implications of the recent spread of veggie choices among Italian consumers. In fact, dietary choice is not simply a way of eating but an art of living, strictly linked to culture and tradition. As Feuerbach suggested in 1870, "we are what we eat", which means that food preferences include a mix of values, expectations, and emotions. Nowadays, personal and social identity is increasingly defined by dietary choices. For this reason, the original claim can be changed to "we are what we don't eat": excluding some foods is a way of asserting and communicating aspects of ourselves (Rosenfield & Burrow, 2017).

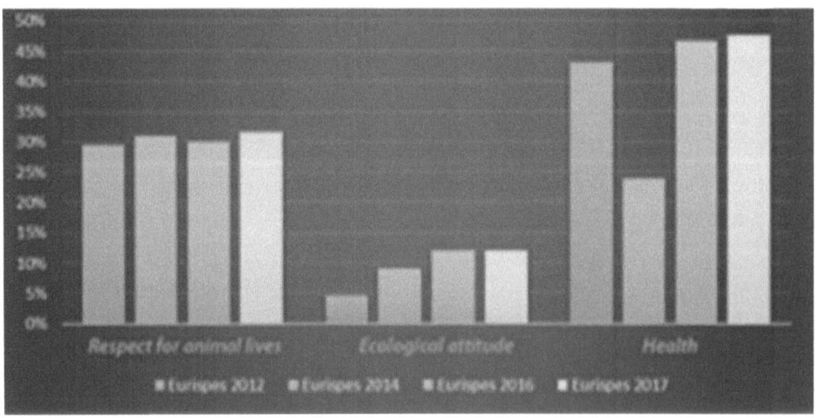

Figure 5.1. Motivations for choosing a veggie-diet

According to this approach, Rosenfeld and Burrow (2017) introduced the concept of "vegetarian identity" to underline the close relationship between plant-based food choices and identity. However, are we sure that it is so simple to label and tell a meat-eater from other types of eaters?

Recent Eurispes (Institute for Political, Social and Economic studies, 2018) data show that the first distinction to make is defining "veg-eaters". Is it actually being a veg-eater or simply behaving like one? More specifically, the market of veggie food has been increasing drastically in the last few years with growth in double-digit percentages (Piccoli, 2018).

More information about the consequences of a healthy diet, more attention to the environmental impact of some food production and more sensitivity to animal rights are the main reasons that push people to adopt veggie food into their diets (see Figure 5.1; Eurispes, 2018). The enhancing of prepared plant-based food, the spreading of information and the introduction of veggie alternatives to the mainstream market also contribute to changing consumer behaviour, even if the number of self-described vegans or vegetarians is still a low percentage of the Italian population.

It is interesting to note that a new label has appeared for people who describe plant-based food as their prevalent choice but not the exclusive one – the so-called "flexitarians" (Santini, 2018). According to the linguistic perspective (Rorty, 1999; Konrad et al., 2018), the new label, introduced by the American Dialect Association in 2003, signaled an important turn in the classic antagonism between meat-eaters and veg-eaters.

In 2016, according to Eurispes, 40 % of the Italian population indicated they preferred vegetarian dishes; however, in 2020 the percentage of people who recognise themselves as veg-eaters is still under 8 % (Figure 5.2). If we compare the vegetarian population in Italy across the last six years, we notice that the percentage remains approximatively the same, with an unstable trend for the vegans.

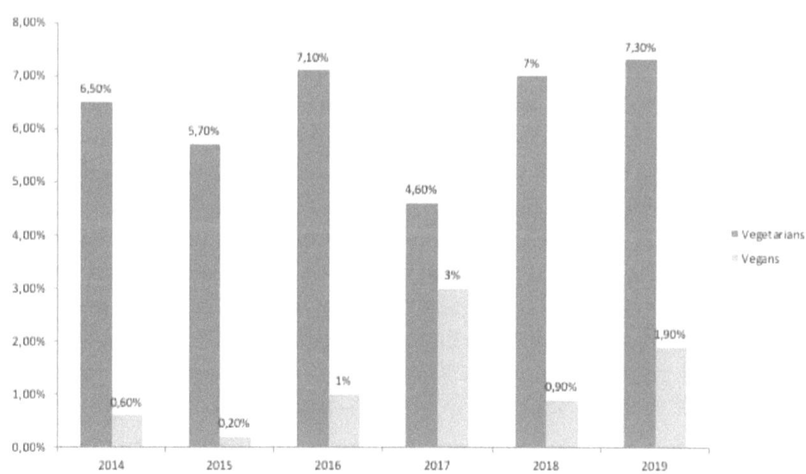

Figure 5.2. The number of vegetarians in Italy from 2014 to 2020

As already mentioned, declaring oneself as part of the veg-eaters community has cultural implications. What is important to highlight in this chapter is the fact that the birth of new words (such as "flexitarians" and others we will show below) is evidence that the borders between meat-eaters and veg-eaters are less strong than we may think. Moreover, this evidence shows that there are at least three hierarchic levels of involvement in vegetarianism/veganism (Figure 5.3) (Micalizzi, 2019).

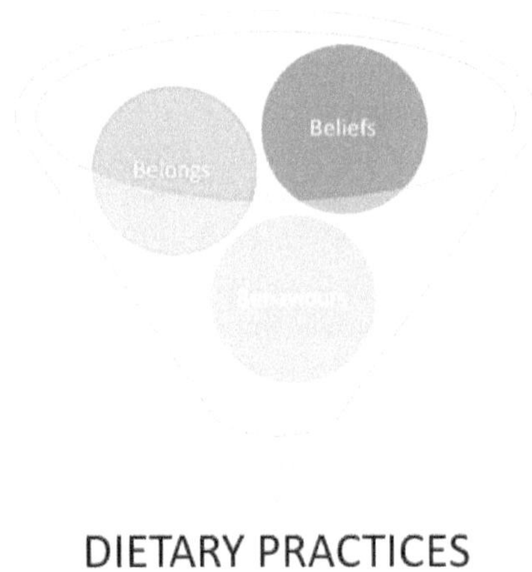

Figure 5.3. The three main levels of Veg-Ideology

The first one, as shown by the high percentage described above, is the level of *behaviours*. Pushed by several not-very-strong reasons, a high percentage of people has discovered that veggie-food is good for one's health and the environment, and therefore they act as if they were vegetarians, united only by their behaviours but not meeting completely the ideology behind it.

The second level is *belonging*. Some groups of people desire to be part of the group of veg-eaters, but they need new labels to define their food choices. Figure 5.4, inspired by a recent article (Schiavazzi, 2015) describes the variety of ways in which people tend to adhere to a veggie diet. The same figure is the expression of *border language*, as Konrad et al. (2018) suggested, inside the community of people who choose to adhere to a plant-based diet.

Figure 5.4. The variety of ways of 'Feeling like Veg-Eaters'

There are four types of veg-eaters: (a) *ovo-lacto vegetarians*, who exclude meat and fish but include eggs, milk and other animal (non-meat) derivatives in their diet; (b) *lacto-vegetarians*, who exclude meat, fish and eggs but consume milk and food with milk as ingredients; (c) *ovo-vegetarians*, who exclude milk but include eggs in their vegetarian diets; and (d) *vegans*, who eat only vegetables and cereals.

Finally, the last level is the one made up of *beliefs*. In that case, choosing to eat only plant-based food is a lifestyle, a new way of thinking about personal consumption in general, and not limited to food choices. As we shall see, this community is less numerous yet more active, especially on the web. This is the population that considers part of their behaviours to be related to evangelisation about the condition of animals, respect for the environment and a drastic change in the collective lifestyle of Western culture.[1]

1 On 23 July 2020 in Milan, there was a flash mob organised by Anonymous for Voiceless and shared by social networks aimed at increasing the awareness about the condition of animals in intensive breeding. For more information, consult https://it-it.facebook.com/anonymousforthevoiceless/

2. Social media and food discourses

The penetration of social media in our everyday lives represents a crucial aspect in the debate about the construction of public opinions (Boccia Artieri et al., 2018; Castells, 2000; boyd, 2010) and of social media representations (Moscovici, 1961). According to Moscovici, social representations are:

> almost tangible entities. They circulate, intersect and crystallize continuously, through a word, a gesture, or a meeting in our daily world.... They impregnate most of our established social relations, the objects we produce or consume, and the communications we exchange. (Moscovici, 1961, p. 40).

Thanks to digital interactive environments, the process of construction and sharing of social media representation is more rapid and more dynamic than in the past. Castells (2000) used to define our age as the one of the Networked societies. With this new label he wanted to identify the dominance of the technological paradigm according to the new digital spaces and tools; these "enhance and accelerate the production of knowledge and information, in a self-expanding, virtuous circle. Because information processing is at the source of life, and of social action, every domain of our eco-social system is thereby (continuously) transformed" (Castells, 2000, p. 15).

In other words, social media and other digital interactive spaces offer new sociocultural contexts where opinions are negotiated, giving visibility to non-dominant positions. Using Habermas's (1992b) words, we can define the new eco-social system as a *digital civil sphere* populated by networked publics (boyd, 2010) and creating a *networked public sphere* (Friedland & Rojas, 2006). Friedland and Rojas (2006) suggest that the Internet represents a secondary lifeworld, strictly linked with the primary one of socialisation, that interact with each other seamlessly, as the communicative and generative sociocultural flow are impossible to separate. The networked public sphere is both defined and constrained by network transformations in the three macrosystems that form the environment of the public sphere: the political system, functional systems, and civil society: "This new networked public sphere systematically increases communicative reflexivity at every level of communication, including the political system, civil society, and the lifeworld" (Friedand & Rojas, 2006, p. 18).

From this perspective, the internet can be considered as a sociotechnical context and not just a platform or a technical artefact (Boccia Artieri, 2013; Boccia Artieri et al., 2018). Moreover, De Carli (1996) argues that the narratives are the main unit of meaning in an online world: for this reason, he defined the Web as a *narrative meta-medium*.

Social network sites are increasingly inhabited spaces where people select information, construct an opinion, and show or perform social behaviours. The generative and shared process deals with language, too: social media are often the sociocultural contexts where new labels or words are coined.

However, besides the opportunity to find many points of view, there is also the possibility to select only the piece of information coherent with our own way of thinking, especially when the argument is controversial. If we look at polarising themes, such as food and dietary choices, the digital interactive media represent ideal spaces to enhance tribal food communication practices, thanks to the searchability of personalised information (boyd, 2008) and the indexing of contents according to users' profiles.

Colleoni et al. (2014) argue that the so-called *echo chamber effect* is due to a tendency of individuals to create homogeneous groups, where there is no space for a debate. In other words, the online social networks might elicit the aggregation of individuals in communities of interest, in which the opinions are coherent and polarized, generating a confirmation bias (Vicario et al., 2016).

In this complex sociocultural scenario, it is interesting to inquire how and if online discourse can orient and change the shared social representations of veggie-eaters in some ways, inside and outside of this specific community, and how they can be marked by labels or linguistic choices.

In the next pages we shall present the design of our research project and a partial analysis of data, integrating the points of view of veggie-eaters inside and outside the digital environments. We know that the discussion is not exhaustive because of its dynamicity and its recent relevance among the civil sphere. However, we hope that the present work can be considered a first milestone, from which may develop wider and more systematic research by increasing the number of interviewees and integrating quantitative tools.

3. Framework and methodologies

Starting from these premises, we conducted empirical research in order to understand the online and offline linguistic borders among veg and not-only-veg-eaters, with the specific point of view of vegetarians and vegans. More specifically, we aimed to describe and analyse:

(a) the sociocultural implications in practices and communication on and offline of veggie-world, and;
(b) how veggies perceive and "label" themselves in a world of meat-eaters, and which is the projected image they perceive of themselves.

We integrated traditional methods with online ones. We carried out 15 narrative in-depth interviews with veg-eaters, selecting both vegetarians and vegans. In addition, we conducted a desk analysis of the main online blogs and interactive sites about veggie topics, using Google, to identify the most active online communities. Finally, we carried out a netnography (Kazinetz, 2019) of about six months in some Italian participative online communities on Facebook. Specifically, we focused our attention on the official page of the *VeganOK* network and of *Il vegano imbruttito* (created and managed by Giorgio Immesi). We focused our attention on the linguistic aspects linked with the self-perception and the self-representation of vegetarians and vegans, inside and outside the community, to explore the linguistic borders (Konrad et al., 2018).

The sample of interviewees included six men (four vegetarians and two vegans) and nine women (five vegetarians and four vegans); altogether there were six vegans and nine vegetarians, The age was variable, ranging from 24 to 62. We identified two categories: the *senior veg-eaters*, who are older and have been vegetarians or vegans for more than 10 years, and the *junior ones*, who have less than 10 years of experience in the veg world and in general are young people who depend on another member of the family to cook.

4. Veggie discourses and their borders: The main results

In order to identify the borders of veggie conversations, we started our field work with a desk analysis of the main results on social media platforms and search engines, using the keywords "vegan*" and "vegetarian*". The results were interesting: we found above all blogs and news websites (digital magazines) focused on cooking veggie food and providing information to spread vegan and vegetarian choices.

The first type of digital context is open-accessed and focused on the author and serves as a testimonial of healthy and good cooking. The second type is made up of both closed and open pages, profiles or groups where users present and discuss more ideological topics. Even in this simple dichotomy the discourse borders are really weak because often, within a recipe, there are ideological positions that open up a debate in the comment section of the page. Or, on the contrary, in ideological groups there is space for information or news about veggie topics reported in mainstream channels.

Using the veg ideology classification (Figure 5.3), we can classify the contents and the relations among the levels in online conversation. More specifically, we distinguished three types of borders: (a) *fragmented borders*; (b) *rigid borders*; and (c) *labile borders*.

Fragmented borders are typically internal borders inside the groups of people who are ideologically involved in their food choices. These borders create subgroups about one specific aspect of veggie beliefs. For instance, one example is offered by the debate whether to eat the so-called "fake burger", a veggie burger tasting of meat, or not, a debate that started on the official page of *Il vegano imbruttito* on Facebook. The community is split between those who support the importance of experiencing the taste of meat, because vegans and vegetarians have positive memories of their childhood linked with that flavour, and those who consider this consumption a hypocritical choice. The owner of this Facebook page and the channel affirmed in an interview that "the problems of vegans are the vegans".

Rigid borders are the those of "in-or-out" communities. In digital discourse these are evident when influencers focus their posts on shameful behaviours of those who have chosen a plant-based diet. Recently, one of the most active figures in the VeganOK community, Renata Balducci, published an angry post about the "false vegan" ("Abbasso I falsi vegan"). One of her followers commented: "I don't like labels. I simply eat natural. Nothing that derives from exploitation and suffering. My foods are alive, colourful, full of energy. I tend not to use stoves. I especially love the fruit". But this post didn't please someone else: "The vegan choice is a leap into the void: once you take the run and jump … it is impossible to go back uI.. If you go back up it's simply because you never made the jump after the run. This is to say that steps back for vegans do not exist".

The influencer's answer to the first comment underlines the rigidity of the borders: "It doesn't depend on labels. It's something that you feel inside".

Finally, we have the labile borders, which are visible in discourse about behaviours. When people share information about what they eat, buy, or simply taste, the affirmation of a veggie identity (Rosenfield & Burrow, 2017) is less strong, and the semantic borders are more flexible.

Using a narrative perspective (De Carli, 1996), we tried to classify the digital narratives according to the aims of the posts. We identified three main types:

(1) *The representative narratives* (e.g., official Facebook pages) aim at constructing a shared narration according to the values and philosophy of veggie-people. They are shared to reinforce, consciously, the reputation.
(2) *Evangelic narratives* (e.g., pages linked with the dietary choices of stars or famous people) aim at promoting the veggie lifestyle. These are part of a content marketing strategy, to enhance the number of people aware of vegan and vegetarian ideology.

(3) *Street narratives* (e.g., peer-to-peer groups, blogs, YouTube comments) are above all spontaneous conversations of everyday veggie-life (how to cook new recipes, direct opinions, sometimes flaming, etc.). In this case the focus is on the practices, and the goal is less explicit. However, the effect is clear: arousing curiosity and attracting the attention of readers.

The in-depth interviews helped us to analyse the process of conversion into a vegan or vegetarian, the main difficulties and barriers met and the role of labels in constructing a self-perception as a part of veggie world. We also explored the borders inside the veggie-community where the distinction between vegans and vegetarians is really clear, more than we expected.

First of all, the decision to change their dietary choices is often linked to a particular episode that generated a drastic end of eating meat. Sauro (55 years old, vegan) pointed out:

> I remember the exact moment that I decided never to eat meat again or any kind of food coming from the exploitation of animals. We were sitting at the table. We were watching the news when the anchorman started to talk about the fur industry and some actions by animalists against it.

At the same time, the conversion to plant-based food is often the result of a social process that involves two main figures: the beginner and/or the mediator. The beginner is someone who has made his/her own decision to change diets, excluding meat, without any external invitations. S/he has had to fight against prejudice and represents a model for others. In some cases, they are public figures, such as in the case of Mara (40 years old, vegetarian), who confessed to becoming vegetarian after her favourite singer made this decision. The mediator is someone close to the interviewees who helps them to relate to omnivores. S/he is a person with a moderate position and open minded, with an inclusive attitude. Sometimes s/he is a member of the family, like in the case of Giuseppe (24 years old, vegan), who used his mother to communicate his choice to his father, who was totally opposed:

> It was hard to explain my choice to my father. For him, it is inconceivable to eat only plant-based food, especially for a sportsman. He said it was stupid and unhealthy.… Nowadays, even though he hasn't accepted it yet, he respects my diet.

The sociocultural barriers are experienced above all in social relations with people with whom vegans and vegetarians share their everyday life, and they are shaped by language too. Most of our interviewees pointed out that they often have to justify their choices with long discussions about the healthiness of a plant-based diet. In addition, they affirmed the existence of negative labels to identify vegans (more than vegetarians): "I hear some people call me a "grass-eater".... They think that my diet is unhealthy. Instead, from the beginning, I started to feel better – lighter and more energetic" (Eleonora, 43, vegan).

The page *Il vegano imbruttito* was born with the idea to overcome the shared narration among vegans to be discriminated and viewed by omnivores as weird creatures, according to us with a fair success in intervening on the peripherical part of the social representation.

More surprisingly, we discovered that there are prejudices by vegans towards vegetarians and vice versa. More specifically, interviews highlighted the existence of some borders inside the veggie community, based on deep values. Vegetarians look at vegans in an aspirational way; they are the point of arrival of a path that is hard to complete:

> I would like to be vegan but it's hard, especially when you have to share your choice with others. I'm a little bit disappointed because some vegans consider me hypocritical and inconsistent. I know perfectly well that the vegan community blames vegetarians, considering them more inconsistent than omnivores. (Serena, 35 years old, vegetarian)

The vegan choice represents an expression of deep values and respect for nature, the environment, and animals, a fully coherent ethical choice. Vegans are harsher with vegetarians than with omnivores. They consider the former as incomplete: they are aware of the risks for the environment and the suffering of animals caused by a meat-based diet, but they are not able to complete the passage. Vegetarians, in the vegans' perception, continue to stay in the middle ground, not respecting their values and not changing the situation.

Vegans, more than vegetarians, underlined the importance of coherence in respecting the principle of equality among living species. Being veg means more than choosing a plant-based diet. It involves several aspects of everyday life, such as mobility, choice of clothing, use of water, and so forth. Their behaviour becomes a way to show that the conversion is possible and easy. Thus, being inflexible is fundamental to "evangelising"; as a consequence, the tiniest exception is not forgiven. Sauro said "It is important to say I'm vegan; however, I don't consider it a divisive label".

Omnivores, on the other hand, are viewed as ingenuous, ignorant (in its literal meaning), people who need to beevangelised. At the same time, the borders between the veggie and meat worlds become barriers when faced with a request for flexibility: interviewees show their morality by keeping a distance when asked to "make an exception" by omnivores, especially during convivial situations shared by friends or relatives.

5. Conclusion

As the discussion of findings as shown, the choice of foods is more than something limited to nutrition: it is an important dimension of one's identity. There are several implications in being "veg"; the adhesion to a specific group defines – more in the perception of others – an invisible space of (conversational) conflict. Social network platforms and other digital interactive spaces, such as blogs, represent new sociocultural contexts in which to share and negotiate aspects of the veggie identity.

On the one hand, we can see an attempt by vegetarians and, above all, by vegans to be more inclusive toward the rest of the world, using the Internet to construct their reputation and a positive social representation linked with attention to health, nature, and the lives of animals. On the other hand, the Web becomes the space for emancipation and legitimation of veggie battles, for which they revendicate the important role played by a strict adherence to their model.

Moreover, the analysis of data has shown interesting dynamics of inclusion/exclusion among veg people with a neat difference in perception, practices, and language use between vegetarians and vegans, with significant perceptive barriers among them. Borders (the fragmented ones described above) are linguistically visible among the same community when the digital discourse tends to touch *choices* that mark a "contamination" of beliefs, sense of belonging or behaviours with the omnivore world. In the previous pages, we mentioned the case of fake burgers, plant-based food tasting of meat.

Finally, the results show how the process of "being veg" involves several aspects of everyday life in one's dealings with others. In particular, junior vegs stress the presence of social barriers in maintaining their diet, especially inside the family but also in peer groups and in social network contexts.

Irony could be a good solution to mediate the debate and reduce the rigid borders: *Il vegano imbruttito* is a good example. Starting from the social representation of veggie people in the eyes of omnivores, the author has been to able present an authentic point of view on vegans and their ideology.

References

Boccia Artieri, G. (2012). *Stati di connessione. Pubblici, cittadini e consumatori nella (social) Network Society*. Milano: FrancoAngeli.

Boccia Artieri, G., Gemini, L., Pasquali, L., Carlo, S., Farci, M., & Pedroni, M. (2018). *Fenomenologia dei social network. Presenza, relazioni e consumi mediali degli italiani online*. Milano: Guerini.

boyd, d. (2008). Social Network Sites: Definition, History, and Scholarship. *Journal of Computer-Mediated Communication*, 13, 210–230.

boyd, d. (2010). *Social Network Sites as Networked Publics: Affordances, Dynamics, and Implications*. In Z. Paracharissi (Ed.), *Networked Self: Identity, Community, and Culture on Social Network Sites* (pp. 39–58). London: Routledge.

Brown, R., & Kulik, J. (1977). Flashbulb Memories. *Cognition*. 5(1), 73–99.

Castells, M. (2000). Materials for an Exploratory Theory of the Network Society. *British Journal of Sociology* 51(1), 5–24.

Colleoni, E., Rozza, A., & Ardivvson, A. (2014). Echo Chamber or Public Sphere? Predicting Political Orientation and Measuring Political Homophily in Twitter Using Big Data. *Journal of Communication*, 64, 317–332.

De Backer, C., & Fisher, M. (2019). Introduction. In C. De Backer, M. L. Fisher, J. Dare, & L. Costello (Eds.), *To Eat or Not to Eat Meat. How Vegetariana Dietary Choices Influence Our Social Lives* (pp. 1–39). London: Rowan Littlefield.

De Backer, C., Fisher, M. L., cDare, J., & Costello, L. (Eds.). (2019). *To Eat or Not to Eat Meat. How Vegetarian Dietary Choices Influence Our Social Lives*. London: Rowan Littlefield.

De Carli, L. (1997). *Internet, memoria e oblio*. Bollati Boringhieri: Milano.

Del Vicario, M., Vivaldo, G., & Bessi, A. et al. (2016). Echo Chambers: Emotional Contagion and Group Polarization on Facebook. *Scientific Reports*, 6, 37825.

Douglas, M. (1987). *Antropologia e Simbolismo. Cibo e denaro nella vita sociale*. Bologna: Il Mulino.

Eurispes. (2018). *Rapporto Italia 2018*. Retrieved September 5, 2023 from http://www.eurispes.eu/content/eurispes-rapporto-italia-2018-vegani-e-vegetariani-sono-il-7-della-popolazione-dai-18-anni

Eurispes. (2019). *Vegetariani e vegani. Le nuove diete si consolidano*. Rapportotereoe Eurispes 2019 – Retrieved September 5, 2023 from https://eurispes.eu/rapporto-italia-2019-vegetariani-e-vegani-le-nuove-diete-si-consolidano/

Fox, N., & Ward, K. (2008). Health, Ethics and Environment: A Qualitative Study of Vegetarian Motivations. *Appetite* 50, 422–429.

Friedland, L. A., & Rojas, T. H. H. (2006). The Networked Public Sphere. *Javonst the Public*, 13(4), 5–26.

Gorter, D. (2018). Methods and Techniques for Linguistic Landscape Research: About Definitions, Core Issues and Technological Innovations. In: M. Pütz, & N. Mundt (Eds.), *Expanding the Linguistic Landscape: Multilingualism, Language Policy and the Use of Space as a Semiotic Resource* (pp. 38–57). Bristol: Multilingual Matters.

Habermas, Jürgen. (1992a). Further Re-ections on the Public Sphere. T. Burger trans. In C. Calhoun (Ed.), *Habermas and the Public Sphere* (pp. 421–461). Cambridge: MIT Press.

Habermas, Jürgen. (1992b). *Between Facts and Norms* (1996 ed.). W. Rehg trans. Cambridge: MIT Press.

Hall, Jemineson K., & Cappella J. (2008). *Echo Chamber: Rush Limbaugh and the Conservative Media Establishment.* New York: Oxford University Press.

Jedlowski, P. (2005). *Un giorno dopo l'altro. La vita quotidiana tra esperienza e routine.* Bologna: il Mulino.

Kazinetz, R. (2019). *Netnography: The Essential Guide to Qualitative Social Media Research* (3rd ed.). London: SAGE.

Konrad, V., Laine, J. P., Liikanen, I., Scott, J. W., & Widdis, R. (2018). The Language of Borders. In: S. Brunn, R. Kehrein (Eds.), *Handbook of the Changing World Language Map* (pp. 2175–2191) Dordrecht: Springer.

Liao, V., & Fu, W.-H. (2014). Can You Hear Me Now? Mitigating the Echo Chamber Effect by Source Position Indicators. In *CSCW '14: Proceedings of the 17th ACM Conference on Computer Supported Cooperative Work & Social Computing* (pp. 184–196). New York: Association for Computing Machinery.

Mannucci, E. J. (2011). *La cena di Pitagora. Storia del vegetartianismo dall'antica Grecia a Internet.* Roma: Carocci Editore.

Micalizzi, A. (2019). Fond of Veg-Food: Tradition, Transition, Transformation. In C. De Backer, M. L. Fisher, C. Dare & J. L. Costello (Eds.), *To Eat or Not to Eat Meat. How Vegetarian Dietary Choices Influence Our Social Lives* (pp. 129–137). London: Rowan Littlefield.

Moscovici, S. (1961). *Social Representations: Explorations in Social Psychology* (Engl. Ed. 2001). New York: New York University Press.

Niola, M. (2015). *Homo dieteticus. Viaggio nelle tribù alimentari.* Bologna: il Mulino.

Piccoli, M. (2018, November 26). Vegani, carnivori e onnivori: il futuro dell'alimentazione spiegato con i numeri, *Il Sole24Ore*. Retrieved September 5, 2023 from https://www.infodata.ilsole24ore.com/2018/11/26/vegani-carnivori-e-onnivori-i-trend-alimentari-spiegati-con-i-numeri/.

Roby, R. (2012). Vegetarianism: A Blossoming Field of Study. *Appetite*, 58, 141–150.

Rosenfield, D. L., & Burrow, A. L. (2017). The Unified Model of Vegetarian Identity: A Conceptual Framework for Understanding Plant-Based Food Choices. *Appetite*, 112, 78–95.

Santini, P. (2018, October 11). Perché la dieta flexitariana è il trend alimentare che cambierà il nostro modo di mangiare? *Elle.it*. Retrieved September 5, 2023 from https://www.elle.com/it/salute/diete/a23595271/dieta-flexitariana-cos-e/

Schiavazzi, V. (2015, September 17). Addio carne e pesce: in aumento il popolo dei vegetariani e vegani in Italia, *La Repubblica*. Retrieved September 5, 2023 from http://www.repubblica.it/cronaca/2015/09/17/news/il_popolo_dei_vegetariani_e_vegani_in_italia_l_infografica-123063811/.

Torriani, L. (2017, February 6). Vegetariani e vegani. Quanti sono in Italia? *Universefood*. Retrieved September 5, 2023 from http://www.universofood.net/2017/02/06/vegetariani-e-vegani-quanti-in-italia/

Paolo Donadio

University of Naples Federico II, Italy

paolo.donadio@unina.it

Chapter 6 Migrants storytelling: An intercultural perspective

Abstract: Narratives are a valuable source when it comes to exclusion. Specifically, this chapter investigates the construction of migrants' identity through spontaneous narration of migration experiences and cultural clashes. During the conversation, multiple identities are constructed for themselves and the "characters" of their story.

Keywords: Narratives, storytelling, migrants, identity

Introduction

Every time we listen to a story, the analysis of discourse is crucial to understand the way in which speaker's subjectivity can be revealed. The category of discourse is assumed as essential to the construction of identity, and not merely a rhetorical frame (Fairclough, 1989). Therefore, any type of transition from a country/culture to another is always to be considered as a *discourse in progress* process, which involves an ongoing redefinition of the self in the relationship between the community of departure and the community of arrival, the land of origin and the chosen destination.

Migrants' experiences are often constructed through stories. The story temporarily embodies a state of mind or a condition, and creates an emotional involvement that drives the subject to reduce his/her control over discourse (Labov, 1972). Any first-person oral narrative, and its temporal sequence of events, allows us to grasp the appearance of a subjectivity that could hardly be detected through more traditional instruments of investigation, such as the questionnaire or the structured interview (see De Fina, 2003). In this sense, language forms may determine the positioning of the self interacting with the interlocutor, the other story "characters" and each one's respective culture (Harré & van Langenhove, 1998). According to Harré (2004):

> Language is the prime instrument of thought social action. In following up the line of argument of the discussion so far, we must abandon a widely held presupposition of much psychological research, namely the stability and transpersonal intelligibility of

language. In so far as there are psychologically significant varieties of language, so there are other dimensions of multiplicity of selves (Harré, 2004).

The aim of this contribution is to investigate the identity construction of the subject through the narration of one's own experience *as a migrant*. Through narratives, we will try to highlight the discursive categories that signal the positioning of the self in relation to the cultural frame (Lakoff, 1987) of the so-called "migrant", and its network of assumptions and stereotypes. We will attempt to demonstrate that the analysis of some discourse features is crucial to see how the subject dynamically constructs multiple identities for himself/herself. We will see that successful integration goes beyond cultural boundaries and depends both on the possibilities to have access to the host culture and migrants' willingness to accept to meet and interact with the host culture.

2. Corpus

The qualitative analysis was possible thanks to 15 interviews, collected in 2014, with migrants living in Italy (Naples) for over 9 years and speaking Italian as a second language. As we can see in the Table 6.1 below, the number of interviees – Senegal (3 interviewees), Ukraine (6 interviewees), Sri Lanka (6 interviewes) – reflects the presence of these communities in the city of Naples, where one out of four immigrants comes from Ukraine (23,2 %), and one out of six is from Sri Lanka (14,6 %), according to a 2019 report by the Italian Ministry of Employment.[1]

Table 6.1. Biographical information about the informants

	Informant	**Age**	**Country**	**Yrs. in Italy**	**Job**
1	Yuri	36	Ukraine	9	Waiter
2	Olga	54	Ukraine	14	Caretaker
3	Stella	39	Ukraine	14	Caretaker
4	Lesia	40	Ukraine	14	Caretaker
5	Alina	36	Ukraine	13	Shop owner
6	Natalia	55	Ukraine	9	Colf
7	Susante	35	Sri Lanka	15	Colf
8	Suril	44	Sri Lanka	12	Colf

1 https://www.lavoro.gov.it/documenti-e-norme/studi-estatistiche/Documents/La%20presenza%20dei%20migranti%20nelle%20aree%20metropolitane,%20anno%202019/RAM-2019-Napoli.pdf

Table 6.1. Continued

	Informant	Age	Country	Yrs. in Italy	Job
9	Susanda	46	Sri Lanka	9	Healthcare worker
10	Sanjeed	37	Sri Lanka	10	Colf
11	Marion	37	Sri Lanka	18	Housewife
12	Tani	23	Sri Lanka	18	Student
13	Amadu	42	Senegal	15	Accountant
14	Ammad	36	Senegal	11	Cultural mediator
15	Pierre	42	Senegal	15	Employee

The interviews, which lasted about one hour, were all planned to get uniform and comparable data, but, at the same time, leave room for the interviewee to speak freely, without being bound to a specific length of the reply. This increased the informal nature of the interview, and the empathy between interviewer and interviewee. The ongoing definition and redefinition of the self would not be discernible through statistical surveys or questionnaires.

3. Theory and methods

Within the vast literature on the theme of "narration and identity", which has interested scholars and disciplines of different orientat–ons – anthropology (Lèvi Strauss, 1963), ethnography (Hymes, 1981), psychology (Rosenwald & Ochberg, 1992), just to name a–few – we will use some methodological ideas from a fieldwork conducted by Anna de Fina (2003) with Mexican immigrants in the United States. The main objective, as in our case, is the detailed reading of migrants' stories in order to elicit their attitude to the host culture:

> To what extent do narrators emphasize their role as individual protagonists within story worlds? Do they stress the *personal* or the *social* meaning of story world actions in which they are involved? An analysis of these levels of representation of the self can throw light on implicit views on the role of *individual* versus the *collectivity* that can in turn be explained resorting to general cultural expectations and/or to the specific social circumstances that the immigrants live (De Fina, 2003, p. 51; italics added).

Although we deal, unlike the aforementioned work, with three different nationalities and cultures, we will check if and how the individual interviewee reacts to the projection onto himself/herself of the stereotypical "migrant" frame, which often means social and professional marginalization, ethnic-racial discrimination, low contractual power, exclusion from rights.

However, a difference between the present study and De Fina's concerns time: in that case, informants had recently passed the border between US and Mexico at the time of the interview, and only one migrant (out of 14) had obtained the documents required to regularise his stay in the US. In our case, instead, the permanence in Italy is longer than nine years and reaches up to 18 years for two informants from Sri Lanka (Marion and Tani). This allowed us to record the interviews in Italian, therefore in the language of the host country, and, above all, gave migrants the possibility to evaluate their experience of migration as a story and not simply as a chronicle (Labov & Waletzky, 1967/1997).

On this ground, three criteria seem to have a certain priority in the construction of the identities against the "migrant" frame:

(a) *identity as a social orientation* through the choice and positioning of pronouns, paying particular attention to the variations between the narrator's self, the collective *we* referring to migrants' community and the category of THEM that designates the host culture;
(b) *identity as lexical categorization*, focused on the lexical choices selected to define the host culture and, conversely, attributed to the self and other group of migrants;I) *identity as narrative negotiation*, in which we try to detect first of all the attitude to narrate and the structuring of the story in terms of number and type of characters and its dialogic na–ure – the category of reported speech in De Fina (2003, p. 93).

4. Migrants from Senegal

The Senegalese informants interviewed residing in Naples are three: Pierre, Ammad and Amadu. Even though this is an extremely small sample, it is quite homogeneous in terms of age (36, 42) and level of education (university studies). Above all, it is useful to start outlining three different variations of the criteria set out above, that is (a) pronominal variations, (b) lexical categories and (c) narrative negotiation.

We observe that Pierre and Ammad tend to use frequently the pronoun *we* that hides the individual speakers in their own community, along with a generic *you* that neutralises the impact of a personal respons

1 Ammad[2]
@EXP: e un giorno hai in mente di tornare in Senegal?
@SUJ: si si si

2 EXP stands for the interviewer, SUJ points to the interviewee. In this example and the following ones, italics are mine.

@EXP: come mai?
@SUJ: vabbè *noi* qua siamo venuti per cercare # oggi va bene non parlo solo come io per esempio parlo come in generale no # *noi* siamo venuti per lavorare e quando *lavori devi* avere come si chiama un piano di dire va bene io lavoro a questa età e devo mh come dire vado in pensione # *noi* siamo qua per lavorare e un giorno *dobbiamo* tornare questo # *io* così la penso

The interview with the third informant, Amud, on the other hand, shows a massive use of an agentive *I/me*, through which he constructs a space in which he is the architect of his own fortune:

2 Amud
@SUJ: perché *io* dico il percorso [/] il percorso l'ho fatto *io io* sono partito del Senegal per venire qua e sta a *me* # # [/] sta a *me* dare la possibilità di integrarsi non è che devo venire imporre la conduzione *io* deve essere in grado di trovare un punto comune sapendo che c'ho una visione esterna XX una richiesta esterna verso un paese verso gente che non sa perché a Napoli c'è gente che non sa nemmeno dove si trova Latina poi si cerca di [//] devi trovare un mezzo per dialogare con quello là non è che porti e imponi la tua cultura non esiste perché se *io* devo imporre la mia cultura *me ne torno* a casa.
@EXP: sei stato chiarissimo.
@SUJ: però crea la ricchezza. *Io* sono diventato qui ricco perché *io* oggigiorno sono capace di sciare tra le acque di essere [//] di cercare di non perdere le mie origini però di cercare anche di adeguarmi di conv [//] di creare una combinazione che mi permettesse di essere felice sia di qua che di là

In terms of lexical categories, Pierre, in particular, constructs the host as a way to *watch* the colour of his skin, emphasising his passive role and a value judgment about the other's propensity to accept the difference, those people with a different skin colour:

3 Pierre
@SUJ: dico si mi aspettavo di questo tutto questo tutto ciò [perchérchè comunque sapevo come se avevo una diversità ovvio # comunque si mi aspettavo la reazione della gente però visto che io sono stato direttamente cioè in un paese non è perchéttà perchè Piana di Sorrento e Sant'Agata sono +… e là seguivano [=?] *con lo sguardo*
@EXP: ti sentivi osservato?
@SUJ: si si mh quasi scappavo nel senso che uscivo per necessità # se dovevo uscire dovevo fare un serviperchéritornare perchè non sopportavo *questo sguardo* di curiosità non è niente di mh però mi dava fastidio

4 Pierre
@SUJ: xperchéo fanno sentire perchè noi vediamo la differenza # guarda ultimamente sono stato in Finlandia # xx seconda volta sono stato anche a Parigi sono stato in altre città e in altri Paesi guardo lo *sguardo* di dire che ci fai qua quando entri in un ristorante quando entri in un bar # quando siamo ricevuti bene cioè tu avverti questa cosa quando poi già tu l'altro lato ha *un occhio discriminante* anche senza parlare te lo senti è molto diffuso

Along with his pronominal choices, Pierre comes to categorise his identity in relational terms, self-defining himself by difference and from the perspective of others, Italian and Neapolitan people, as a *straniero* (foreigner):

5 Pierre
@EXP: non lo so tu ti senti alla pari di un cittadino italiano al momento?
@SUJ: io mi sento sempre *straniero*

Ammad, on the other hand, categorises his identity as a migrant in the more typical terms of national and geographic-cultural origin (Senegal, Africa):

6 Ammad
@EXP: tu ti senti alla pari di un cittadino italiano?
@SUJ: no per esempio io avevo la fortuna di fare la cittadinanza l'hperchéutata per dirti
@EXP: perchè hai rifiutato?
@SUJ: io mi sento *senegalese* e morirò come *senegalese*

7 Ammad

@SUJ: perciò io la mia filosofia no io vivo in Europa
@EXP: ma pensi africano
@SUJ: però dormo in *Africa* questa è la mia filosofia

In terms of narrative negotiation, the split between Pierre and Ammad on one side and Amud on the other is quite apparent, in line with their respective selection of pronouns and lexical categories. Pierre tells stories whose purpose is to build up a conflicting relationship with the host country. In the following example, the Italian host performs an action (in italics) that challenges Pierre's status as a traveller and transforms him into the "migrant" stereotype. The Italian character is represented as a policeman, through whom Pierre constructs the standard point of view of the average Italian who meets a young guy from Senegal:

8 Pierre
@EXP: cosa ti ricordi del giorno in cui sei arrivato in Italia?

@SUJ: allora quando sono arrivato in Italia da Roma sono sceso # beh il paesaggio e ho incontrato un agente [=?] non capivo benissimo l'italiano diciamo quando parlavano veloce e il fatto # *questo qua mi fa "senegalese? E' atipico"* non capivo xx perchè ha detto atipico e lui ha detto "*di solito i senegalesi non [=?] vengono qua a studiare*" # allora già a primo impatto +... poi dopo quel stesso giorno da Roma mi sono venuti a prendere e dovevo andare fino a Sant'Agata # vabbè tutto bello ad un certo punto cioè a Sant'Agata quando vai c'è tutto mh c'è tutto il verde tutto un po' buio perchè il tragitto cioè non so se sei pratica di queste zone

The intercultural dialogue is fictitious, as it allows the informant to construct the other through his attitude towards migrants. Reported speech allows Pierre to sum up a dialogue with an impersonal and threatening interlocutor, who embodies the stereotyped social evaluation that Italians have about people from Senegal.

Amud, on the other hand, while resorting only once to a narrative that conforms to the minimum requirements of a story (temporal sequence, characters, sequence of events, protagonist's response, final solution), allows the host culture to emerge as an autonomous point of view, without using it to construct a judgment that follows sterotypes:

9 Amud

@SUJ: Claudia mi ha detto "guarda stanno cercando un ragioniere" perché io aveva dei paletti sulla mia vita diceva "entro sei mesi se non trovo il lavoro mio me ne torno a casa" tutt'ora c'ho il mio lavoro la mia [//] il mio mestiere. Quindi io sono venuto e ho detto – avevo uno scarso italiano – "guarda se si tratta di contabilità lo so fare se cerchi un contabile ti posso dimostrare che lo so far"" e lui diceva "a me non interessa il colore" perché io sono rimasto con lui fin quando XX perché mi ha dato fiducia mi ha dato ha detto "non mi interessa che sei immigrato a me interessa qualcuno che sappia portare avanti".

Amud's narrative, which includes individual voices of the Italian community, and not institutional roles or functions, can be said to be based on a true dialogue. The other is represented as an autonomous point of view and in a position that is symmetrical to narrator's.

5. Migrants from Ukraine

The group of Ukrainian informants is larger, but equally homogeneous in terms of education levels and age, although two informants are older than others (Olga is 54 and Natalia 55). From a professional point of view, the only significant difference concerns a single informant (Alina), who opened a grocery store with her husband and lives in a condition of economic wealth which is not comparable to other informants. Another difference to notice is the almost total presence of female informants, with the exception of only one male informant, Yuri.

In this series of interviews, the opposite approaches, at least in terms of our criteria, are represented by Alina and Olga: the former offers a highly individual response to the experience of migration, with a self constructed as decisional and strong:

10 Alina
@SUJ: *Io* sono una diciamo che mi piace tantissimo ascoltare e sentire consigli tutto quello che vuoi sempre consigli ascolto tantissimo la decisione la prendo *Io* consigli di tanti però la decisione è *mia* a un certo punto mi è mancato poter parlare con qualcuno ancora più saggio di *me*.

Olga, on the contrary, offers a response to migration in terms of a confrontation between a nationalist and collective US – we Ukrainians – against an explicit THEM, the Italian citizens:

11 Olga
@SUJ Vorrei dire cosa i figli vengono per 10–20 minuti e poi se ne va non c'è pazienza però da *noi* vogliono togliere pelle Io già detto "volete togliere pelle? Purtroppo non si può". "che volete *da noi*?" ho detto *noi* facciamo troppo già anche molto e non dovete giudicare o dire "questo non è buoni o questi non è vero" *noi* siamo buoni perché *noi* venuti qua a lavorare non devo giudicare *noi stranieri*. *Loro* devo dire grazie *a noi* cos[//] cosa *noi* siamo come devo dire [//] siamo di gente come *noi* venuti qua dare mano aiuto

For Alina, the pronoun *we* refers only in a few cases to the Ukrainian community, nor does it take on the sense of a 'national'–alignment – most occurrences refer to an extended self to her husband, with whom Alina shared the idea of setting up a business activity:

12 Alina
@SUJ: [...] *Abbiamo fatto* un altro passo oltre cioè *non sapevamo* se va bene va male come va in che modo e avendoci tre bambini non potevo più giustamente andare a lavorare a ore perché era impossibile e *io e mio marito <abbiamo fatto>* [//] *<abbiamo deciso>* [//] *abbiamo fatto* questa decisione di *proviamo facciamo* quel negozio tanto documenti *abbiamo* il permesso di soggiorno ci permette di fare questi passi diciamo così.

It is Yuri who uses "we" in a contrastive and almost nationalist key, to underline cultural differences between his own nation and Italy, and often construct a cultural superiority to which he seems to belong:

13 Yuri
@SUJ: perché arrivato a piazza Garibaldi riguardando tutto quel casino [//] era notte era l'una di notte e guardando tutti quelli sai neri cos' perché *da noi* non vedi spesso persone di colore poi albanesi *sporchizia* all'inizio io "ma che è? Dove sono finito!" [ridono!]

In terms of lexical categories through which migrants identify themselves, the definition of *straniero* ("foreigner") is the most recurrent, even if it is meant in a contrastive key that highlights te cultural gap between the two countries and cultures. For Stella, the condition of being a foreigner is an ineliminable one, which does not allow her to have a symmetrical relationship with an Italian citizen:

14 Stella
@SUJ: no non potresti mai diventare italiana sarai sempre *straniera* anche se ti trovi bene

Olga goes even further and provides the most nationalistic and confrontational group representation, as she is the only one to use and generalise the term *schiavo* ("slave"), in order to describe her relationship with the Italians and project Italians' approach to migrants as deeply racist:

15 Olga
@SUJ: "sì noi venuti per soldi non hai sentito?! Cosa siamo *schiave*!" tu non mi comprato giusto? [si rivolge all'intervistatrice] con mio carattere quando io non trovo con famiglia o con mia signora io devo sentire in casa come dentro di famiglia ma non cosa io devo sentire *schiava*, io *schiava* nemmeno là non sono stata anche noi siamo signore voglio dire non come pensano loro.

As for the others, identification occurs more frequently through nationality (the Italians) or work relationship ("the lady"), with the exception of Natalia who is the only one to have a very rich cultural life, and therefore represents the host according to the interactional contexts in which she is involved – the teacher of Italian language, and the poets and artists of the cultural centre that she regularly attends. Natalia is the only one to know and mention some names that represent Neapolitan culture (Totò, Eduardo de Filippo).

On the other side, Olga constructs a narrative negotiation that is rich with voices, but embedded in a monologuing context. This is instrumental to assert a point of view based on cultural and national conflict.

16 Olga
@SUJ: Da me è capitato mio lavoro lo sapete come ha detto una volta figlia? Dice "*allora quest'anno io non ti do tredicesima*" ho detto "*perché*?" "*e perché*

> *io senza lavoro crisi e tredicesima prendo io*" io detto "*Veramente? e dove questo scritto*?" e ho detto "*cara mia prendi mio posto di lavoro stai vicino a sua mamma e prendi mie *stipendie* e tu dopo prendi tredicesima provi mio pane*" che cosa io detta. Ecco questa non mi piace cosa *loro* vuole XXX che questo *loro* non gli pagano questo mi è molto molto doloroso però io non lo so cosa questo lei non fare con me così però pensava può darsi una stupida che dire "*sì sì va bene*", no non mi va bene.

This type of representation clarifies the meaning of narrative negotiation: it is not the mere presence of several and different voices that constructs a dialogic story, but the way in which these voices are exploited by the narrator: if these voices are instrumental to speaker's ideology, as in this case, we have a sort of monologue dramatisation, in which the distance between the narrator and story he/she tells is extremely reduced.

6. Migrants from Sri Lanka

In the case of the Sri Lankan community, we deal with interviewees who generally have a low degree of social and cultural integration, but are not in a disadvantaged position from an economic point of view. The seven informants have different ages, since this group includes the youngest informants, aged 27 (Tani) and 23 (Nathan); moreover, the interviews also reveal the only case of an explicit internal conflict with the migrant community, as emerges from the interview with Susanda (44).

Tani and Nathan's situation cannot be assimilated to that of other migrants, as they joined their families at the age of 4 and 11 respectively. Both Tani and Nathan say that they feel more integrated into the Italian culture and mentality, as demonstrated by their linguistic mastery and frequent references to conflicts with their "conservative" parents:

17 Tani

@EXP: e ora con tua madre com'è il rapporto ora?

@SUJ: ora ora niente mi capisce ci capiamo ha capito che *io sono così come sono* [ride!] nel senso ehm # che non faccio niente di male nel comportarmi sì nel *sentirmi e vivere come un'italiana* non voglio dire vivere come un'italiana perché comunque sembra che [//] cioè *avere le stesse abitudini di una ragazza italiana*

Therefore, the pronominal distribution, in these cases, is of little relevance, even if Nathan adopts a national *we* when comparing the Italian and Sri Lankan school systems.

However, we do not find the expression of a sharp difference between US and THEM, as described by some migrants from Senegal (Pierre) or Ukraine (Yuri, Olga). Among the informants, it is Susante who refers to a collective *us* and introduces a personal stance, but just to outline a cultural distance from the host country, rather than a conflictual relationship:

18 Susante
@EXP: ma secondo te la crisi colpisce più gli italiani o più gli immigrati?
@SUJ: mh penso gli italiani più perché *noi* o almeno *io io* non è non ce l'ho crisi tengo però *io* non rimane sempre qui # perché *io* qualche dopo due anni tre anni cinque anni massimo *io* vado Paese # quindi *io* non interessa invece italiani sempre rimane qua in loro Paese questo e *loro* interessa molto cosa *io* non guardo questo # questo è vero perché è inutile *io* deve guardare mio Paese # quindi *io* non ci penso molto diciamo # non lo so perché mio tempo *io* lavorando guadagnare qualcosa *io* vado Paese # quindi *io* non guardo questo invece molto xx per italiani è il loro Paese le loro cose e *loro* guardano # diciamo per stranieri chi rimane qua non vuole partire Paesi vuole cittadinanza *loro* deve pensare questo *per me* no non c'è problema.

With the exception of the youngest informants, Tani and Nathan, the informants from Sri Lanka reveal a very high degree of agency in relation to the desire to come back to Sri Lanka (as shown by the "I" of the previous example), but a very low degree of agency in the relationships with Italian employers. Susanda is strongly critical of the Sri Lankan community precisely because of its excessive closure to contact with the Italian community and its isolation.

19 Susanda
@SUJ: no e ti dico proprio la verità sincera mi sono deluso troppo dai srilankesi
@EXP: hai avuto questo brutto impatto
@SUJ: brutto perché *io* ho vissuto anche a Napoli qualche mese con gli srilankesi mi hanno trattato proprio male *io volevo* andare a scuola *loro* mi hanno detto delle parolacce mi hanno detto "dormi che vai a fare!"
@EXP: è strano
@SUJ: ma forse geloso
@EXP: ma forse perché tu +...
@SUJ: forse perché *mia intenzione* di studiare di imparare e *loro* non hanno fatto questo quindi non volevano facevano gli altri srilankesi molto permalosi [...]

Susanda demonstrates a degree of agency ("I wanted to go to school", "my intention to learn") which is highly dynamic and does not conform to the customs of the community to which he belongs.

In the case of the Sri Lankan community, we can see that the recurrent nominal category does not concern the identification of the self ("foreigner", "Tamil", "Sri Lankan"), but a *function* of the self: "work", which is one of the most recurrent words in the interviews. Italy, for these informants, seems to be instrumental in the search for work and a relative improvement of their economic conditions, a necessary condition before coming back to their own countries (the average time of stay of migrants from Sri Lanka in Campania is 9.2 years, see de Filippo & Strozza, 2014, p. 31).

20 Sanjeev
@EXP: cosa ti aspettavi venendo qua? Qual'era il tuo sogno?
@SUJ: diventare non molto ricco una vita normale # una bella casa una # per me *qualsiasi lavoro* io *lavoro* qualche cosa da fare solo io non pensavo molto diventare ricco non lo voglio voglio una vita però +... però comunque *io # può lavorare* ancora e credo di arrivare a quello che penso io

The story as a strategy of identity construction is naturally dialogic in reporting the voice of the Italian host, since migrants from Sri Lanka get exactly what they want from Italy, a job as remedy to poverty:

21 Sanjeev
@EXP: e qual è stata la tua impressione? [all'ingresso in Italia]
@SUJ: [...] qualche volta carabiniere pure controllato a me che hanno detto *"permesso di soggiorno?"* io detto *"io non c'è permesso di soggiorno senza permesso di soggiorno siamo poveri non voglio rientrare e così"* però hanno mi liberato non è detto niente detto *"non ti preoccupare però cerca di non girare per la strada uscire senza permesso"* così perché io è spiegato la mia situazione così non voglio tornare # quello importante no? se vai in Germania loro mandano via subito! Guarda come fatto carabinieri che ha detto *"vai a casa non girare la notte"* perché io stava andando da mio fratello sorella a trovare una Domenica

For the Sri Lankan community, however, a dynamic narrative negotiation has a different meaning from what we have noticed in some cases of the Senegalese (Amadu) or Ukrainian (Alina, Natalia) communities. If the dialogue indicates an open minded attitude towards the host culture for the migrants from Senegal and Ukraine, the dialogue here becomes just a neutral discursive element, which reflects the community's self-isolation within the city territory.

7. Conclusion

By analysing migrants' stories, several and different representations and constructions of the self and the *others* have emerged. The analysis, guided by the criteria of pronoun positioning, lexical categorisation and narrative negotiation has allowed us to observe if and how the single interviewed subject produces a social response to the stereotypical "migrant" frame or is able to provide an individual and personal response to intercultural challenges (De Fina, 2003, p. 51).

The group of Senegalese informants shows in Pierre and Amadu the two sides of identity construction, with Pierre's conflictual position in opposition to Amadu's orientation towards cultural integration. In the case of the migrants from Ukraine, this imaginary line between socio-cultural conflict on the one hand and individual integration on the other is radicalised. In Yuri's and Olga's stories, the cultural clash between the country of origin and the host country is frequently mentioned. However, the cases of Alina and Natalia show how the individual response and a high degree of constructive agency can pave the way to a successful integration process.

In the case of migrants from Sri Lanka who are who are fully integrated into their community (Marion, Susante and Sanjeev), the focus on work and the need to improve their economic conditions overshadows any abstract representation of intercultural interaction.

References

de Filippo, E., & Strozza, S. (Eds.) (2014). *Indagine sulla presenza straniera e il livello di integrazione degli immigrati stranieri presenti nella regione Campania.* Servizio Regionale di Mediazione Culturale, Rapporto di ricerca, Napoli.

De Fina, A. (2003). *Identity in Narrative: A Study of Immigrant Discourse.* Amsterdam: John Benjamins.

Fairclough, N. (1989). *Language and Power.* London: Longman.

Harré, R., & van Langenhove, L. (Eds.) (1998). *Positioning Theory.* Oxford: Blackwell.

Labov, W., & Waletzky, J. (1966). Narrative Analysis: Oral Versions of Personal Experience. In J. Helm (a cura di), *Essays on the Verbal and Visual Arts* (pp. 12–44). Seattle: University of Washington Press.

Lakoff, G. (1987). *Women, Fire, and Dangerous Things.* Chicago: Chicago University Press.

Stavros Assimakopoulos, Rebecca Vella Muskat

University of Malta, Malta

stavros.assimakopulos@um.edu.mt, Rebecca.vella@um.edu.mt

Chapter 7 The negotiation of minority inclusion and exclusion in the participatory web

Abstract: This chapter analyses online comments to news reports about migrant and LGBTIQ issues with a focus on explicit and implicit discursive strategies in the communication of positive and negative attitudes. The results show that while indirectness is used to support both inclusion and exclusion, explicitness is used more in defences of inclusion.

Keywords: Migration, News Discourse, participatory web, Social Media Critical Discourse dies.

1. Introduction

The critical analysis of discriminatory discourse has a long and particularly rich history, whereby scholars who are "sociopolitically committed to social equality and justice" have focused their efforts on identifying how "discourse (re) produces social domination, that is, the power abuse of one group over others, and how dominated groups may discursively resist such abuse" (van Dijk, 2009, p. 9). As evidenced by the vast literature in the area of Critical Discourse Studies (CDS), looking at different *discourses* – as "different perspectives on the world, [...] associated with the different relations people have to the world, which in turn depends on their positions in the world, their social and personal identities, and the social relationships in which they stand to other people" (Fairclough, 2003, p. 124) – can provide significant insight into the particular ideological stances that underlie discriminatory attitudes. This is customarily done through detailed textual analysis which, in combination with a careful assessment of the socio-political context in which a text under study is produced, allows the analyst to draw conclusions about the ways in which some minority group is disparaged and stigmatised in a particular community. Along these lines, it has repeatedly been shown that, apart from constituting an inextricable part of our more general social practices in their own right, our discursive practices can additionally reveal the dominant ideologies that justify and – by extension – perpetuate social injustice.

At the same time, in a relatively recent development, researchers in CDS have enriched their methodological arsenal with the additional implementation of tools and methods traditionally used in corpus linguistics. The main motivation behind this move has been the need to reduce researcher bias in a field that has often been criticised for relying on what are perceived to be subjective interpretations of the analysed data (see, for example, Baker et al., 2008). This has led to a number of attempts to analyse datasets much larger in size than the ones traditionally used for CDS work, following an approach that combines the rigour and objectivity of quantitative analysis with the in-depth nature of qualitative research. In this regard, an added benefit of this approach has been that it has made it possible to measure in more concrete terms the extent to which discriminatory remarks tend to crop up in texts from diverse sources that can potentially affect the public outlook towards a particular social group.

The research recently undertaken under the auspices of the EU-funded C.O.N.T.A.C.T. project (cf. Assimakopoulos et al., 2017) is a case in point, since it provided some initial insight regarding the pervasiveness of xenophobic and homophobic attitudes in comments posted online in reaction to articles published in news portals across a number of European countries. This was made possible through the collective annotation of a representative sample of comments as communicating a positive, negative or neutral attitude towards migrant and LGBTIQ minorities,[1] which, in turn, allowed for a more direct comparison of discriminatory attitudes across the different national contexts under study. The results of this process painted an interesting picture in which xenophobic attitudes were in most cases markedly higher in proportion when compared to homophobic ones,[2] while comments identified as negative toward

1 It is important to note here that, given the scope of the project, all comments were evaluated according to their stance toward (members of) the specific minority groups under investigation. So, comments that revealed other discriminatory attitudes (e.g., ageism, ableism, etc.) or contained axiological information pertaining to other social actors, such as political parties or other individual commenters were marked as 'irrelevant' in the process.

2 Naturally, exceptions to this pattern also arose, as in the case of Cyprus, where negative comments targeting members of the LGBTIQ community significantly outnumbered negative comments targeting migrants, as well as that of Italy and Lithuania, where the negativity towards both minority groups appeared to be in a relative equilibrium (for the full table of the results obtained across the C.O.N.T.A.C.T consortium, see Assimakopoulos et al., 2017, p. 13).

both migrants and members of the LGBTIQ community outnumbered those marked as positive almost across the board.

The sole exception in this last respect was that of Malta, where in the case of comments targeting the LGBTIQ community the exact opposite trend was noted, with comments viewing (members of) this group in a positive light outnumbering those revealing a negative outlook by a proportion of 24.2 % over 18.7 %. At first sight, this could be seen as pointing to a society that is far more accepting of minorities in general, but the results obtained from the analysis of comments targeting the topic of migration suggested otherwise, since the comments annotated as negative in this case were almost double in number in comparison to their positive counterparts, with a respective proportion of 32.3 % over 16.3 %. While these results have already been reported and elaborated on in previous work focusing specifically on the Maltese context (Assimakopoulos & Vella Muskat, 2017, 2018), we believe that the unique pattern that emerged from the analysis of the Maltese data could potentially lend itself to investigating more closely a main reason why, by virtue of its design and particular affordances (Hutchby, 2001), the participatory web can be both a platform for the dissemination of discriminatory attitudes and a space where such attitudes are resisted.

Given C.O.N.T.A.C.T.'s original aims, our previous research focused mainly on those comments that reveal a negative stance towards the two minority groups under question, independently of the thread in which each of these comments was originally posted, and did indeed uncover – through a combination of textual analysis and the administration of supplementary questionnaires and focus group interviews – a number of discursive strategies and ideological standpoints that underlie the communication and justification of xenophobic and homophobic attitudes locally. Building up on this earlier work, what we return to examine in this paper are the transition patterns that can be identified in comment threads discussing the two minorities at hand, while juxtaposing the axiological polarisation within each one of the different news portals that populated the Maltese C.O.N.T.A.C.T. corpus. Our motivation for this lies in the premise that "[p]eer attitudes [...] have a strong influence on individual perception [...], while social networks, including online social networks, are known to heavily influence opinions and behaviour in many [...] areas of human activity" (Williams et al., 2015, p. 127; see also, Centola, 2010). On these grounds, we believe that an investigation of the concentration of pro- and anti-minority attitudes in an online discursive space should provide a more nuanced perspective regarding the distribution and pervasiveness of discriminatory attitudes therein. Given the clear indication then, from our original analysis, that the comments collected for the purposes of the C.O.N.T.A.C.T. project are polarising in opposing directions with respect to the two minority groups at hand, our corpus seems ideal for this purpose.

In this vein, following a justification of our rationale against the background of current research in the areas of CDS and Computer-Mediated Discourse (CMD),[3] and after a presentation of the corpus used for this study and some main results of our analysis in relation to the individual news portals under investigation, we will demonstrate how, despite the "complex, multi-threaded structure" (Wang et al., 2008, p. 152) of conversational data therein, news portal comment threads can give rise to coherent discourses that can be shown to mediate the promotion and demotion of discriminatory stances.

2. Critical discourse analysis and attitude negotiation in the participatory web

The relevance of CMD for socially oriented research had been recognised from quite early on. Even before the emergence of Web 2.0, Herring (2001, p. 625) affirmed that CMD "can be a tool of either oppression or resistance," noting that "the discursive negotiation and expression of social relations in cyberspace, including asymmetrical relations, constitutes one of the most promising areas of future investigation". Indeed, in a more recent overview of the field, Herring and Androutsopoulos (2018, p. 140) reiterate that "the performance of playfully framed social identities is [...] pervasive" in CMD, and review a number of studies that investigate it in detail. That being said, most of this research seems to focus either on the users' individual self-presentation or on the ways in which "interactants negotiate the relational aspect of language use in computer-mediated contexts" (Locher, 2010, p. 1). So, while the discursive construction of the identities of social media users themselves has received some attention in the relevant literature, the critical evaluation of how ordinary internet users negotiate the identities of minority groups in the participatory web has not been as straightforward an affair as one would correspondingly expect.

There are of course various reasons for this, but a central impediment in the process has been the traditional engagement of CDS with particular kinds

3 We have opted to use this term in this paper, mainly for convenience, as, alongside computer-mediated communication, it seems to be the one more widely used in the relevant literature. It should, however, be acknowledged that there is still substantial disagreement as to how to call the type of digitally-mediated interaction that we are interested in here (cf. Jucker & Dürscheid, 2012).

of discourse. As KhosraviNik and Unger acknowledge, research in this field has "generally focused on the analysis of elite texts" (2016, p. 231), such as (traditional) media talk or political speeches, where "there is a predominantly one-way flow of content from a few elite producers to masses of ordinary recipients" (KhosraviNik & Unger, 2016, p. 210). It was actually not until fairly recently that "the increasing availability and growth of digitally mediated linguistic data and the impact of social media in various aspects of social, political and economic processes" led scholars to recognise that "a socially oriented critical approach such as CDS cannot remain oblivious to these changes, in terms of material communication concentration or the changes in norms of production and dissemination of social discourses" (KhosraviNik & Unger, 2016, p. 206).

It is this realisation that has effectively led to the inception of the more specialised field of Social Media Critical Discourse Studies (SM-CDS), which, keeping in line with the main principles of CDS, is again dealing with questions of power, in the sense that it is "not only interested in what happens in [social] media per se but in how it may shape and influence [the] social and political sphere of our life worlds" (KhosraviNik, 2018, p. 586). Given this commitment, the main theoretical preoccupation of scholars in the field has been to address the questions of who controls the information flow in social media and how this information flow can be exploited by various actors to either nurture or fight social injustice in a "discursive environment [...] in which the loci of power are much more diffuse and the instruments of ideological control and discipline are more subtle and complex" (Jones et al., 2015, p. 1).

Within this same spirit, the majority of existing case studies that could be broadly taken to belong to SM-CDS appear to concentrate on social media discourse that either seeks to question and resist social injustice (e.g., Chiluwa, 2012; Shirazi, 2013) or denigrates and stigmatises (e.g., KhosraviNik & Zia, 2014; Brindle, 2016). Again though, this is not coincidental. The polarisation that is typically noted in the relevant literature is to a large extent justifiable, given the way in which the participatory web has been commercially designed. Since their main source of revenue is advertising, most social media platforms make use of algorithms that actively push content expected to appeal to their users in order to encourage all the more consumption which will in turn increase advertising revenue. This inevitably leads to a substantial proportion of social media interaction taking place in what are commonly referred to as *echo chambers*, "whereby the architecture of the media tends to favor and encourages like-mindedness and intensification of feelings and beliefs with little or no critical scrutiny" (KhosraviNik, 2017, p. 64; see also Pariser, 2011).

Be that as it may, the extent to which some online space can be taken to constitute an echo chamber, or at least fairly insular to critical scrutiny, is ultimately an empirical question that should in principle be approached through a careful examination of the discourse it encompasses. In this regard, the aforementioned results of the axiological analysis of the Maltese C.O.N.T.A.C.T. corpus point to a mixed-attitude online community of commenters, since both pro- and anti-minority comments in relation to the two minority groups under study were identified across the board. Still, this is only part of the full picture, which, given the fact that "social media are by their nature interactive, inherently and substantially multimodal and user-centred" (KhosraviNik & Unger, 2016, p. 211), additionally depends on a closer look at the particular ways in which individual users negotiate their attitudes towards migrants and (members of) the LGBTIQ community within the individual comment threads of each news portal in our corpus.

Against this backdrop, our working hypothesis in our subsequent analysis is that the more issues of social injustice are debated in a participatory online space, the less polarising this space itself should be taken to be. With this in mind, we can now engage in a closer investigation of the attitude polarisation present in our corpus, with a particular focus on the extent to which and direction in which users negotiate their relevant stances.

3. Ideological polarisation in the Maltese C.O.N.T.A.C.T. corpus

Given the more general "practical and ethical issues connected to the elicitation of non-public CMD data" which are to a considerable extent responsible for the often noted "scarcity of language-focused social network research" (Herring & Androutsopoulos, 2015, p. 140), the data we opted to collect and analyse for the purposes of the C.O.N.T.A.C.T. project belong to the publicly-available comment sections that accompany articles in online news portals. All in all, the Maltese C.O.N.T.A.C.T. corpus (see Table 7.1) consists of two balanced subcorpora of articles reporting on migration- and LGBTIQ-related news respectively over a six-month period in 2015–2016, as well as two further subcorpora comprising a representative sample of the comments that were posted below each of these articles in the original news portal in which they were published.[4]

---

4 A detailed outline of the methodological approach that was followed for the compilation of the corpus and the steps that were taken to ensure the representativeness of its contents can be found in Assimakopoulos and Vella Muskat (2018, pp. 27–29). For a

Table 7.1. Overview of the Maltese C.O.N.T.A.C.T. corpus (English language[5])

Domain	Article subcorpus		Comments subcorpus	
	Number of articles	Word count	Number of comments	Word count
Migration	78	39799	1130	41020
LGBTIQ	80	42273	1109	40924

Naturally, even in this context, there are various factors that could be conducive to the creation of echo chambers. The most pertinent of these is the political or ideological orientation of some particular news portal which is often considered a determinant of the portal's readership on the grounds that "politically opinionated individuals primarily use information sources that best suit their own belief-system" (Leruth et al., 2017, p. 98). Still, in the absence of an algorithm that promotes and demotes content on the basis of a user's tracked preferences,[6] as in the case of other social networking sites, echo chambers are expected to be primarily formed in the case of news outlets that adopt a rigid ideological line, especially on the radical ends of the political spectrum, which either way leaves little room for objective evaluation and constructive criticism (Hardin, 2002). On the basis of their political affiliation then, the three news portals that were included in the corpus at hand could be generally characterised as centrist, with the *Times of Malta* falling squarely in the centre, *MaltaToday* belonging to the centre-left and *The Malta Independent* to the centre-right. This centrist orientation was also corroborated during our critical evaluation of the collected articles, which did not reveal any particular tendencies towards an inclusionary or exclusionary ideology with regard to the two minority groups at hand for any of the news outlets under study.[7] Even so, as already mentioned

---

presentation of the common methodology used across the C.O.N.T.A.C.T. consortium, see Assimakopoulos et al. (2017, pp. 17–20).

5 Since our search in local news platforms that publish in the Maltese language did not yield enough comments to complement in equal measure the data retrieved from the major English-language local news outlets, we have excluded them from the present discussion.

6 That being said, it should also be noted that user participation is to a certain extent equally important for the business model on which news portals operate, since, by allowing it, "news organisations seek to increase performance measures such as click rates or re-visits" (Weber, 2014, p. 954).

7 This is probably also due to the fact that the majority of the collected articles were mere reports of local and international events, with only eight in total being editorial or opinion pieces and thus more ideologically-charged in the relevant sense. Either way,

above, the analysis of the comments accompanying these articles revealed a strong anti-migrant and a marked pro-LGBTIQ stance, which in itself calls for a closer look at the distribution of polarising comments within individual news portals, all the while taking into account each portal's ideological orientation.

3.1. Echo chambers or spaces for deliberation?

The results obtained during the original quantitative analysis of comments in our dataset would certainly not justify characterising the relevant online discursive space as an echo chamber; yet, looking at the distribution of polarising and non-polarising comments in each portal in Figure 7.1, we can see that this does not apply in equal measure to all three news outlets under study. More specifically, we can observe that in the case of *The Malta Independent* there are more negative than positive comments in relation to both minority groups under question. On the other hand, *MaltaToday* appears to attract a far more liberal pool of commenters, since, even in the otherwise notorious discussion of news relating to migration, the percentage of comments that reveal a positive stance towards migrants is not that far behind that of comments marked as negative. Finally, the *Times of Malta* clearly stands between the two other news portals in terms of axiological polarisation in its comment sections. Given their aforementioned political affiliations, this picture is largely consonant with our expectations regarding each portal's readership, but what clearly stands out in this picture is that, despite the rather centrist orientation of *The Malta Independent*, the discussion of migration there overwhelmingly attracts comments that communicate an exclusionary attitude toward migrants.

In order to assess the extent to which the comment sections of *The Malta Independent* can be taken to constitute echo chambers when it comes to the communication of xenophobic attitudes, we decided to take a closer look at the distribution of attitudes towards migrants within individual comment threads from each portal. An obvious challenge for this is that, in the particular context of social media talk, "with multiple actors, each with their own goals and discourse intentions, it cannot be assumed that the conversation proceeds with a single focus at a time" (Wang et al., 2008, p. 152). Indeed, as evidenced by the high percentage of comments marked as "irrelevant" during the annotation of our dataset, the Maltese C.O.N.T.A.C.T. corpus is no exception in this regard. Here too, commenters often veer off from the article's topic and engage in commentary

---

our dataset was compiled using the most commented-on articles as the main criterion (Assimakopoulos & Vella Muskat, 2018, p. 28), which in itself suggests that it may be current affairs reporting that tends to attract more user engagement in this context.

related to other matters; most notably, the discussion of political partisanship or the passing of character judgements with regards to their peers' personalities. Therefore, since there is, to the best of our knowledge, no established framework for reporting on the axiological polarity of single comment threads comprising both ideologically-charged and irrelevant posts, we decided to proceed as follows: after counting the number of comments that view the two minority groups in a positive and in a negative light per thread, we calculated their distribution in the two categories – positive and negative – as the percentage they represent out of the total of the relevant ideologically-charged posts in that thread.[8]

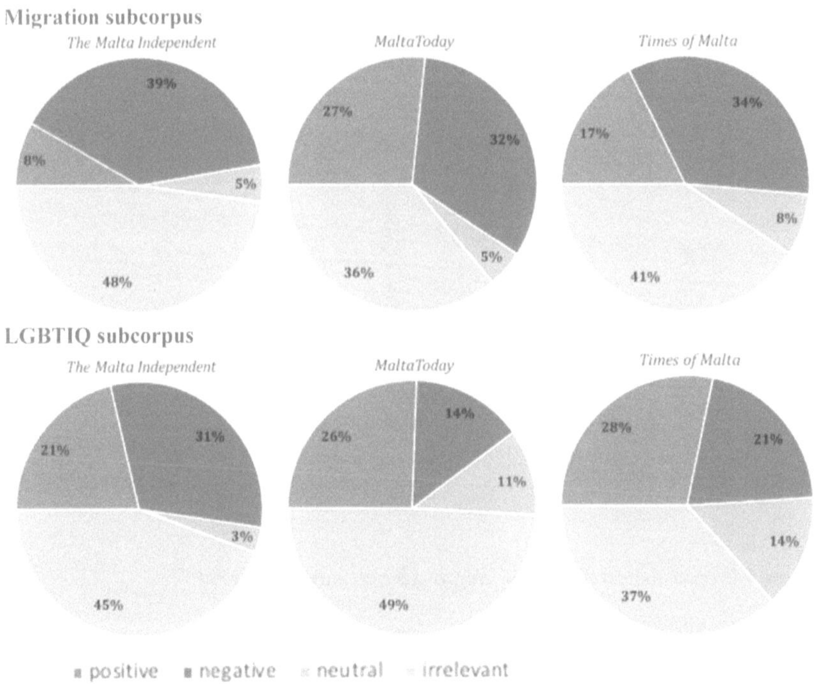

Figure 7.1. Axiological polarity of comments per news portal

8 Since our present interest is in the actual negotiation of inclusionary and exclusionary stances toward migrants and members of the LGBTIQ community, we only took into account comment threads comprising at least two comments that reveal an attitude towards these specific groups.

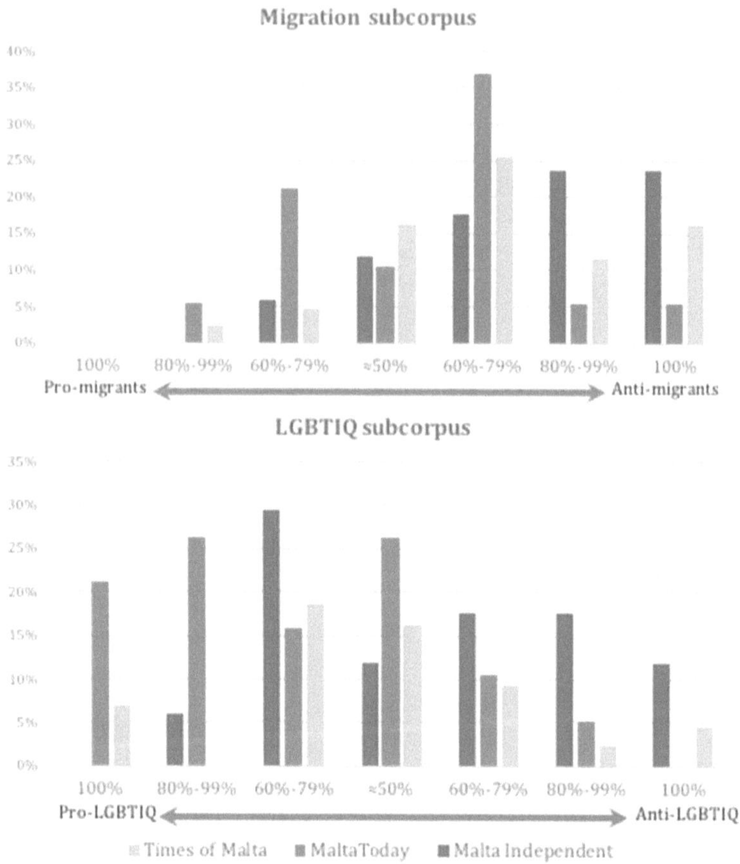

Figure 7.2. Axiological polarity of comments per comment thread

In line, again, with the expectations raised on the basis of each news portal's political affiliation, the results of this measurement, which can be found in Figure 7.2, indicate that there is significantly more agreement towards a positive representation of the two minority groups, and especially the LGBTIQ one, among commenters of *MaltaToday* than among commenters of *The Malta Independent*, with those of the *Times of Malta* holding the middle ground in this regard. What these results additionally reveal, however, is that even in the case of *The Malta Independent*, where the overall percentage of comments that view migrants in a positive light was particularly low, some commenters are still resisting the generally negative outlook in a considerable proportion of the relevant comment threads. This effectively suggests that there is, to varying degrees of course, genuine deliberation regarding attitudes towards both minority groups in the discussion threads of all three news portals at hand, including *The Malta Independent*.

Even so, this measurement is still based on a raw count of polarising comments per thread, and hence says little about the patterns of interactivity that different commenters of the same article participate in when debating their relevant positions. So, in order to further probe into the negotiation of inclusionary and exclusionary attitudes towards the two minority groups under question, we needed to specifically look at the way in which commenters react to individual posts that either resist or engage in othering (members of) the migrant or the LGBTIQ minorities.

3.2. Inclusionary and exclusionary attitudes in interaction

Trying to establish a method for evaluating the direction in which stances towards migrants and (members of) the LGBTIQ community are negotiated in the collected data, a further complication that arose, on top of the aforementioned existence of irrelevant comments intercepting ideologically-charged interaction, was that, much like most social media talk, our dataset predominantly consists of long polylogues where the attitudes towards each minority group can and often do sway from one direction to the other. Seeing then that, in this specific setting, axiological interactivity could present itself in myriad possible configurations, not only in terms of varying transition patterns, but also with respect to the number of participants involved in each polylogue, we opted to provide a rougher quantitative measure of it by looking only at the transition patterns between polarising posts and subsequent comment(s) reacting specifically to them. In this vein, we took note of those instances where a post is explicitly marked on the platform as a response to a preceding comment and is also ideologically-charged in the relevant respect.

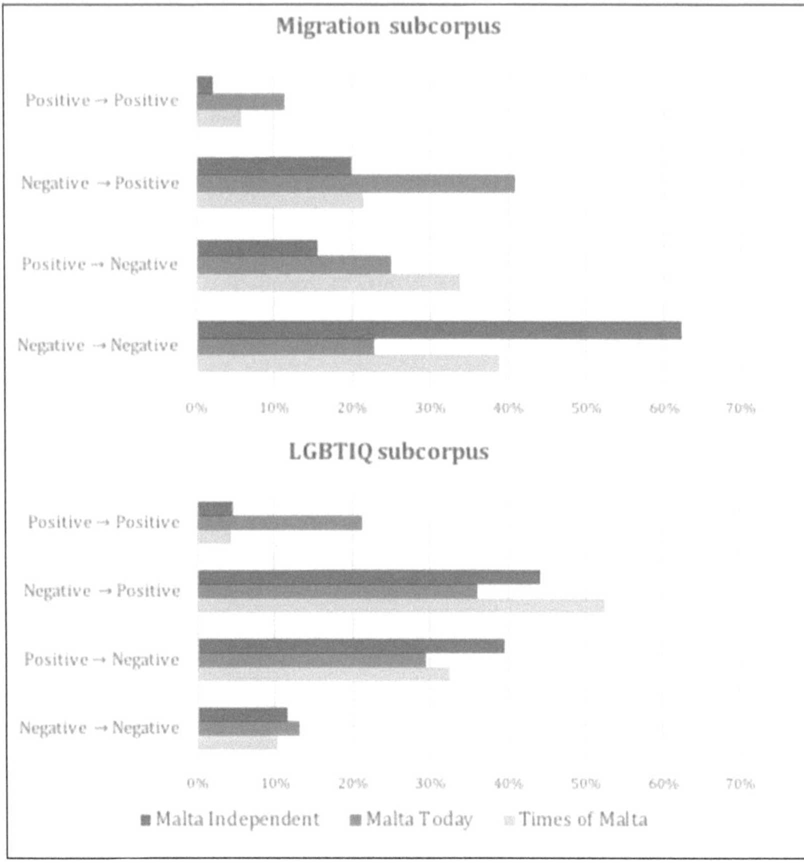

Figure 7.3. Attitude negotiation in single comment responses

The rationale behind going for this categorisation model was that it would offer us further insight with regard to the kind of reactions that positive or negative comments tend to attract in the three discursive spaces at hand, complementing in this way our initial findings reported above. Indeed, as Figure 7.3 shows, within the Migration subcorpus, the most frequent type of transition in the *Times of Malta* and especially *The Malta Independent* is from negative to negative comment, while the most frequent interaction pattern noted in the annotated comments of *MaltaToday* was that of responding to a negative comment with a positive one. These results reinforce the conclusion that the discourse pertaining to migrants and ethnic minorities is overwhelmingly negative in our dataset, but they additionally reveal that *MaltaToday* is an online space where exclusionary attitudes towards migrants have a slight tendency to be challenged and resisted. Conversely, in the LGBTIQ subcorpus, the most frequent type of interaction is from a negative to a positive comment pretty much across the board, which indicates that, even though discriminatory discourse crops up in this context too, there is a higher likelihood for commenters to defend the LGBTIQ community than to condemn it. This is notably the case even in the context of *The Malta Independent*, where the initial count of all messages' ideological orientation pointed to a marked anti-LGBTIQ sentiment, which effectively suggests that even in this otherwise more insular space, there is a fair amount of deliberation and defence of this particular minority.

While these results are certainly indicative of the trends of axiological interactivity within our corpus, there are obvious limitations to the method we employed to obtain them. For one, our categorisation model does not really take into account the multi-threaded structure of social media interaction, which in conjunction with the conversational bifurcation that inevitably comes in this setting (see Marcoccia, 2004) can raise the chance of obtaining skewed results. Clearly, online interaction of the sort we are looking at here is not typically well organised, especially since internet users may not always use the dedicated "reply" option to respond to a peer's comment. So, even though we double-checked the collected data to make sure that those comments structurally marked as responses to an initial post are indeed reactions to it, there is still no guarantee that further comments responding to it were not accidentally posted outside this particular thread, and inadvertently left out of our corpus during our initial sampling process. Then, given the size of our annotated sample, it is hard to determine whether some commenters in it are "internet trolls" or "partisan hacks" who systematically target a particular minority, or, from the opposite end of the spectrum, internet activists who seek to dominate the discussion in order to promote a more inclusive attitude. Finally, and perhaps most substantially, our classification glosses over the significant distinction between single-turn interactions, whereby a commenter merely reacts to the attitude of a previous post, and the polylogues that clearly dominate our dataset, where on top of doing that, all commenters additionally co-construct a stance towards the minority groups at hand through their ongoing interaction.

With regards to this last limitation though, a significant merit of our method was that it provided an important first step towards a closer, more critical evaluation of the particular patterns of interaction that arise in our data. It was this closer examination of each exchange within the polylogual setting at hand that enabled us to identify those configurations through which news portal commenters manage to build coherent perspectives regarding the two minority groups under study, in a process that can significantly influence the way in which the overall discourse of the online participatory space at hand is perceived and consumed. In the next section of this paper, we will turn to these configurations, in an attempt to show, through the discussion of representative examples from our corpus, how the concentration of ideologically adjacent attitudes in a social media setting can solidly promote and demote inclusionary and exclusionary stances.

4. Interactionality and stance in news portal comment threads

Following Tran and Ngo's (2018) preliminary attempt to provide a detailed description of reader-reader interaction in Web 2.0 commentary, one can approach viewpoint polarisation by distinguishing between three types of exchanges that can take place among users who post ideologically-charged comments; namely "*support*", "*confrontation*" and "*alternation*" exchanges. Matching these categories with the transition patterns used in our study is a rather straightforward affair. Those single- or multi-turn exchanges with a positive to positive or negative to negative attitude transition pattern would qualify as support exchanges, while those featuring positive to negative or negative to positive attitude sequences would fall under the confrontation category. The alternation characterisation, on the other hand, would apply specifically to multiple-turn interactions that comprise a sequence of posts expressing varying stances; that is, the types of sequences that were notoriously difficult to meaningfully group together for our quantitative analysis above. Since, then, in Web 2.0 sites, "stance is not taken by one single speaker or writer, but is constantly created and renegotiated collaboratively by a networked public" (Barton & Lee, 2013, p. 31), the driving force behind the establishment of an inclusionary or exclusionary attitude as dominant in a participatory online space should be the high concentration of posts with a single ideological orientation and the lack of posts that challenge them.

Against this backdrop, one would expect ideological insularity to primarily present itself in spaces that are dominated by support exchanges. In this setting, even though a continuous transition from negative to negative comment may on the surface appear rather different from a corresponding positive to positive transition, and does indeed serve a completely different purpose, they both seem to perform the same additional function: that of establishing compatibility between the different users' views and values in either opposition to or defence of a particular minority group. On top of that, the longer the exchange at hand, the more pronounced the sense of *rapport building* among commenters that we appear to be getting at.

The excerpt of a polylogue in (1)[9], for instance, which follows an article headlined "Four held after boss is beheaded in France" (*Times of Malta*, 26/6/2015) clearly displays solidarity between users espousing a negative stance towards migrants.

(1) **User 1:** [This comment was deleted.]
User 2: Yes ... I think that we have come to this, now.
User 3: The fact is that if you kill them, you are doing them a favour since they believe that this way you become a hero and go direct to heaven. So it is a win win for them.
User 4: They could use a woman to execute them because they believe that if they are killed by a woman they will not go to heaven to enjoy their 77 virgins. That's why they are terrorized by the women Peshmerga.

Even though the comment of User 1 was deleted from the online platform, indicating that it was deemed too inappropriate by moderators to remain online, the rest of the thread provides enough context to safely assume that it is in some way referring to killing Muslims, with subsequent participants in the interaction making explicit reference to killing and even using sarcasm to further degrade this minority group. In this regard, despite not having had their comments removed, these users do not only defend the stance of the first commenter, but also appear to directly endorse and legitimise it.

At the other end of the spectrum, we can look at an article headlined "US court ends same-sex marriage ban" posted on the same date and platform as the previous one (*Times of Malta*, 26/6/2015), and whose accompanying comment thread is reproduced in (2) in its entirety.

(2) **User 1:** Wonderful news.
User 2: Well done US but Malta beat you to it.
User 3: Happy days for millions of humans, that had their love discriminated! Well done! :)
User 4: Finally the land they call the free is catching up to our own continent, great news, on a day where hatred seems to dominate the headlines.

The exchange here begins with a comment that directly responds to the news with a positive stance toward the LGBTIQ community stating that this is "*wonderful*

9 For the sake of transparency, all examples provided in this section and the next have been reproduced in their exact original form; hence the presence of typographical and/or expression mistakes.

news". Subsequently, other users continue the thread by incrementally adding their own positive messages, with both User 2 and User 3 using the positively-charged adjective "*well done*" and User 4 resonating User 1 by calling the news "*great*". So, much like in the previous example but in the opposite axiological direction, apart from building a strong sense of community within the virtual platform, the users' positive stances engender additional comments that further legitimate the minority group at hand.

Turning to threads that comprise confrontation exchanges, a similar situation appears to arise. Again, in the presence of multiple posts that challenge a polarising comment, we bear witness to a similar sense of comradery which steers the collectively-formed attitude towards a minority group in a particular direction. The exchange in (3), for instance, is an example of an inclusionary attitude with regard to the LGBTIQ community being met with backlash on the grounds of religious ideology.

(3) User 1: If more priests were like him, our churches will be full on Sundays.
User 2: I prefer them to be empty and yet faithful to the teachings of the Lord.
User 3: "Tridux tmorru intom ukoll" qal Kristu lill-appostli. Kristu mhux ifittex il-kwantita. Ahna nimpressjonaw ruhna mill-folol. Il-folol mhux se jimpressjonaw lil Kristu. Kienu l-istess folol li grew wara Kristu ghall-mirakli li ghajtu sallbu, sallbu. ["You don't want to go as well, do you?" said Christ to the apostles. Christ is not looking for quantity. We are impressed by the masses. The masses will not impress Christ. It was the same masses that ran after Christ for miracles that shouted crucify him, crucify him. Leave us in peace.]
User 4: Do you think so User 1? Our churches should be full by faithful who obeys God's teaching and not Montebello's. When St. Peter told Jesus that those are around him are leaving because they cannot understand his teaching Jesus replied.' Would you also go away' For those who refuse the Gospel there is no place in the church.

In this example, following an article about a priest, Fr Mark Montebello, getting rebuked by the archbishop over the blessing of the rings of a gay couple (*The Malta Independent*, 13/4/2015), User 1 expresses the opinion that the church should generally be more open-minded and accepting of the LGBTIQ community, by implicating that its current position on the matter has led to several people missing Sunday masses. In direct response to this, User 2 contradicts the previous elucidation about filling up churches, thereby implicating a negative stance towards the acceptance of LGBTIQ individuals within the religious community. User 3 takes this a step further by using strong language to refer to Fr Montebello as a "rebel priest" and, much like user 2, takes a negative stance towards the

LGBTIQ community by indicating support for the church (and, by extension, the archbishop) and the condemnation of Fr Montebello. Moreover, User 4 escalates this even further, again by directly responding to User 1's comment. Employing language like "*faithful, obey, no place*" as well as making reference to St. Peter and the Gospel, User 4 makes clear the position that religious doctrine (or at least what is perceived to be this doctrine here) should be "*obeyed*" and, on these grounds, directly ostracises the LGBTIQ community who have "*no place*" among the "*faithful*". This exchange is thus a clear example of users rallying together in what can be ideologically characterised as a *collective attack* on a comment that endorses a minority group; a pattern that can again be taken to serve the legitimisation of the anti-minority sentiment, leaving very little room for expressing any kind of support to the minority group in question.

The example in (4), on the other hand, reproduces a threaded discussion that follows an article about the Irish referendum on gay marriage being predicted to have a positive outcome (Times of Malta, 5/2015).

(4) **User 1:** There will be no peace for men & women the way of Sodoma is very near men-kind have chosen his way to abomination he has become worse than an animal.

User 2: I am pleased and happy about the results. A great day for equality and democracy. We must be proud. It is wonderful.

User 3: Well considering man is an animal and that the city of Sodom never existed I think you've got to dream up something else to scare the masses. The world is maturing, yes to human rights to all the people of the world.

User 4: User 1, if you bother to read the Holy Bible, the story of Sodom and Gomorrah has nothing to do with same sex relations. In fact the opposite is true. God punished the 2 cities because: 1. they contravened the value of hospitality due to strangers, 2.Straight men wanted to defile the daughters of Lot, who pleaded for God for forgiveness! PS: there are many animals in Nature who indulge in same sex. Are you implying that the Almighty is flawed in HIS/HER eternal scheme of things or in HIS/HER creative process? How very dare you to question the Eternal!

Here, User 1 begins the discussion by using religious doctrine to imply the calamity of the expected outcome of the vote and solidifies his position against gay marriage by using the extremely negatively-charged word "*abomination*" and explicitly denigrating LGBTIQ individuals by suggesting that they are "*worse than animals.*" In their confrontational responses, the 3 users that follow collectively defend the LGBTIQ community by not only countering the originally expressed negative stance but also by increasingly using this very argumentation against User 1. In this regard, User 2 may not engage in a direct discussion of User 1's comment, but counters the attitude expressed therein by a whole host of positively-charged vocabulary ("*pleased*", "*happy*", "*a great day*", "*proud*", "*wonderful*") which expresses complete solidarity with the minority group in question. Then, User references User 1's allusion to the animal kingdom by contending that indeed humans are part of it and thus rendering User 1's assertion redundant before going on to directly confront the original negative post. User 4 continues this trend by using the actual reference of Sodom and Gomorrah in the bible to dismantle User 1's claim by rectifying the original misquotation, again rendering the initial argument null and void of any real substance. In addition, User 4 also addresses the allegation that humans are worse than animals by making reference to actual behaviour observed in nature and contradicting in this way User 1's view, before launching a sarcastic spin which serves to further invalidate it. All in all, what we are witnessing here could correspondingly be characterised ideologically a *collective attack* to some initial disparaging attitude which could again be taken to readily communicate that the expression of an exclusionary disposition towards the LGBTIQ community in this comment thread is very likely to be met with a defence *en masse*.

5. Concluding remarks

According to Giles et al. (2015, p. 46), "it is important to be able to track the spread of ideas or opinions through hundreds of thousands of [social media posts…], but to ignore the interactional dynamics at the local level would be losing sight of the trees in order to understand the wood". In line with this observation, the main objective of this paper has been to elucidate, through the presentation of a corpus-based case study, the central role that online interactivity can play for the dissemination and confrontation of discriminatory discourse. To this end, we developed a preliminary framework for assessing whether some participatory online space constitutes an echo chamber or a forum for more democratic stance deliberation. In the particular case of the three news portals that populated the Maltese C.O.N.T.A.C.T. corpus, our analysis suggested that both inclusionary and exclusionary attitudes are to a certain extent debated across the board, which suggests that none of the portals at hand could be characterised as harbouring a potential echo chamber. On top of this, however, this exercise enabled us to additionally pinpoint the main interactional patterns that underlie ideological insularity within a social media polylogual context.

While the eventual outcome of this process might appear self-evident, we believe that our discussion showcases in more concrete terms how interactivity lies at the very core of SM-CDS and its specific focus "on the form, processes, and projected meanings of the [social media textual] content itself and their calculated impacts in society" (KhosraviNik, 2018, p. 587). Unfortunately, we do not have the space to discuss this specific impact in detail here, but the general consensus in this regard seems to be that "online audience feedback not only guides news organizations' editorial decisions concerning what to report and how to report it, but also tells news readers what to read, how to read, and how to respond to it" (Lee & Tandoc, 2017, p. 445). Perhaps, as a compromise, we can ask you, the reader of this paper, to have a closer look at the comment exchanges provided in the four examples above and consider the extent to which a continuous interaction along the lines set out therein would entice you to engage in that discussion or even have a bearing on you deciding on whether to keep reading the news on the platform that hosts each exchange. It will probably not take you much time to select those sequences that appeal to you the most, but no matter what your choice ends up being, it is bound to be tied to your own stance towards migrants and LGBTIQ individuals.

Now, while you are taking part in this thought experiment, we might as well bring in, just for the sake of comparison, the example of an alternating exchange in (5). To provide you with some context, this is an excerpt of the comment thread that follows a news article (*Times of* Malta, 17/1/2016) that reports on a protest against Muslims praying in the open air, during which members of the far-right political party Ghaqda Patrijotti Maltin distributed pork sandwiches.

(5) User 1: I strongly agree with the Patrioti Maltin keep it up. they have enough where to pray if they want. we can't afford to have a fundamental institution here. we can learn from what is happening in England where certain schools were being run by muslim fundamentalists.

User 2: Welldone User 1,you are correct in your comments. Do we really want this country being over run,first they want to pray where they want. What next ban bacon,ban feasts.The quicker the government does something to stop this the better.

User 3: The problems arise from people like you who shy away from confronting problems with those you do not agree it.It takes discipline, effort and understanding to live with someone you are not accustomed to.

User 4: We are not shying away – we are protecting our country from losing our culture, language and most important of all – freedom.

User 3: Nobody's threatening your culture, language and freedom and people like you keep making myths up instead of coming out and have the guts to say that you're bigots.The Ghaqda has attacked a 19 year old student for promoting EQUALITY. What's wrong with equality?Grow up and stop this nonsense of children a ban on ham in schools, of lampuki with

> ebola, and of persecuting people that differ from you.People like you want a theocracy and stop others from expressing themselves and their religion.You would probably even be scandalised if you saw a woman breastfeeding in public.
>
> User 5: No need to be scandalized cause the way things are going beastfeeding babies can be hidden under burkas soon……
>
> User 6: On what do you base your argument? I have seen many Maltese women and many more in Germany breast feeding in public all western all white and because of probabilities all christians. Non wearing a Burka.
>
> User 4: no I would not be scandalized and I am not a bigot either. I have helped a few immigrants find jobs too – if you must know. But I do not expect that they would overcome my country either. The fact is you are a bigot against your own people – that is what!

Even after stimulating you with an example that encompasses pure stance negotiation, chances are that, when it comes to your own personal engagement with the news, you would still rather stick to a news portal that would feature the exchanges you chose from the previous options. That is highly likely because, as it has long been established, people "tend to enjoy interacting with others of like opinions" and that "such interaction tends to polarise their attitudes and prejudices" (Parsell, 2008, p. 43). Seeing then that we cannot realistically seek to change a fundamental pattern of human behaviour, we can and should, in our aim – as critical discourse analysts – to fight social injustice, expose discriminatory discourse in all its forms, even if that means dealing with social media data that are noisy pretty much by default.

References

Assimakopoulos, S., Baider, F. H., & Millar, S. (2017). *Online Hate Speech in the European Union: A Discourse-Analytic Perspective.* Cham: Springer.

Assimakopoulos, S., & Vella Muskat, R. (2017). Exploring Xenophobic and Homophobic Attitudes in Malta: Linking the Perception of Social Practice with Textual Analysis. *Lodz Papers in Pragmatics,* 13(2), 179–202.

Assimakopoulos, S., &Vella Muskat, R. (2018). Xenophobic and Homophobic Attitudes in Online News Portal Comments in Malta. *Xjenza Online,* 6, 25–40.

Baker, P., Gabrielatos, C., KhosraviNik, M., Krzyżanowski, M., McEnery, T., & Wodak, R. (2008). A Useful Methodological Synergy? Combining Critical Discourse Analysis and Corpus Linguistics to Examine Discourses of Refugees and Asylum Seekers in the UK Press. *Discourse & Society,* 19(3), 273–306.

Barton, D., & Lee, C. (2013). *Language Online: Investigating Digital Texts and Practices*. London/New York: Routledge.

Brindle, A. (2016). *The Language of Hate: A Corpus Linguistic Analysis of White Supremacist Language*. London/New York: Routledge.

Centola, D. (2010). The Spread of Behavior in an Online Social Network Experiment. *Science,* 329, 1194–1197.

Chiluwa, I. (2012). Social Media Networks and the Discourse of Resistance: A Sociolinguistic CDA of Biafra Online Discourses. *Discourse & Society,* 23(3), 217–244.

Fairclough, N. (2003). *Analysing Discourse: Textual Analysis for Social Research.* London/New York: Routledge.

Giles, D., Stommel, W., & Paulus, T. M. (2017). The Microanalysis of Online Data: The Next Stage. *Journal of Pragmatics,* 115, 37–41.

Hardin, R. (2002). The Crippled Epistemology of Extremism. In A. Breton, G. Galeotti, P. Salmon, & R. Wintrobe (Eds.), *Political Extremism and Rationality* (pp. 3–22). Cambridge: Cambridge University Press.

Herring, S. C. (2001). Computer-Mediated Discourse. In D. Schiffrin, D. Tannen & H. E. Hamilton (Eds.), *The Handbook of Discourse Analysis* (pp. 612–634). Oxford: Blackwell.

Herring, S. C., & Androutsopoulos, J. (2018). Computer-Mediated Discourse 2.0. In D. Tannen, H. E. Hamilton & D. Schiffrin (Eds.), *The Handbook of Discourse Analysis* (2nd ed., pp. 127–151). Oxford: Wiley.

Hutchby, I. (2001). *Conversation and Technology*. Cambridge: Polity.

Jones, R. H., Chic, A., & Hafner, C. A. (2015). Introduction: Discourse Analysis and Digital Practices. In R. H. Jones, A. Chic & C. A. Hafner (Eds.), *Discourse and Digital Practices: Doing Discourse Analysis in the Digital Age* (pp. 1–17). London/New York: Routledge.

Jucker, A H., & Dürscheid, C. (2012). The Linguistics of Keyboard-to-Screen Communication: A New Terminological Framework. *Linguistik Online*, 56(6/12), 1–26.

KhosraviNik, M. (2017). Right Wing Populism in the West: Social Media Discourse and Echo Chambers. *Insight Turkey*, 19(3), 53–68.

KhosraviNik, M. (2018). Social Media Critical Discourse Studies (SM-CDS). In J. Flowerdew & J. E. Richardson (Eds.), *The Routledge Handbook of Critical Discourse Studies* (pp. 582–596). London/New York: Routledge.

KhosraviNik, M., & Unger, J. W. (2016). Critical Discourse Studies and Social Media: Power, Resistance and Critique in Changing Media Ecologies. In R. Wodak & M. Meyer (Eds.), *Methods of Critical Discourse Studies* (3rd ed., pp. 205–233). London: SAGE.

KhosraviNik, M., & Zia, M. (2014). Persian Nationalism, Identity and Anti-Arab Sentiments in Iranian Facebook Discourses: Critical Discourse Analysis and Social Media Communication. *Journal of Language and Politics,* 13(4), 755–780.

Lee, E.-J., & Tandoc, E. C. (2017). When News Meets the Audience: How Audience Feedback Online Affects News Production and Consumption. *Human Communication Research,* 43(4), 436–449.

Leruth, B., Kutiyski, Y., Krouwel, A., & Startin, N. J. (2017). Does the Information Source Matter? Newspaper Readership, Political Preferences and Attitudes towards the EU in the UK, France and the Netherlands. In M. Caiani & S. Guerra (Eds.), *Euroscepticism, Democracy and the Media* (pp. 95–120). London: Palgrave Macmillan.

Locher M., A. (2010). Introduction: Politeness and Impoliteness in Computer-Mediated Communication. *Journal of Politeness Research,* 6(1), 1–5.

Marcoccia, M. (2004). On-Line Polylogues: Conversation Structure and Participation Framework in Internet Newsgroups. *Journal of Pragmatics,* 36(1), 115–145.

Pariser, E. (2012). *The Filter Bubble: What the Internet Is Hiding from You.* London: Penguin Books.

Parsell, M. (2008). Pernicious Virtual Communities: Identity, Polarisation and the Web 2.0. *Ethics and Information Technology,* 10(1), 41–56.

Shirazi, F. (2013). Social Media and the Social Movements in the Middle East and North Africa. *Information Technology & People,* 26(1), 28–49.

Tran, G. H., & Ngo, X. M. (2018). News Comments on Facebook: A Systemic Functional Linguistic Analysis of Moves and Appraisal Language in Reader-Reader Interaction. *Journal of World Languages,* 5(1), 46–80.

van Dijk, T. A. (2009). Critical-Discourse Studies: A Socio-Cognitive Approach. In R. Wodak & M. Meyer (Eds.), *Methods of Critical Discourse Analysis* (2nd ed., pp. 62–86). London: SAGE.

Wang, Y. C., Joshi, M., Cohen, W., & Rose, C. (2008). Recovering Implicit Thread Structure in Newsgroup Style Conversations. In E. Adar et al. (Eds.), *Proceedings of the 2nd International AAAI Conference on Weblogs and Social Media* (pp. 152–160). Menlo Park, CA: The AAAI Press.

Weber, P. (2014). Discussions in the Comments Section: Factors Influencing Participation and Interactivity in Online Newspapers' Reader Comments. *New Media & Society*, 16(6), 941–957.

Williams, H. T. P., McMurray, J. R., Kurz, T., & Lambert, F. H. (2015). Network Analysis Reveals Open Forums and Echo Chambers in Social Media Discussions of Climate Change. *Global Environmental Change*, 32(1), 126–138.

Federica Formato

University of Brighton, UK

F.Formato@brighton.ac.uk

Chapter 8 How is gendered language commented on and explained? An overview of speakers supporting or rebelling against a gendered system-justification frame in Italian

Abstract: The chapter presents the debate on gendered forms in interactions among speakers on social media and provides a comprehensive overview of what goes wrong and right when discussing gendered language. Drawing on recent events, for example the FIFA Women World Cup, Formato shows how personal and social perspectives are strictly intertwined.

Keywords: Gender, Italy, ideology, gendered language.

1. Introduction

There is not a day that goes by that social media does not provide linguists, and those interested in gendered language, with some interesting interactions on the topic of (sexist) language. While English speakers are arguably more trained to spot sexism (in all its forms, visual as well as in the language), speakers of other languages, especially grammatical ones, are still battling with this. In working on the Italian language (Formato, 2014, 2016, 2017, 2019; Formato & Tantucci, 2020) and, acknowledging the grass-root initiatives on the topic of (non)sexist language, I noticed some telling practices of how gendered language is used to express a wide array of: (a) ideological positionings about culture/society, (b) one's own view of terminology, and (c) political stances, or the three together. Before explaining how this happens in linguistic terms, *the* gendered arrangement in Italy sees women to continuing to be subject to imbalances in public and private spaces. While in appearance this seems to improve – for example the female composition of the two chambers rose to 33.46 % in the current parliament[1] – sexist attitudes

1 Official data can be seen here: http://www.senato.it/leg/18/BGT/Schede/Statistiche/Composizione/SenatoriPerEta.html, and here https://www.camera.it/leg18/564?tiposezione=C&sezione=1&tabella=C_1_2 [accessed on 04/06/2020].

towards female politicians have continued (if not escalated through the use of social media, see Formato, 2019; Spallaccia, 2017). Other detrimental imbalances can be seen in: a) the gendered crime of *femminicidio* – women killed by their ex/partner, 142 in 2019, b) the workforce, a divide of 19.8 % between men and women[2], c) the unemployment rate (8.9 % for men and 9.8 % for women[3]), and d) the expectations of labour during the recent Covid-19 pandemic.

With this in mind, I here attempt to reflect on questions about how speakers choose language to re-interpret *this* society and culture and I develop my argument from the notion of system-justification (Jost & Banaji, 1994). I first present a brief overview of grammatical and social gender in Italian; I then introduce some reflections about personal ideology and the implications of advocating and supporting masculine generics through the aforementioned system-justification frame (Jost & Banaji, 1994); in Section 4, I present some examples of how the system-justification works and who confronts it. In Section 5, I draw some conclusions.

2. A brief overview of linguistic and social gender in Italian

To provide the readers with a linguistic guide for the following sub-sections, I present a very brief overview of gender in Italian (for a full overview, see Formato, 2019). Italian is a grammatical gender language, this means that gender is visible through:

- Lexical forms (e.g., ***donna***/woman – ***uomo***/man);
- Singular and plural morphological inflections attached to the root (these specific for each grammatical gender, e.g., *bambin-*, *bambin**o***/male child, *bambin**a***/female child);
- Epicene inflections, where the vowel attached to the root is the same to refer to both women and men, for example president-, presidente/speaker-chair. Gender is here specified through articles, adjectives and other masculine or feminine elements matching, for example **la**.FEM president**e** italian**a**.FEM and **il**.MASC president**e** italian**o**.MASC). There are also exceptions to these, for instance, those I labelled semi-epicene (Formato, 2019), as they are

2 https://www.openpolis.it/wp-content/uploads/2019/04/Report-occupazione-2020.pdf [accessed on 04/06/2020].

3 https://www.agi.it/fact-checking/tasso_disoccupazione_lavoro_giovani_italia-6769043/news/2019-12-20/ [accessed on 04/06/2020].

epicene in the singular form (**il**.MASC/**la**.FEM pediatra/pediatrician) but have gendered morphological inflections in the plural, for example pediatr**e**.FEM and pediatr**i**.MASC.
- Words that have a grammatical gender but not a referential one, for example **persona** (person), **membro** (member); they are grammatically feminine or masculine (respectively in the examples above) but, those they refer to can be anyone.

From what I discussed above, one could think that the Italian language provides *enough* choices to be clear about the gender of the referent/s. The picture is complicated by what can be referred to as "social gender" that is the view/s that speakers hold about gendered arrangements in society. Linguistic choices are, therefore, *motivated* (Abbou, 2011). *Use* and *availability* are two terms I employed (Formato, 2019) to explain speakers' *motivation*. For instance, the choice of (unmarked) generic masculines; these are grammatical masculine forms used to address, refer to and talk about women, preferred over (marked) feminine forms for job-titles (see Formato, 2016 on the use of *ministro/a* and Nardone, 2018 for terms used in job adverts). One can then say that social gender shifts the focus from language to speakers; specifically, the motivation in choosing the masculine forms to refer to women is to be found in how the speakers conceptualise language and how they conceptualise society, each on their own and together. The rationale beyond linguistic choices needs to be carefully interpreted but also tentatively found in a landscape that sees only some speakers favouring 1. feminine forms to refer to women (e.g., *ministra, sindaca*/minister, mayor.FEM), 2. neutral forms (e.g., *corpo insegnante*/teaching body) or 3. Split forms (e.g., *professoresse e professori*/female and male teachers/professors). Some others fiercely advocate for the use of masculine generics and, in some cases, "personalised masculines" (Formato, 2019, p. 69, see definition of the term below). To further complicate this scenario, some epicene forms are considered generic masculines by some speakers. It will become clear in the following sections that the debate is concentrating mainly on job-titles; however, an array of grammatically masculine terms are widely used in Italian in a generic fashion. For instance, the term *operatore* (agent) to refer to somebody working in a call centre or the greeting *benvenuto* (welcome) on billboards or when opening the Microsoft Windows operating system. Similarly, impersonal forms are widely used as generics (see Formato & Tantucci, 2020 on the use of *uno*).

Scholars continue to research these linguistics imbalances. A recent collection titled *Il Sessismo nella lingua italiana. Trent'anni dopo Alma Sabatini* (edited by Somma & Maestri, 2020), aimed at gathering the voice of those who have worked on these topics, starting from the legacy left by ground-breaking documents of Alma Sabatini (1987, 1993), who was the first to present lists of linguistic imbalances between feminine and masculine terms.

3. Personal ideology-ing

In this section, I provide an in-depth reflection on how speakers exhibit power through linguistic choices. Research has been and continues to be interested in variationist sociolinguistics – that is the use of standard and non-standard features by speakers divided into groups, divided into, for instance, social class, age and gender. Here, the main argument takes a different route, the question is not *what choices speakers make in order to construct their social identities?* but *how do they use the available linguistics options to build an understanding of societal gender arrangements?* The "how" question wishes to reflect upon the interpretations of speakers' ideas and the interaction about those in relation to what terms are preferred and possibly why. Hence, the issue at hand here is attempting to reflect on power, ideology and resources used by the speakers, in a broader context of available forms and uses (see Schiefflin et al., 1998 and Johnson & Milani, 2010). To attempt to explain these, I argued that speakers have, consciously or unconsciously, an *ad personam sociolinguistic imagination* (Formato, 2019, p. 28), that is a personalised exhibition of ideology-ies of socially appropriate (or not) terms. Most speakers seem to be inclined to discuss and debate the choices they make or the choices that are made to describe themselves and the others, being these inextricably tied to reproducing or changing gender(ed) stereotypes. The sociolinguistic imagination derives from gendered and stereotyped (self-) narratives – i.e., divisions into roles, statuses – that are constant, pervasive and reproduced in the media, in family traditions and in institutions. On the notion of stereotyping from a social psychology tradition (with no focus on language), Jost and Banaji (1994, pp. 1–2) argue that people are in search of justification for social events, their own feelings, thoughts and behaviours, their status or position, the status or position of others and prevailing social conditions. Their theoretical framework is an interesting one in order to reflect on how speakers explain language used by and for themselves but also used for and by the others, particularly in relation to high-ranking and male-dominated spaces, for example politics. Jost and Banaji (1994, p. 2) summarise the justification in:

- *Ego-justification*, "refer[ing] to the notion that stereotypes develop in order to protect the position or behaviour of the self";

- *Group-justification* "assum[ing] that stereotyping emerges in the service of protecting not just the individual ego, but also the status or conduct of the social group as a whole";
- *System-justification*, for which "existing social arrangements are legitimized".

I concur that the notion of system-justification has potential in discussing language used and conceptualised by those that do not seem to encapsulate a wider and more open gender experience (e.g., the preferred use of generic masculines for women). System-justification transcends the ego (which cannot be completed disregarded but seems more difficult to prove), and my interpretation of *ad personam*. More specifically, It emerges from "information processing in an ideological environment" (Banaji, 1994, p. 4), where stereotypes have the consensus of many people and are "undisputed or widely accepted as valid" (Banaji, 1994, p. 9). To further enhance this point, Berzonsky postulates that "meaning is considered to be construed and constituted within culturally based symbolic systems, metaphors and practices" (Berzonsky, 2005, p. 127), providing an explanation as to why stereotypes (in language choices and otherwise) are rarely challenged. Hence, language forms a bridge between the starting point – an ideological environment – and what world is rebuilt, as well as degrees of who is included/excluded. But how is this ideological environment voiced and evaluated? In her seminal work (Berzonsky, 1995), Cameron argues that verbal hygiene refers to the "urge to meddle in matters of language" (Berzonsky, 1995, p. VI) rather than, as simplistically thought, an appeal for employing correct language. Starting from this, speakers who discuss language become "active shapers of discursive structures" (Motschenbacher, 2016, pp. 153–156), that is they convey their social experience (Heath, 1989) and become dedicated language *mavens* (Cameron, 1995). The louder voices can be found when speakers dislike the policing of their words against their will (Cameron, 1995) and feel forced to change their linguistic habits (Sapegno, 2010). It is not a coincidence that the terms that suffer from widespread confusion are those referring to roles that were stereotypically male and are now seeing more female professionals obtaining them.

4. The workings of system-justification in language use

Following the theoretical background, I want to operationalise the system-justification frame in this section. This is an attempt to move past previous work concerned about the reasons why speakers use forms that are reproducing a systemic sexist order. For instance, I investigated a questionnaire run in 2015

(Formato, 2019), classifying 4 reasons as to why speakers prefer one form over the other, that are: (a) opposition to traditions of language, (b) un-aesthetic nature of the forms, (c) misunderstanding of grammatical gender, (iv) *there are more important things to deal with*). With a similar goal, Vergoosen, Renström, Lindqvist, and Sendén (2020) classify 14 reasons for speakers' resistance to the neutral pronoun *hen* in Swedish, among which (a) defending linguistic status quo, (b) change is too difficult and unnecessary, (c) appeal to authority, tradition, sexism and cisgenderism, and so forth. The aim set for this section is to problematise how non-sexist and gender language is used and conceptualised by some speakers.

4.1. Politics-related terms

I have already anticipated that political terms are those who are capturing the attention of the speakers and those interested in gendered language. I here collect examples that present a complex overview of how job-titles are believed to be either neutral or highly gendered or, in a telling fashion "personalised" forms.

I begin with an interesting explanation offered by a right-wing politician (Deputy Head of the *Forza Italia* party in Emilia Romagna), Alberto Ancarani. On a local newspaper, he published an editorial titled *Perchè "assessora" non va* (why assessora.FEM does not work) where he suggests some reasons as to why grammatically feminine job-titles should not be used in Italian. In his (incorrect) grammatical overview, he argues that: 1. masculine generics are neuter in Latin 2. The use of feminine terms is part of a dictatorship of the politically correct and 3. morphological inflections should not contain any information about gender, sexuality and disability. This explanation provides incorrect information (e.g., neuter terms in Latin) as well as an arguably common and simplistic problematisation of politically correct as a term and notion. It seems to reproduce what O'Neill (2011) argues, that is using other terms than the ones we are accustomed to has a focus on language rather than intent. However, his ideological and firm position against feminine terms can also be seen in his Twitter account[4] that is when prompted by other users, he frequently dismisses the use of feminine forms such as *Ministra* (minister.FEM) and *Prima Ministra* (Prime Minister.FEM). Ancarani, in his editorial, also suggests that feminine terms might be used against female politicians. While his piece is overall extremely critical of feminine terms, I found in my research that this could possibly be a valid argument (Formato, 2019, p. 161, see derogative re-semantization).

---

4 https://twitter.com/albertoancarani [accessed on 20/07/2020].

Similarly, right-wing Augusta Montaruli[5], in an intervention in the Lower Chamber of the Italian Parliament (on 21 June 2019), asked the Speaker not to use the feminine form *deputata* (MP.FEM) to refer to her. Her argument is that *in questo mondo arcobaleno, dove tutti possono definirsi come vogliono, io voglio ancora avere il diritto di auto-definirmi deputato, almeno fino a quando la Camera resterà dei deputati e non diventerà Camera dei deputati e delle deputate o addirittura Camera dei deputat* con l'asterisco.* (in this rainbow world, where everybody can refer to themselves with the labels they want, I want to have the right to define myself *deputato*.MASC, at least until the Chamber will be of the *deputati*.MASC and not of the *deputati*.MASC and *deputate*.FEM or, even, *Camera dei deputat** with the star). Specifically, the female MP resorts to a versatile masculine (Formato 2019, p. 58), that is a masculine form also used to refer to gender-mixed groups: *deputati* (MPs) is used to support her claim that only grammatical masculine job-titles (also used as generics when needed) can find room in this political arena. She sarcastically remarks the use of the plural feminine form in the title of the chamber and makes a reference to the use of the *, which some speakers use as a neutralisation strategy. Comments on how gendered language is or should be used are not rare in the Italian parliament: in the past, Laura Boldrini, former Speaker and an advocate for the use of feminine job-titles, was referred to as *Signor Presidente* (Mr Speaker) by right-wing politician Roberto Simonetti[6]. In that circumstance, she interrupted the MP to suggest that the correct form is *Signora Presidente* (Ms Speaker), adding *perché sono una donna* (because I am a woman), while the male MP insisted referring to her with the male title (Mr) followed by the epicene *presidente*. She ironically continues the interaction by saying *Allora io la chiamo deputata*.FEM (then I'll call you MP.FEM) and the male MP nervously suggesting that he can say what he wishes and has the right to address the chair as he pleases. Boldrini attempts to re-establish a fairer linguistic order as well as an institutional one. These three episodes, together with the others narrated below, all tend to justify the masculine form as a neutral generic one that no one should oppose to. These episodes tend to go beyond the ego-justification – legitimising the self, in status and conduct in relation to the other (Jost & Banaji, 1994) – and a

---

5 https://video.corriere.it/politica/voci-dal-parlamento/camera-onorevole-fdi-fico-mi-chiami-deputato-non-deputata/0566a3fe-94d6-11e9-b462-499d272481c8 [accessed on 10/07/2020].

6 https://www.ilfattoquotidiano.it/2015/12/20/simonetti-lega-nord-vs-boldrini-grazie-signor-presidente-se-io-sono-signore-lei-e-la-deputata/455209/ [accessed on 10/07/2020].

group-justification that "defend[s] the actions of others with whom [the speaker] shares a social identification" (Jost & Banaji, 1994, p. 6). In fact, these system-justification strategies present how "an individual perceives, understands and explains an existing situation or arrangement with the result that the situation or arrangement is maintained" (Jost & Banaji, 1994, p. 10).

The support to a sexist system is a particularly crucial one in Italy and in formal interactions, such as interviews, some politicians rebuild the social grammar. A former minister of justice, Giulia Bongiorno, interviewed in moderate newspaper *Il Corriere della Sera*[7], was asked which form she prefers. To the question *Ministro o Ministra?* (minister.MASC or minister.FEM), she provides the following answer: *Ministro. È un ruolo. Mi pare una deminutio declinarlo in base al genere. Avvocato, non avvocata* (Ministro.MASC. It's a role. I think choosing the gender inflection is undermining. Avvocato.MASC, not Avvocata.FEM). Driven by similar understandings of gendered language, the current minister of Public Administration, Fabiana Dadone has the job-titles in the generic masculine form in her Twitter bio[8], that is *ministro.*MASC and *deputato.*MASC. From the same perspective, councillor Dorota Kusiak[9] from right-wing Lega (in Ferrara) asks to *essere chiamata assessore perché è la forma adeguata e corretta rispettosa del ruolo che ricopro* (be referred to as *assessore.* MASC because it's the correct and most suitable form which shows respect to the role I hold). Kusiak is not the only one, Stefania Segnana, from the same party, wrote an official document in her role as councillor (in the city of Trento) suggesting that the council should promote collegiality through *l'utilizzo del linguaggio comunemente usato, privo di inutile e ridondanti declinazioni al maschile e al femminile, in grado di determinare unicamente storture e incomprensioni* (the use of a language that is in everyday use, devoid of redundant masculine and feminine endings, which are only leading to distortions and misunderstanding). Her point was aimed at being address *assessore* (councillor.MASC) instead of *assessora* (councillor.FEM), yet disregarding that the former is a grammatically masculine term.

The system justification approach convincingly argues, as it is shown in the previous and following examples, that the stereotypes, and in this case

---

7 https://www.corriere.it/cronache/19_marzo_07/giulia-bongiorno-a-tutte-donne-destra-dico-lottare-la-parita-52717d66-4118-11e9-8d4c-9b3b6b114344.shtml [accessed on 13/07/2020].

8 https://twitter.com/DadoneFabiana [accessed on 14/07/2020].

9 https://www.estense.com/?p=858953&fbclid=IwAR3hbNSxVT2JinZrhwPjN14sxTQzyAynSzkvP-TEV27VkiNMaZs7kSMcnSk [accessed on 13/07/2020].

explanation of stereotypical sexist use of language, is also put forward by those that are considered as inferior in the defended *status quo*. More specifically, some female politicians (as in the case of Montarulo, Bongiorno, Dadone, Kusiak and Segnana), seem to *work* against fairer forms that would also benefit them. This seems to mainly happen in right-wing parties, making it un-coincidental that female politicians are supported and helped in navigating political arenas[10]. It is for this reason that in reviewing how social gender appears in language, I coined a category that takes this view into account. I labelled it "personalised masculine" (2019), where the personal experience in a role is foregrounded with respect to the gender of the person. In Italian grammar there is no such understanding, as in all dictionaries *ministro* is classified as a masculine (and singular) noun. The examples above seem to lead to the notion of false consciousness, that is, some speakers fail to acknowledge the grammatical and, mainly, social nature of masculine generics. This is also reproduced in newspaper articles – for example, the masculine form is mostly used when referring to female ministers in the period 2012–2014 (Formato, 2016). For these reasons, I argue that some of the speakers who conceptualise a system-justification are those who would benefit from a change.

Furthermore, the perceived neutrality of some terms also creates grammatical incongruences (mainly for those speakers advocating feminine forms), as in the case of Dadone giving birth to her second son and still referred with the masculine term, for example *Il ministro Fabiana Dadone sarà ancora mamma*[11] (the *ministro*.MASC will be a mum again). This is not new, mum-to-be Giulia Grillo (former minister of Heath – Conte cabinet I) was referred to as *ministro*.MASC in several headlines. For instance, the newspaper *Il Messaggero* writes *Il ministro Grillo è diventata mamma*[12] and, similarly, former minister Madia

10 At the moment, the only female leader of a party in Italy is Giorgia Meloni, a right-wing populist politician leading *Fratelli d'Italia* (Brothers of Italy). The name of the party seems to suggest her way of supporting and maintaining the *status quo*. Newspapers have been found to use masculine generic forms to report her political roles (Formato, 2019).

11 https://www.targatocn.it/2020/06/04/leggi-notizia/argomenti/attualita/articolo/il-ministro-fabiana-dadone-sara-ancora-mamma-maschietto-in-arrivo-a-fine-giugno.html [accessed on 14/07/2020]. Congratulations for the birth of her second child were given to the *ministra*.FEM from fellow minister Teresa Bellanova and Prime Minister Giuseppe Conte. The other female ministers, except Lamorgese who does not have accounts on social media, have all chosen the feminine term.

12 https://www.ilmessaggero.it/politica/giulia_grillo_mamma_ministro-4095949.html [accessed on 17/07/2020].

(Renzi cabinet 2014–2016) was referred to as *ministro* when her child was born. Incongruence can also lead to misunderstandings: differently from those described above (seen the relationship with motherhood), newspaper *La Stampa* addresses the prime minister of New Zealand with the generic masculine *primo ministro,* using all elements needing gendered inflections in their masculine forms, for example *acclamato* (acclaimed), *allontanato* (sent off). Called out by some users on Twitter[13], the newspaper *fixed* some misgendered items but left some others; at the moment of writing the article reads: *[I]n Nuova Zelanda il primo ministro Jacinda Andern, acclamata durante la pandemia di coronavirus, è stata allontanata da un bar insieme al marito perché considerato troppo affollato per le linee guida che lui stesso aveva dettato*[14] (In New Zealand, the primo ministro. MASC Jacinda Andern, acclaimed.FEM during the corona virus pandemic, has been sent off.FEM from a café, together with the husband because considered too crowded following the guidelines that he himself.MASC had issued). There seems to be a legacy of the mistakes, more specifically the *lui* (he himself) that suggests that it is the husband who has issued the guidelines.

The relationship between availability and use of generic masculine and feminine forms transcends gendered groups, as we saw in some of these previous examples, building in- and out- groups which are characterised by their distance or closeness to (waves of) feminism, being this the social identification for choosing to be inside or outside categories of speakers who would prefer one form over the other. The defence of the interests, mainly from right-wing supporters, also passes through the term *boldrinate,* originating from the surname of Laura Boldrini (mentioned above), to refer to trivial linguistic matters advocated by those who prefer and defend the use of feminine forms.

However, there are more complex cases. In late 2019, Italian politics was faced with another change: the coalition *Movimento 5 stelle* (M5S) and *Lega* stepped down in favour of a coalition between the M5S and left-wing parties *Partito Democratico* (PD) and *Liberi e Uguali* (LEU). The cabinet changed (while the Prime Minister remained the same, Giuseppe Conte), and 7 women (8 from 2020) were invested of a ministerial role (out of 22 ministers). The day before Elena Bonetti became the minister of equal opportunities, her Twitter bio reported the

13 https://twitter.com/crialicata/status/1262036936086237185 [accessed on 17/07/2020].

14 https://www.lastampa.it/esteri/2020/05/17/news/coronavirus-in-grecia-e-francia-riaprono-le-spiagge-drammatica-escalation-in-brasile-1.38855312 [accessed on 17/07/2020].

masculine generic *professore di analisi matematica* (professor of mathematics)[15], while the day after, *professore* had been shortened to *prof* and the new role was reported with the feminine morphological inflection, *Ministra* (minister.FEM)[16]. Similarly, the minister of labour and social policies, Nunzia Catalfo (in the Conte II government), used the generic masculine *ministro* in her bio on Twitter, accompanying it with the feminine *senatrice*[17] (senator.FEM). Such confusion also seems to occur in institutional pages. As for the Conte II government (2018–2020), one of the official webpages of the *Presidenza del Consiglio* (the cabinet) used the generic masculine *ministro* for female ministers Pisano and Bonetti and the generic masculine *sottosegretario* for female undersecretaries Malpezzi and Agea, but the feminine *ministra* for minister Dadone[18]. In the webpage where the ministers were presented, the generic masculine was the only form used[19].

Similarly, a recent issue (July 2020) of the magazine *IO DONNA* (offered weekly with the broadsheet *Il Corriere della Sera*) gathers the voice of women from the music scene, politics and the media. The MP Valeria Valente is described as *senatrice* (senator.FEM) but also as *assessore* (councillor.MASC) and *candidato sindaco* (candidate.MASC to become mayor.MASC).

Other ways in which confusion is generated refer to how job-titles are used in newspapers. For instance, Marco Travaglio, journalist and founder of newspaper *Il Fatto Quotidiano* shares on his Facebook page one of this outlet's article changing the feminine form *assessora* (used in the heading) to the generic masculine *assessore* for Councillor Catalfamo[20].

Cases such as these show that the scenario is much more complex than just choosing between the feminine inflection or term and the masculine (generic) ones. This might reflect an intricate understanding of personal positioning (ego-justification) within the *status quo* hierarchy, which leads into the wider understanding of group-justification language stereotyping.

---

15 *Professoressa*.FEM is widely used, maybe her the speaker wanted to signal that she is a university professor rather than a high school one, where teachers are referred to as *professore*.MASC and *professoressa*.FEM.

16 https://twitter.com/elenabonetti [accessed on 13/07/2020].

17 https://twitter.com/CatalfoNunzia [accessed on 14/07/2020].

18 http://presidenza.governo.it/AmministrazioneTrasparente/Organizzazione/OrganiIndirizzoPolitico/index.html [accessed on 13/07/2020].

19 http://www.governo.it/it/ministri-e-sottosegretari [accessed on 13/07/2020].

20 https://www.facebook.com/marcotravaglio/posts/10151515672759990/ [accessed on 17/07/2020].

4.2. Other job-titles: Architett- and avvocat-

It is not only in politics that speakers seem to defend the *status quo*, the linguistic outcome of this can also be found in other working environments. Debates and interactions about generic masculines such as *avvocato* (lawyer.MASC) and *architetto* (architect.MASC) are not rare. These are fuelled by choices made by speakers and advertised through the affordances of social media or traditional media such as newspapers/magazines. Starting from these, a group of female architects explain that they want to be addressed and referred to as *architettrici*[21], firmly explaining that this is the appropriate term. *Architettrici*, though, is seen in relation to the masculine *architettori*, an archaic form of architett+morphological inflection. On the same term and moving to social media, the post[22] of the *Ordine Architetti PPC Reggio Emilia* (a register that gathers the architects of the city of Reggio Emilia, in the North of Italy) attracted the interest of many Facebook users. The female counterparts of the *ordine*, published a picture on their facebook page where they write *Architetto o Architetta? Noi preferiamo "un'architetto" con l'apostrofo* (Architetto.MASC or Architetta.FEM? we prefer "un'.FEMarchitetto.MASC" with the apostrophe). This needs a detailed grammatical explanation before delving into the social one. In Italian, the determiner *uno, una, un, un'* (*a/an* in English) are classifiable in terms of gender: *uno* and *un* are used for masculine nouns (or adjectives), depending on how the word begins (*un quaderno, uno zaino*/a blocknote, a backpack), while for feminine forms *una* is mostly used with words beginning with consonant (*una*.FEM *rosa*/a rose) and *un'* used with feminine words starting with a vowel (*un'.FEM amica*/a friend.FEM). The choice of these female architects, therefore, is to have a hybrid term[23], where the article is feminine but the job-title is masculine (and generic). The comments to the post reproduce the scenario that sees opposing those who resort to the idea that job-titles are neuter (or, as I postulated, personalised masculines) and those who criticise their linguistic preference (also a novel one). Those who

---

21 https://www.elledecor.com/it/people/a31220705/donne-architettura-intervista-ernesta-caviola/?fbclid=IwAR0ypY5YVa9KyWFycNkOkBkFkcgLyOWbWWT46QTaxQHA6efXB3me8gSfPJU [accessed on 22/07/2020].

22 https://www.facebook.com/219085911528908/photos/a.219091971528302/2583979738372835/ [accessed on 13/07/2020].

23 I refer to forms similar to these as semi-marked, e.g., *Signora*.FEM *Ministro*.MASC (Formato, 2014) or *candidata*.FEM *sindaco*.MASC (Formato, 2019). One can note that the job title, which is arguably the most important information, is in its masculine forms and elements surrounding these are given the benefit of being grammatically feminine.

created the post, possibly taken by surprise, justified their message by underlying their sarcasm and self-irony, suggesting that they were not seriously considering this option. The trivialisation of gendered language seems to be another crucial aspect of the group-justification strategy, one that is widely used on social media (Formato, 2019).

The same destiny is found in the job-title *avvocat-*, for which the masculine form – *avvocato* – seems to be preferred over the feminine – *avvocata*. The feminine itself is found to be problematic by Italian speakers, it ranges from *avvocata* to the (semantically incorrect) *avvocatessa*[24]. In the previous section, we read that Bongiorno (a lawyer and a former minister), suggests that the job-title should be used in its masculine (but perceived neutral) form as it refers to the role rather than the gender of the referent. Similarly, Maria Elena Boschi, a former minister of the Renzi Government (2014–2016) seems to prefer the generic masculine *avvocato*, as indicated by her profile on the social network Twitter[25]. Valente, interviewed in IO DONNA (see Section 3.2. for a detailed account of the magazine) is similarly referred to as *avvocato* (lawyer.MASC)[26]. This is reminiscent of what I discussed before: the justification is put forward also by those who are to lose from reproducing a *status quo* that has historically been and still is detrimental and unfair to them. On the topic of *avvocata* or *avvocatessa*, websites such as *la legge per tutti*[27], seem to be sceptical as to why using a gendered fairer language could promote a different view of women in the profession. The reason used to support this is the higher number of female lawyers with respect to the male counterparts.

To conclude, generic masculines are not only found in politics but in a range of professional spaces where women co-habit with men, and while numbers of female professionals are growing, sexist attitudes still seem to prevent them to fully experience their careers.

24 Alma Sabatini (1987, 1993) suggests that the suffix *–essa* has been used to mean "the wife of" and therefore is problematic. However, feminine terms such as *professoressa* (high school teacher, professor) and *dottoressa* (doctor) are widely used and accepted.

25 https://twitter.com/meb [accessed on 20/07/2020].

26 The same scenario is found in fiction, where female having leading roles in TV series as lawyers are referred to as *avvocato* and, in some cases, *avvocatessa* (in the case, for instance, of *Non dirlo al mio capo*, a TV series aired on RAI 1, 2019) or *Sorelle* (RAI 1, 2019).

27 https://www.laleggepertutti.it/210133_si-dice-avvocata-o-avvocatessa [accessed on 16/07/2020].

4.3. Rebelling to the system-justification frame

In the previous sections, with the aid of examples, I provided an overview of how speakers, unconsciously or consciously, recreate a justification that reproduces and bolster a male-oriented and sexist *status quo*. While this seems a prominent discourse in Italian media, politics and other environments, one should not disregard the efforts taken to counteract these strategies. Nowadays, many city councils (and other institutions) have adopted guidelines that promote a non-sexist use of the language, for exampleMilan[28]. Among these, I have recently kept in touch with the person in charge of the Facebook posts[29] of the council of my hometown, to ask what guided the choice of a non-sexist use of language, for example assessora rather than the generic masculine *assessore* when reporting news about female councillors. The answer[30] did suggest an interesting trend, for which speakers seem to ground their choices in accordance to the *Accademia della Crusca* (an academy of independent linguists thought to have authority on language) or dictionaries such as *Il Treccani*[31]. Similarly, in the episode of the architects of the region Emilia Romagna, another group of architects under the name of *Rebel Architette* (rebel architects.FEM) rebuked the choice of *un'architetto* (see Section 3.2), mentioning the linguists of *La Crusca*. On 12 June 2020, they also published a note on their Facebook page to specify which forms they prefer, writing: *siamo architette non architettrici né archittetti donne* (we are architette.FEM, not *archittettrici*.FEM? nor women *architetti*.MASC)[32].

That of reflecting about the connections between speakers' choices and the perceived authority of dictionaries and linguistic institutions has been a previous concern (see Formato, 2019). *La Crusca* is frequently mentioned as a life buoy when criticisms are directed at the use of feminine terms. This seems to reproduce a search of institutional and authoritative support for linguistic choices, such as feminine forms, aimed at ideologically counteracting the group-justification. However, *la Crusca* still has contrasting voices in relation to newer inclusive forms such as the use of the asterisk or the use of the schwa.

---

28 https://www.comune.milano.it/-/pari-opportunit%C3%A0.-la-parit%C3%A0-di-genere-nelle-comunicazioni-ufficiali-del-comune [accessed on 15/07/2020].

29 https://www.facebook.com/ComunediBenevento/ [accessed on 20/07/2020].

30 Personal communication. 15 July 2020.

31 http://www.treccani.it/ [accessed on 15/07/2020].

32 https://www.facebook.com/architettearchiwomen/photos/a.1623823844298585/3505420616138889 [accessed on 17/07/2020].

From a *scholarly* point of view, academic literature on the topic (most notably the work by Fusco, 2012; Cavagnoli, 2013; Nardone, 2016, 2018) not only presents how language is used but convincingly focus on the need of a revitalisation of a language that should include women. Many speakers seem to take on board feminine terms. Advocating for feminine forms should not been seen as a way to recreate the battle of the sexes, or to prescriptively suggest that grammar is a monolithic entity that should be respected without an in-depth reflection. On the contrary, it should be seen as an effort to reframe a society and a culture that continues to construct a taxonomy of (fixed) roles, traits and attitudes, all unfavourable to women.

5. Conclusion

The aim of this chapter was not to prescriptively tell speakers that using feminine forms is *better*, more correct or, to observe statistical significance of most used form. With necessary elements of these, the aim was to show how speakers use and conceptualise language and how it can be explained through historical sexist stereotyping (through the notion of system-justification, Jost & Banaji, 1994).

More specifically, a grammatically masculine language stems from a given construct of reality that sees, and linguistically refers to, women as invisible, and sometimes as "interlopers" (Cameron, 2006). (Some) speakers seem to have personal and political views, based on a society that tends to consistently disadvantage one gender group (women) over the other (men). However, Italian speakers would never confront the grammatically feminine of words such as *ragazza* (girl) or *infermiera* (nurse.FEM). Yet, as shown, some would easily use and comment on grammatically feminine terms such as *ministra, sindaca, avvocata, architetta*. What is interesting is that feminine terms describing traditional female oriented working environments have been unproblematically used with masculine inflections; for instance, terms such as *maestro* (teacher of elementary schools.MASC) or *infermiere* (nurse.MASC). Similarly, *mammo* is used to refer to men *acting as traditional mothers* (e.g., looking after their children, cooking or stay-home dads): while this is semantically challenged by feminists, the terms is never commented on in relation to how it sounds, its grammatical incorrectness and according to other explanations offered for feminine inflections.

One can link this to what Berzonsky (2005, p. 128) convincingly argues, that is "within a particular frame of reference – a set of values, goals, or standards – some choice, options, or ideas can be deemed to be better or more preferable than others. Pragmatic consideration such as utility, predictive power or problem-solving effectiveness play a role in determining which theoretical constructions are considered to be more intelligible or believable than others". With no direct reference to language, this quote suggests that choices, options and ideas are used (and sometimes, I argue, manipulated) to frame how we perceive the world, about us and about the others. In Section 4, I provided examples that show this problematization, with speakers consciously and loudly suggesting that grammatically feminine forms are incorrect and have no space in the Italian language. One could argue that for some, this is a matter of terminology rather than intending to maintain the *status quo*, yet it seems very likely that the social legacy has an active role in what language is chosen. Based on this, I only touch upon the notion and implications of the term *politically correct* throughout the chapter; politically correctness, as in the words of O'Neill (2011, p. 280), has the benefit of "discourage[ing] the reflexive use of words that impart a negative stereotype thereby promoting conscious thinking about how to describe others fairly on their merits" (O'Neill, 2011, p. 280). However, it is interesting that disagreement directed at *politically correct* language, as a notion, is used as forming part of the system-justification aimed at maintaining the sexist *status quo*[33].

The notion of system-justification enhances what suggested above and puts forward the idea that the frame of reference is embedded, in many cases, in stereotypical views of people. Stereotypes are not embraced only by those who seem to benefit from those constructions, but also by those to whom these are detrimental. Shown through examples, I argue that female professionals using generic masculines and criticising the use of grammatically feminine terms, contribute to justify the sexist *status quo* (see also Formato, 2014, 2016, 2019), specifically in relation to a *suitable* division of labour (see Hoffman & Hurst, 1990). Another point that seems to emerge from the analysis of terms used and explained, is that right-wing politicians are those who frequently comment against a fairer use of language, demonstrating the complexity of the intertwine of personal experience and political alignment.

This chapter only marginally looks at the wider experience of gender as it is concerned with women and men only, disregarding other linguistic and cultural aspects such as sexuality and gender as a much wider spectrum. I do not intend

33 Recently, the journalist Mattia Feltri wrote two editorials against the use of the asterisk and schwa, and more broadly, showing his disagreement of a politically correct language (starting from an interaction occurred with a former member of *La Crusca*). https://www.lastampa.it/topnews/firme/buongiorno/2020/07/25/news/allarmi-siam-fasciste-1.39122109 [accessed on 31/07/2020].

to overlook language that refers to, addresses or is used by those outside the (possibly heterosexual) binary men/women. Language used by and for outside the binary is as complex, and scholars are beginning to work on this in the Italian language (see Santonocito, 2019; Zawacki, 2018).

References

Abbou, J. (2011). Double Gender Marking in French: A Linguistic Practice of Antisexism. *Current Issues in Language Planning*, 12(1), 55–75.

Berzonsky, M. D. (2005). Ego Identity: A Personal Standpoint in a Postmodern World. *Identity*, 5(2), 125–136.

Cameron, D. (1995). *Verbal Hygiene*. London: Routledge.

Cameron, D. (2006). Theorising the Female Voice in Public Contexts. In Baxter, J. (Ed.), *Speaking Out: The Female Voice in Public Contexts* (pp. 3–20). London: Palgrave-Macmillan.

Cavagnoli, S. (2013). *Linguaggio giuridico e lingua di genere: una simbiosi possibile*. Alessandria: Edizioni dell'Orso.

Formato, F. (2014). *Language Use and Gender in the Italian Parliament*. Unpublished PhD thesis. Retrieved September 5, 2023 from https://eprints.lancs.ac.uk/id/eprint/71736/1/2014formatophd.pdf

Formato, F. (2016). Linguistic Markers of Sexism in the Italian Media: A Case Study of Ministra and Ministro. *Corpora*, 11(3), 371–99.

Formato, F. (2017). 'Ci sono troie in giro in Parlamento che farebbero di tutto': Italian Female Politicians Seen through a Sexual Lens. *Gender & Language*, 11(3), 389–414.

Formato, F. (2019). *Gender, Discourse and Ideology in Italian*. London: Palgrave Macmillan.

Formato, F., & Tantucci, V. (2020). Uno: A Corpus Linguistic Investigation of Intersubjectivity and Gender. *Journal of Language and Discrimination*, 4(1), 51–73.

Fusco, F. (2012). *La lingua e il femminile nella lessicografia italiana. Tra stereotipi e invisibilità*. Alessandria: Edizioni dell'Orso.

Heath, S. B. (1989). Language Ideology. *International Encyclopedia of Communications*, 2, 393–395.

Hoffman, C., & Hurst, N. (1990). Gender Stereotypes: Perception or Rationalization?. *Journal of Personality and Social Psychology*, 58(2), 197–208.

Johnson, S., & Milani, T. (Eds.). (2010). *Language Ideologies and Media Discourse: Texts, Practices, Politics*. London: Continuum.

Jost, J. T., & Banaji, M. R. (1994). The Role of Stereotyping in System-Justification and the Production of False Consciousness. *British Journal of Social Psychology*, 33(1), 1–27.

Motschenbacher, H. (2016). A Poststructuralist Approach to Structural Gender Linguistics. In J. Abbou & F. H. Baider (Eds.), *Gender, Language and the Periphery* (pp. 65–88). Amsterdam: John Benjamins.

Nardone, C. (2016). Asimmetrie semantiche di genere: un'analisi sull'italiano del corpus ItWaC. *Gender/Sexuality/Italy*, 3.

Nardone, C. (2018). *Lingua, genere e lavoro in Italia e in Germania: un'analisi comparativa su annunci di lavoro, sui corpora itWaC e deWac e sulla stampa.* Unpublished PhD thesis, Università di Bologna and Heinrich-Heine-Universität Düsseldorf.

Ochs, E. (1992). Indexing Gender. In A. Duranti & C. Goodwin (Eds.), *Rethinking Context: Language as an Interactive Phenomenon* (pp. 335–358). Cambridge: Cambridge University Press.

O'Neill, B. (2011). A Critique of Politically Correct Language. *The Independent Review*, 16(2), 279–291.

Sabatini, A. (1987). *Raccomandazioni per un uso non sessista della lingua italiana.* Commissione nazionale per la realizzazione della parità tra uomo e donna, Presidenza del Consiglio dei Ministri.

Sabatini, A. (1993). *Ricerca sulla formulazione degli annunci di lavoro.* Commissione Nazionale Per La Parità E Le Pari Opportunità Tra Uomo E Donna.

Santonocito, C. S. (2019). LGBT People in the Speeches of Italian and British PMs: A Corpus-Assisted Critical Discourse Analysis. *Critical Approaches to Discourse Analysis Across Disciplines*, 11(2).

Sapegno, M.S. (ed). (2010). *Che genere di lingua? Sessismo e potere discriminatorio delle parole.* Roma: Carocci.

Schieffelin, B. B., Woolard, K. A., & Kroskrity P. V. (1998). *Language ideologies: Practice and theory*. Oxford: Oxford University Press.

Somma, A. L., & Maestri, G. (Eds.). (2020). *Il sessismo nella lingua italiana. Trent'anni dopo Alma Sabatini.* Pavia: Blonk.

Spallaccia, B. (2017). *Misogynistic Hate Speech on Social Networks: A Critical Discourse Analysis.* Unpublished PhD thesis. University of Bologna.

Vergoossen, H. P., Renström, E. A., Lindqvist, A., & Sendén, M. G. (2020). Four Dimensions of Criticism Against Gender-Fair Language. *Sex Roles*, 1–10.

Zawacki, S. (2018). Fuori dal Binario: Linguistic Gender in the Italian Context. *Inquiry*, 22, 82.

Stefania M. Maci

University of Bergamo, Italy

stefania.maci@unibg.it

Chapter 9 "stop . mansplaining . my . rights . to . me ." *#mansplaining* on Twitter: A pilot study

Abstract This study investigates the phenomenon of mansplaining, by means of an analysis of tweets containing the hashtag #mansplain. The aim is to detect whether the hashtag measures societal beliefs or whether it has become an ideological weapon revealing processes of identity building.

Keywords: mansplain, hashtags, gendered discourse, social media discourse, sociosemiotics.

1. Introduction

Social media, and Twitter in particular, play a fundamental role in providing a public space for people to discuss contemporary social issues, ranging from terrorist attacks to domestic violence, from (online) misogyny to science and politics (Lutzky & Lawson, 2019). Moreover, in recent years, online revelations of sexual abuse and harassment in most fields of society (journalism, politics, film industry) have evidenced more than ever lines of male privilege and power imbalance vis-à-vis women, leading to online discussions of gender relations and inequalities, while the hashtag #metoo has become a password to reveal sexual abuse, assault and harassment faced by women (Lutzky & Lawson, 2019, p. 1).

Within this context, this contribution studies the hashtag *#mansplain** (deriving from the substantive *man* + the verb *explain*, with the wild card standing for any suffix after the verb *explain*), a neologism originally used on Twitter to indicate men's socially problematic behaviour to detect whether this term actually represents effective politically (in)correct communication or if it reveals a wider range of meanings and uses on Twitter. Using Corpus Linguistic analysis, we will discuss the pragmatic function of this term on Twitter, drawing on a corpus of 192,217 running words (6,972 types) from 1 January 2017 to 31 July 2019.

In order to achieve this goal, this paper will proceed as follows: Section 2 introduces the background to the rise in popularity of the term, followed by a relevant literature review and the research questions; Section 3 describes the data and methodological approach, as well as the ethics applied in order to carry out an analysis of the findings explained in Section 4, in which data interpretation is also discussed. A conclusion is offered in Section 5.

The results suggest that although the term does not seem to be used as a "catch-all" expression underlining the gender war on the Internet, it can be used to indicate power inequalities.

2. Background, literature review and research questions

According to the Oxford English Dictionary online (OED), the term *mansplain* is a verbal compound deriving from the substantive *man* plus the verb *explain* and has the meaning of "to explain (something) needlessly, overbearingly, or condescendingly, esp. (typically when addressing a woman) in a manner thought to reveal a patronising or chauvinistic attitude". The term was first recorded by OED on 21 May 2008 as a coinage created by Ann Larimer (nickname: phosfate) in her post "On statistics", in which she replied: "Oh, gosh, thank you so much for mansplaining this to us", while commenting on an article entitled "Women Who Hate Dean Hating Women Hating … wait", posted by themadscientist on *Fandom Wank Blog* (themadscientist, 2008).

The notion of *mansplaining* seems, however, to have been coined by Rebecca Solnit in her blog on 13 April 2008, though the word *mansplaining* was never mentioned. In the blog *TomDispatch. A Regular antidote to the mainstream media*, and later in her book, *Man Explain Things to Me* (Solnit, 2014), the writer explains her personal experience as well as women's awareness of men unnecessarily explaining things to women:

> Men explain things to me, and other women, whether or not they know what they're talking about. Some men. Every woman knows what I'm talking about. It's the presumption that makes it hard, at times, for any woman in any field; that keeps women from speaking up and from being heard when they dare; that crushes young women into silence by indicating, the way harassment on the street does, that this is not their world. It trains us in self-doubt and self-limitation just as it exercises men's unsupported overconfidence. (Solnit, 2008)

In 2010, *The New York Times* included *mansplainer* in its Words of the Year list,[1] with the meaning: "A man compelled to explain or give an opinion about

1 Retrieved from: https://archive.nytimes.com/www.nytimes.com/2010/12/19/weekinreview/19sifton.html [15/7/2020].

everything – especially to a woman. He speaks, often condescendingly, even if he doesn't know what he's talking about or even if it's none of his business. Old term: a boor."[2]

Ever since then, the term has been used by journalists to describe actors, TV characters, musicians and even politicians – one of the most notable examples being in 2018, when Ilana Kaplan reported that "Stephen Colbert accuses Trump of trying to 'mansplain the Midterms' to female voters".[3] At the beginning of 2016, the term provoked a discussion between two Members of a committee of the Australian Senate, Katy Gallagher and Mitch Fifield (italics added):

Senator GALLAGHER:	The process you have just outlined is slightly different to the process that is outlined in the *Cabinet Handbook* about the way in which matters are dealt with.
Senator Fifield:	Sorry can I just –
SG:	Well, you had finished. That is why I restarted. Okay, you have restarted. Fair enough.
SF:	Let me stop you so you don't waste your line of questioning.
SG:	*I love the mansplaining. I'm enjoying it.*
SF:	You are loving what?
SG:	*The mansplaining that is going on.*
SF:	What do you mean?
SG:	By not answering the question. By repeating processes which are not related to the question that I have asked.
SF:	*What is 'mansplaining', Senator?*
SG:	*It is the slightly patronising and condescending way that you are responding to my questions.*
SF:	*I would suggest, Senator, that if you are putting the word 'man' in front of some description of what I am doing, you are doing that which I am sure you are very much against – that is, making a sexist implication about how I am conducting my role as a man. Is that what you are saying, Senator?*
SG:	*What I am saying is that the way you have been responding to me has been patronising and condescending and I have responded to that. The easier way to deal with this –*
SF:	*By saying I am mansplaining.*

2 Although the term *mansplain* has recently been introduced, the act of mansplaining is unfortunately not recent. For a cultural history of mansplaining, see Rothman (2012) at: https://www.theatlantic.com/sexes/archive/2012/11/a-cultural-history-of-mansplaining/264380/ [17/7/2020]

3 Retrieved from: https://www.rollingstone.com/tv/tv-news/stephen-colbert-trump-mansplain-the-midterms-female-voters-745095/ [15/7/2020].

SG: *is not to have that way in responding to the questions I have asked.*

SF: *Imagine if I said you were 'womansplaining'. Imagine the reaction if I said you were 'womansplaining'. You are saying that I am mansplaining.*

SG: Well, it is a term that is used when –

SF: Is it? By whom? By rude senators.

CHAIR: Doesn't make it any less offensive.

SF: By senators who are seeking to make gender an issue.

SG: *I am not. I am just saying that your answers to me have been condescending and patronising and I have responded to that. The way not to have that is not to have that approach in the way you have answered your questions.*
(https://parlinfo.aph.gov.au/parlInfo/search/display/display.w3p;query=Id%3A%22committees%2Festimate%2F9ebf9471-a8f5-45dd-90dd-6c25d49f9cd5%2F0002%22 [15/7/2020])

The situation here is clear: instead of answering a political question properly, SF simply explains processes not relevant to the question itself in a patronising and condescending tone; in a word, by using mansplain. A similar clash occurred in 2018, when, on the UK Parliament's floor, the Prime Minister, Theresa May, confronted the Government opposition leader, Mr Corbyn, for having explained International Women's Day:

Corbyn: Tomorrow is International Women's Day to celebrate how far we have come but also to reflect how far we have to go […] As she makes her arms sales pitch, will she also call on the crown prince to halt the shocking abuse of human rights in Saudi Arabia?

May: *First of all, can I thank the right honourable gentleman for telling me it's International Women's Day tomorrow. I think that's what's called mansplaining* […] that does not mean we should be pulling our punches and I agree, which is why I will be raising concerns about human rights with the crown prince when I meet him and can I just say, as the right honourable gentleman started, I welcome the fact that the crown prince will be sitting down with, as the guest of, a female prime minister.[4] [italics added]

As Kinney (2017) underlines, not only has the word begun to be included in major dictionaries, such as, as we have already seen, the OED and the *Maquarie* Dictionarie, but also in the *Dictionary of Social Justice*, which explicitly underlines the fact that to *mansplain* is not simply intended to refer to an explanation given by a man, but rather to an explanation given by a man "without checking the credentials of anyone else in the conversation, assuming his were better than anyone else's in the room – i.e., that he was the expert by default"[5] – the reflex of a

4 Retrieved from: https://www.youtube.com/watch?v=QCEJ6y5heq4 [17/7/2020].

5 Retrieved from: https://medium.com/the-establishment/your-global-mansplaining-dictionary-in-34-languages-a5e44bf682ba [17/7/2020].

culture that devalues non-men, and, especially, non-white non-men individuals. For this reason, the action of *mansplaining* is perceived by women as a set of actions performed by men who consistently interrupt and talk down to them, for the simple reason of showing off (unwanted) knowledge as the basis of power in their relationship (Buerkle, 2019), which evidently contributes to creating, in women, a feeling of frustration and disregard, particularly in matters concerning women's careers (Bridges, 2017; Kidd, 2019).

The phenomenon of *mansplaining* is quite popular in blogs and on social media. Interestingly, the topic of *mansplain* is particularly evidenced on Twitter by means of hashtags. As suggested by Heyd and Puschmann (2017), hashtags are semiotic typesets which, in the 19th century, were used to indicate "number", a symbol that gained semiotic importance in the 20th century to "denote semantics of enumerating or numbering elements" and went "on a trajectory of popularization with the emergence of widespread and popular communication via the Web in the early Nineties" (Heyd & Puschmann, 2017, p. 53). As indicated by Lutzky and Lawson (2019), a hashtag is a combination of a hash symbol (#) and a word or set of words integrated into a tweet (for instance, #goodmorning, #thestruggleisreal), and this is a textual practice introduced on Twitter to help Twitter users easily find relevant topics. According to Zappavigna (2018), hashtags are semiotic metadata (i.e., they visually represent data about data). Furthermore, precisely because hashtags have experiential, interpersonal and textual functions (Zappavigna, 2018), they mark the topic of a tweet and at the same time become a means to evaluate or add semantic context to the tweet's content. In addition, they act as hypertext, linking a tweet's content to the same topic dealt with by this hashtag and, therefore, to other tweets with the same tag, embedding them in a wider discussion, where hashtags become evaluative metacommentary in the sense that they create intra- and intertextual references to tweet content to express emotive and moral attitudes and evaluations (cf. Martin & White, 2005).

Previous studies related to the use of hashtags, starting from their deictic function (Heyd & Puschmann, 2017), have increasingly concentrated on the role they have in creating visibility for Twitter users (Page, 2012) and facilitating topic retrieval as they convey contextual information and help derive implicit and explicit information (Scott, 2015), or even act as a storytelling device, while aspects related to hashtags' pragmatic use as self-praise, (positive) self-presentation and audience management strategies are evidenced by Matley (2018a, 2018b) and Coesemans and De Cock (2017), whereas Scott (2018) stresses how hashtag use is rapidly evolving from written to spoken, face-to-face communication and considers populist attitudes towards it. This is clearly linked to Computer-Mediated Communication (CMC), seen as a form of communication realised in a social space where deliberate discursive choices are made by individual to communicate beliefs and ideologies and to establish their cultural knowledge and construct their social identities (Jacknick & Avni, 2017). For decades, CMC has been regarded as allowing equal access to communication, given its alleged ability to democratise communication through Internet anonymity, thanks to which a participant's gender, race, social status, age or education level are not visible in interactions (Morikawa, 2019). Early studies on CMC have, on the contrary, demonstrated that CMC reveals the same discursive strategies as those found in spoken interaction, which undermines the hypothesis that the inherent anonymity of Internet language prevents a connection between gender, race, social status, age or education level and language use being repeatedly undermined (Morikawa, 2019). This probably means that, on Twitter, use of the term *#mansplain* may depend on sociolinguistic factors. What is clear, however, is that the term itself has changed in meaning. As Hart (2014) puts it, "along the way, *mansplaining* has morphed from a useful descriptor of a real problem in contemporary gender dynamics to an increasingly vague catch-all expression that seems to be inflaming the Internet gender wars more than clarifying them". This new connotation can be found, for instance, in the *Urban Dictionary*'s definitions: while in 2010 *mansplaining* was defined as the patronising tone men have towards women, as from 2015 *mansplaining* also includes the derisive tone women have when referring to a man they are speaking to.

Although *#mansplain* is a popular hashtag on social platforms, it has to date received scholarly enquiry from a feminist perspective but, to the best of our knowledge, few studies have focused on it from a linguistic and sociolinguistic perspective (cf. Bridges, 2017); the only study that offers a corpus linguistic analysis is by Lutzky and Lawson (2019), showing broad pattern uses of *#mansplain*, *#mansinterruption* and *#manspreading*, particularly in the technological and political fields, and metadiscursively linked to evaluations Twitter users make of "proper" gender behaviours.

Given this broad introduction and gap in the literature regarding the investigation of *#mansplain* on Twitter in general discourse, the research questions of this study are:

- Does *#mansplaining* represent the dynamics or a war between the genders?
- Does *#mansplain* represent effective politically (in)correct communication or does it reveal a wider range of meanings and uses on Twitter (*is it a catch-all expression*)?

In the next sections, we will describe the methodological approach before discussing the results obtained.

3. Methodological approach

In order to answer the research questions posed in the previous section, a background survey was carried out, and 150 questionnaires administered, to understand the extent to which the phenomenon of *#mansplain* is understood and experienced on social media. The results of this questionnaire are supported by a pilot study in which a sentiment analysis was carried out with SocialBearing.com, Twitter analytics software: a small corpus of tweets containing the hashtag *#mansplain** was downloaded from 22 to 31 July 2019 (1,298 tokens; 347 types); the wildcard stands for all possible desinences – so, for instance, all hashtags such as *#mansplaining*, *#mansplainer*, *#mansplains* and so forth. have been considered in the study.

On the basis of the background survey results and sentiment analysis, the second step of the investigation was carried out. The second part of the linguistic investigation was both quantitative and qualitative. Linguistic quantitative analysis was carried out with WMatrix (Rayson, 2008) to detect key semantic domains, to which a CDA approach was applied for a qualitative interpretation of the resulting data.

First, a corpus of tweets containing #mansplain* was downloaded with ScrapeStorm, a free web scraping tool, from 1 January 2017 to 31 July 2019 – this formed a corpus of 192,217 running words (6,972 types). All tweets were then read to better contextualise the posts, understand cross-references, inter- and intra-textuality, so as to avoid ambiguity and semantic misunderstandings. Since in the download process both retweets and mentions were collected, a manual check allowed me to disregard retweets that were duplicates of what had already been said, while mentions were considered because they were replies to tweets starting with the name of the Twitter user.

A semantic analysis of all then tweets was then conducted using WMatrix4.[6] The purpose was to have a more comprehensive account of the key themes in the data collected. In key semantic domains, what is analysed is not keywords in context but the context of the semantic prosody of words grouped under

---

6 Wmatrix is a web-based tool for corpus analysis. Through its web interface it offers tools for Constituent Likelihood Automatic Word-tagging System (CLAWS) and UCREL Semantic Analysis System (USAS) corpus annotation, besides standard corpus-linguistic methodologies such as frequency lists, keyword lists, collocation and concordances.

semantic fields characterising the corpus under investigation, by collating all members detected within the semantic domain. A semantic domain can be defined as a cluster of terms and texts that have a high level of lexical coherence. Key semantic domains are such because they are identified with keyness computation. WMatrix4 detects key semantic domains through the Lancaster University Centre for Computer Corpus Research on Language's (UCREL's) semantic analysis system (USAS), based on Tom McArthur's Longman Lexicon of Contemporary English (McArthur, 1981). The semantic tagset used by USAS "has a multi-tier structure with major discourse fields (shown here on the right), subdivided, and with the possibility of further fine-grained subdivision in certain cases" (cf. Rayson, 2008); see also: http://ucrel.lancs.ac.uk/usas/ [24/7/2020].

The number of key semantic fields detected was 289; key semantic field analysis granted a more comprehensive account of the key themes in the data collected, necessary to answer the research questions posed in Section 2.

Permission to download tweets is covered by Twitter Terms of Agreement (https://developer.twitter.com/en/developer-terms/agreement) and any sensitive data from Twitter users were erased from the posts collected. For the purposes of the research, only verbal elements were collected from tweets, given that the visual part of tweets, if present, is not relevant for this study.

4. Results

4.1. Pilot study: Background survey and sentiment analysis

In order to understand whether the term *#mansplain* is commonly used by social media users, a background survey was constructed on Google Drive at https://forms.gle/FfmV8RbfMouKxq5X7 and reached 150 people (18 years of age or over), mainly in the UK, US, Australia, Germany and Italy, via the most popular social media, Facebook, Twitter and Instagram (cf. Berera, 2019).[7]

The questions in the survey were the following:

1. Have you ever heard the term *mansplaining*?
2. If yes, where?
3. Do you think the term *mansplaining* is a sexist word?
4. Do you feel offended by the word/do you think that the word may offend someone?

7 I acknowledge Dr Jenny Berera for the creation of the background survey and her help in resuming the quantitative analysis of the resulting data.

5. Have you ever experienced *mansplaining*?
6. Do you think that *mansplaining* really occurs in everyday life?
7. Have you ever been a **splainer*?
8. Age (–25; 26–49; 50+)
9. Sex (male/female)

Of the 150 respondents, 67.3 % were women. Of the three age groups identified (question 8), 47.3 % of the population belong to the first group; 35.3 % to the second; and 17.3 % of the population are over 50. Most respondents, therefore, are young women aged between 18 and 25 years of age.

Fifty per cent of the respondents do not know the term *mansplain*; 17.3 % are not sure about its meaning, while 32.7 % do know it and have primarily seen or heard it in web-blogs, on social media, on TV shows or during conversations with friends. For those people not familiar with the term, an explanation was provided with a definition from the OED. The replies to question no. 3, *Do you think the term mansplaining is a sexist word?*, show that 41.3 % of respondents think the word is a sexist one, which means that even those who do not know the word intuitively assign a negative connotation to it (39.3 % of respondents think the word is not sexist, while 19.3 % are not sure). The question *Do you feel offended by the word/do you think that the word may offend someone?* was answered positively by only 37.2 % of respondents, who also add that a lot depends on the context: not only can men be offended if they are addressed with this term, but they can also feel manipulated. If asked whether an alternative term should be used rather than *mansplain*, 53.2 % of the respondents think that there is no need to use an alternative. However, 43 % of the respondents replied that a new lexical item should be used. Interestingly, one woman replied that:

> …most men [don't] care about the word *mansplaining*. However, if we would have to address the issue following the equal sexes rhetoric, then women should not use that world as it is indeed sexist. Furthermore, it would be seen as a much greater issue if men were to use the world *womansplaining*.

Fifty per cent of the respondents have never experienced a *mansplaining* situation, 16.7 % are not sure, but 33.3 % confirmed that they have experienced it, mostly women and mostly at work from male colleagues and/or male bosses, male relatives (father, brother, husband, boyfriend) or from men in general in various daily situations, for exampleshops, at filling stations, gyms and so forth. This was confirmed by the next question, *Do you think that mansplaining really occurs in everyday life?*, to which 61.3 % confirmed the phenomenon does occur daily, with one person clarifying that "it happens in both directions. Let's say there is also a certain amount of *womensplaining*" – only 34.7 % believe that *mansplaining* does not exist. However, when asked to reflect whether they themselves were **splainers*, only 9.4 % of the respondents admitted they are, while 23 % think they might be and 67.5 % think they are not.

Overall, one third of the respondents know what the phenomenon of *mansplaining* is and have experienced it. After reading the definition of the word *mansplaining*, almost half of the respondents think the word is sexist and more than half believe the phenomenon permeates our society.

The analysis conducted on the corpus (55 tweets; 1,298 tokens; 347 types) of tweets containing the hashtag *#mansplain** collected with Socialbear.com revealed that the hashtag *#mansplain* is mainly employed in the US, Canada, the UK, Germany and Australia (see Figure. 9.1, below), which roughly corresponds to the countries of origin of the respondents to the background survey described above.

Figure 9.1. Pilot study – #mansplain* diffusion on Twitter. Tweets by country.

The sentiment analysis carried out automatically by SocialBear.com on the pilot corpus revealed the data indicated in Figure 9.2, below:

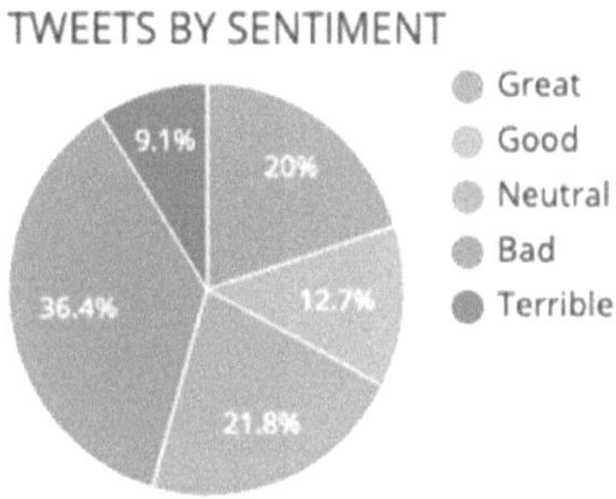

Figure 9.2. Pilot study – #mansplain* sentiment analysis on Twitter.

As can be seen, 36.4 % of the collected tweets are classified as "bad" and 9.1 % as "terrible", overall reaching a 45.5 % of negatively connoted tweets, while 54.5 % consider the term in a positive (20 % as "great"; 12.7 % as "good") or neutral (21.8 %) way. This seems to confirm the data of the background survey related to a sexist consideration of the term.

4.2. Results: Main corpus

Analysis of the corpus collected from 1 January 2017 to 31 July 2019 (579 tweets; 192,217 running words; 6,972 types) was carried out with WMatrix4. This allowed the detection of 181 key semantic fields, which are listed in the Appendix. Each key semantic domain (SemTag) was detected by comparing the corpus against the British National Corpus (BNC) sampler Corpus – spoken (990,704 words).[8] For $p \leq 0.01$ and 1 degree of freedom (1 d.f. is when two corpora are compared), the resulting cut-off point for log-likelihood statistics is 6.63. This also indicates that all the USAS tags are positively overused. Of these, the top 37 key semantic domains are used significantly. For the purposes of this study, only the top 10 significant key semantic domains are analysed. They are listed in Table 9.1, below:

8 See http://ucrel.lancs.ac.uk/bnc2sampler/sampler.htm [23/7/2020].

Table 9.1. Overview of the top 10 key semantic domains

#	SemTag	O1	1 %	O2	2 %	Use	LL	Definition
1	Z99	1514	21.72	5684	0.58	+	7680.24	Unmatched
2	S2.1	82	1.18	875	0.09	+	265.35	People: Female
3	C1	77	1.10	896	0.09	+	237.44	Arts and crafts
4	S2.2	83	1.19	1829	0.19	+	165.37	People: Male
5	Q2.2	117	1.68	5794	0.59	+	92.00	Speech acts
6	S1.2.4+	14	0.20	103	0.01	+	54.51	Polite
7	I1	48	0.69	2197	0.22	+	42.68	Money generally
8	Q3	30	0.43	1105	0.11	+	35.76	Language, speech and grammar
9	S1.2.3+	9	0.13	102	0.01	+	28.17	Selfish
10	X3.2	26	0.37	1139	0.12	+	24.65	Sensory: Sound

As can be seen in Table 9.1, above, each semantic domain is identified by a letter and a number (e.g., Z5 – second column), and by a description of the detected semantic domain (ninth column). For each semantic domain, the frequency observed in the corpus (O1, third column) and in the reference corpus (O2, fifth column) are indicated, as well as their relative frequencies in the text (fourth and sixth columns, respectively). The positive overuse of the semantic domain compared to the reference corpus is shown in the seventh column. Log-likelihood statistics (cf. https://ucrel-wmatrix4.lancaster.ac.uk/wmatrix4.html) are indicated in the eighth column.

In the Z99 semantic field (1,514 items) appear all the unmatched words, that is all those items that could not be tagged and grouped under other semantic domains. This is an umbrella class mainly containing the hashtag *#mansplain**, and the terms *Twitter*, *www*. Similarly, SemTag I1 – Money (48 occurrences), includes the item *http*, which indirectly explains why a manual reading of all tagging is necessary.

The second significantly used key semantic domain is the one tagged as S2.1 and defined as "People: Female" (82 items). Words included are "women" (41 hits), "woman" (16 hits), "female" (11 hits), "girls" and "lady" (4 hits each), "feminism" and "feminist" (2 hits), and other hapax. The occurrence of this semantic class does not come as a surprise, as one would expect that a corpus dealing with mansplaining has to do with men and women. The concordance lines of *women*, as a matter of fact, not only reveal women's voice on Twitter as far as #mansplaining is concerned, but also the fact that mansplain is done to women: they unwillingly become the patients of an unwanted action, as some excerpts from Figure 9.3, below, suggest:

```
plaining and 'savior' approach . As  women  in the #MiddleEast , we know EXACTLY
ansplaining : When Trudeau yells at  women  , it 's because he cares . When he s
s or how to deal with interruption   women  face from men also termed #Mansplain
 is the right winner : mansplaining  women  s anatomy to a woman who is a gynaec
hould be calling our campaign about  women  's experiences in the workplace . Ap
ity All men should watch ; also all  women  who love men/work w men #ThreeMythsO
 101 : Why Do Men Explain Things To  Women  ? https : // feminisminindia. **34;46
what a panel of confident , capable  women  look like when facing , yet again ,
TOOLONG &; At a Tunis conference on  women  in prisons , w/a panel mostly of wom
en in prisons , w/a panel mostly of  women  , 2 of the few men in audience shout
mendrinkwhiskytoo We need more #GOP  women  except those that think on their own
s : that men know better , and that  women  are always ready to be helped and ta
0;TOOLONG &; So @AtnafB knows all Z  women  who r angry @BilleneSeyoum &; all r
se stop trying to explain things to  women  who ride bikes and then get offended
 talking enduring challenges facing  women  , esp #BAMEwomen #womenofcolour in t
 without insulting or #mansplaining  women  , please steer clear of my mentions
ng , #equalpay and the struggles of  women  I too am guilty of TaqMansplaining #
 of men sexually **27;88679;TOOLONG  women  , feel free to come back and lecture
exual harassment to people ( read :  women  ) who are sexually harassed on a dai
ogant men only did #mansplaining to  women  https : //twitter. **38;88847;TOOLON
acceptable to a woman . . while the  women  watch on #Mansplaining #Humpday blue
c. twitter. com/deGS7qRhFs How many  women  just screamed #Mansplaining at the t
k you @RepJayapal ! Unfortunately ,  women  experience #mansplaining in other se
OLONG &; Condescending responses to  women  's experiences and knowledge perpetu
#mansplaining and instead listen to  women  . By @LorenRaeDeJpic. twitter. com/Q
bu " #Mansplaining is a reaction to  women  s articulation of their experiences
t to be confused with men mentoring  women  . #flipthescript https : //www. glam
nding the author are irritated that  women  who disagree are being firm and not
right to bear arms . " Paul Ryan on  women  : " Bare arms are indecent. " #doubl
e a linguistic phenomenon , helping  women  to define an experience that had lon
oneil47pic. twitter. com/nKVF848fY2  Women  on Twitter Are Sharing Their Worst E
 they need to include the excellent  women  and physicians in their party #radxx
 sentence ! Talking over the top of  women  on @InsidersABC is terrible #Insider
awilliams #Mansplaining " Christian  women  are telling us they hear **29;91495;
announces a series meant to amplify  women  's voices . Suddenly lots of male ch
sly amok . Thx , @brokeymcpoverty !  Women  share infuriating stories. http : //
n even know what #mansplaining is ?  Women  are sharing their experiences with m
he other difference between men and  women  is having periods. . . #mansplaining
alize anti-choice oppression . PS :  Women  's lives are human lives. https : //
tual , admitted Peeping Tom telling  women  what will make them feel safe in the
 #nottoday Well , if you show up to  Women  in STEM groups and start #mansplaini
```

Figure 9.3. Concordance lines of *women* in S2.1–People: women.

Even the words *feminism* and *feminist* are used ironically in tweets to represent #mansplain:

1. Today we 'll gather 4 men to explain to you what is *feminism* #Mansplaining #shittypress
2. Mexico's UNAM university has taken #mansplaining to a new level by organising a conference on *feminism* with 11 speakers, all of them male
3. Just ENDURED pilot episode of the new #Charmed &; it's a pile of crap. It was meant to be *feminist*, but includes a lot of #Mansplaining, its patronising &; just pathetic

The third most significantly used semantic domain, C1 – Arts and crafts (77 items), has nothing to do with #mansplain because it includes words such as *pic.*, *pictures*, *photos* and therefore explicitly refers to the pictures accompanying tweets.

The semantic domain S2.2 – People: Male (83 items) is the fourth most significantly one used and, exactly like the *Female* semantic domain, was to be expected in a corpus dealing with *mansplaining*: it is mainly found in *women's* talking (sarcastically) about men who mansplain them, as can be seen in Figure 9.4, below:

void #Mansplaining . Unlike how some	men	treated Dr Anna Watts on Friday . See
&; Hey girls ! Today we 'll gather 4	men	to explain you what is feminism #Mans
l with interruptions women face from	men	also termed #Mansplaining when they s
#mansplaining here . We love it when	men	tell us what we should be calling our
ansplaining vs real #Masculinity All	men	should watch ; also all women who lov
; also all women who love men/work w	men	#ThreeMythsOfMasculinity @SharonneHay
st read ! #Mansplaining 101 : Why Do	Men	Explain Things To Women ? https : //t
archive would go on to be ignored by	men	throughout the 20th century. pic. twi
s . She also doesn t constantly need	men	to tell her what lesson she needs to
panel mostly of women . 2 of the few	men	in audience shouted out asking whethe
a symptom of two ugly beliefs : that	men	know better , and that women are alwa
riage is success ? He is sure &; all	men	who are angry are frustrated blha blh
//twitter. **37;1251;TOOLONG &; Dear	men	who ride bikes : Please stop trying t
ity #Mansplaining #microagressions +	men	who are donutspic. twitter. com/uvnSs
veryone choosing to wear black . The	men	wearing the badges. #OprahWinfrey spe
utting down the ridiculous amount of	men	that have been crying all day about a
r. **40;88638;TOOLONG &; I love when	men	in sports media who have played recre
ng I hear so often is egregious Dear	Men	of Twitter : When you have solved the
When you have solved the problem of	men	sexually **27;88679;TOOLONG women , f
/twitter. **41;88707;TOOLONG &; When	men	want to define what is sexual harassm
e beach in Jazz Singer episode . The	men	were all #emotional but June was calm
QorFWdD In case you thought arrogant	men	only did #mansplaining to women https
l Great talks @AMERSAtweets . but to	men	in audience walking to . #mansplainin
#Newsnight Hilarious watching these	men	argue about what is acceptable to a w
witter. com/ydVE7qULex I am tired of	men	(always , always older successful wh
TOOLONG &; A brief twitter story for	men	. Let s learn to stop #mansplaining a
ile we 'll just follow your advice .	Men	always know better https : //twitter.
ubject most worthy : #mansplaining .	Men	who think they can govern when they h
&; #Mansplaining the #city : Why are	men	driving the conversation about the fu
nsplaining , not to be confused with	men	mentoring women . #flipthescript http
ter. com/w9NeXRTXT8 Ironically , the	men	defending the author are irritated th
/2rrr8JO The Universal Phenomenon of	Men	Interrupting #Women #womenincardiolog
lection of gender relations in which	men	s voices &; knowledge are given prior
NG . WUMQOOqnZJo. twitter &; Strange	men	constantly explain to me how to do my
tter. **45;91840;TOOLONG &; How many	men	even know what #mansplaining is ? Wom
ells me the other difference between	men	and women is having periods. . . #man
NewYorker by @WillMcPhail helping us	men	understand #Mansplaining #HeForShe #R

Figure 9.4. Concordance lines for *men* in S2.2 – People: Men

Even the other items included in this key semantic domain, that is male (13 hits), guy (7 hits), guys (2 hits,) and all the hapax, are used with this function.

The semantic tag Q2.2 – Speech Act (117 items) mainly includes such verbs as *explain** (17 hits), *tell** (16 hits), *interrupt** (4 hits) and the noun *advice* (2 hits), plus many other hapax, that is items that indicate the action of mansplaining:

4. Why Do Men *Explain* Things To Women?
5. We love it when men *tell* us what we should be calling our campaign about women 's experiences in the workplace. Apparently, our name is "stupid" and we should call ourselves something that evokes more seriousness. Thanks for the help
6. Woman reading a book about #mansplaining *interrupted* by a #mansplainer
7. Don't give *advice* to a Woman unless she requests it

While in (4) the question seems genuine (it is actually the title of Solnit's essay included in her book written in 2014), and clearly indicates that there is no need for men to explain things, which is, in a way linked to the imperative expressed in (7), in (5) and (6) the tweets are more sarcastic: in (5) women clearly do not love any intrusions by men in their professional lives; in (6) the absurd situation is underlined by the intrusive presence of the man who interrupts a woman – clearly to explain her what she is reading.

This semantic domain seems similar to Q3 – Language, speech and grammar (30 items), it is mainly formed by the verb *read** (12 hits) and the item *word** (8 hits), plus 10 additional hapax. Interestingly, *read* refers to what women should read: the book by Solnit (2014) about mansplaining:

8. #Mansplaining A must read! #Mansplaining 101: Why Do Men Explain Things To Women?

Even the item *word* is linked to the realm of *mansplaining:*

9. Today 's *word*: mansplain

Needless to say, all semantic tags are related. Even the SemTag S1.2.4+ – Gratitude (14 items), which seems to have nothing to do with #mansplaining, is connected to it, as we can see in examples (10) and (11):

10. We love it when men tell us what we should be calling our campaign about women's experiences in the workplace. Apparently our name is "stupid" and we should call ourselves something that evokes more seriousness. *Thanks* for the help
11. I love being mansplained by a male doctor about how hormones work. Hmmm, I have a Masters in Biochemistry, but *thanks*. #Mansplaining

Gratitude is ironic: women sarcastically thank men for explaining things they already know, either because they are directly involved in it, as in excerpt (10), or because of their profession, as indicated in example (11).

With these premises, the semantic domain S1.2.3+ – Selfish (9 hits) could only refer to men: they are indeed described as *narcissistic*, *patronising*, *condescending* and *arrogant*, as examples (12)–(14), below, show:

12. #Mansplaining taking another *egotistical* step 2 far
13. Not the *narcissistic* ignorant orange buffoon
14. He pivots from sexist *patronising* to claim "Speaking truth to power" as if the topic, not the #mansplaining is the problem. Which is the pivot being made by misogynists everywhere.

In this SemTag there is interestingly the voice of a man – a politician – who complains about having being mansplained by another man – a journalist:

15. In case you thought *arrogant* men only did #mansplaining to women:
    A: Germany tonight in its biggest political crisis since late 1940s. Bigger even than UK's current ongoing political crisis.
    B: You have not got a clue. One of four parties walked out of coalition talks. It might take a while to find a solution. Big. F**king. Deal.
    A: Guess you're not reading/watching German media
    B: I LIVE in Germany. I am a member of a German political party and am a delegate to its party congress. I follow German politics for my job. And, just maybe, I might know a thing or two about it?

It is in this type of tweet that we can see a turning point in the use of #mansplain, going from a term originally used in a gender battle to a term being used with a wider range of meanings as a catch-all expression.

The items included in the semantic domain X3.2 – Sensory: Sound (26 hits), are *listen** (11) items and *hear** (13 items), plus other two hapax. When *listen* is used, the Twitter user normally wonders why women are never listened to; when the verb *hear* is used, it normally refers to what women hear from men:

16. stop #mansplaining and instead *listen* to women
17. when @NYGovCuomo's staff mansplain you on the phone and you can't believe what you're *hearing* #mansplaining #noidcny

Interestingly, the use of these two verbs is not by chance: while *hear* conveys an idea of perceiving or having a sensation of sounds, *listen* suggests the idea of paying attention (cf. OED). Therefore, men do not listen with attention to what women have to say, and women perceive mansplaining as done with noise.

5. Discussion and conclusion

As indicated at the beginning of this contribution, the RQs posed as the basis of this preliminary research aim to detect whether *#mansplain* is used to emphasise the social dynamics hindering effective interaction between men and women, or whether the term is used as a catch-all expression to emphasise a war between the genders.

The background survey carried out with 150 respondents (from the US, the UK, Canada, Australia, Italy and Germany) revealed that only one third of the population involved in the study know the phenomenon and 50 % of them – mainly women – have experienced it in everyday situations.

The pilot study conducted with SocialBear.com revealed that the phenomenon of mansplain is mainly present in the US, the UK, Canada, Australia, China and German. The sentiment analysis carried out on the collected tweets suggests that about 45 % of Twitter users regard the phenomenon as a negative one – confirming the data that emerged in the background survey.

The investigation carried out with WMatrix4 revealed interesting data. Among the SEMTAGs detected by WMatrix4 are some peculiar uses, as they underline a peculiar attitude women have in relation to the phenomenon of mansplaining. They describe a world in which dialogue and its potential have been turned off: the act of mansplaining becomes a sort monologism (cf. Bakhtin, 1981), or better, "a monologically understood world [...] an objectified world, a world corresponding to a single and unified authorial consciousness" (Hays, 2005, p. 9). What women complain about is the presence of one-way truth as indicated by men, who do not listen to women. This lack of interaction has an impact on the interpretation of the world – which ultimately depends on the speaker's viewpoint (Harts, 2014). While instances of mansplaining may pass unnoticed, it is on Twitter that these types of behaviour are observed, discussed and condemned (Lutsky and Lawson, 2019). People who want to take part in this sociocultural discussion express their viewpoint *and* their stance through the hashtag #mansplain. The audience who take part in this Twitter discussion seem to mainly (but not necessarily) comprise women. Indeed, women's posts underline the fact that:

- they are unnecessarily educated about / have explained things;
- they wonder why this occurs;

- they underline that men have a patronising attitude;
- they want people (and men, more precisely) to stop mansplaining things to them.

In this description of the phenomenon, they are never derisive but rather sarcastic, as seen, for instance, in the *Gratitude* SemTag. This is not simply a criticism. As Lutsky and Lawson (2019, p. 10) claim, a woman "contests and challenges the sexist nature of these terms or their restriction to the male gender". This could be true in the absence of male discourse. Different from Lutsky and Lawson (2019), we found at least one tweet in which the hashtag #mansplaining is used to refer to an episode in which a man is being patronised by another man. Therefore, it seems that the term is beginning to be used as a "catch-all" expression, thus underlining not only the gender war on the Internet and the dynamics between the genders as described by women, but also any dynamics where power relations are being established.

Given these results, and given the presence of other parallel constructions found on Twitter, such as *#womansplaining*, *#whitesplaining*, *#blacksplaining*, *#rightsplaining* and even *#mumsplaining*, our future research will focus on the hashtag **#*plaining** to look at a wider range of meanings and uses and evaluate the appropriateness of Twitter users' discourse and to reflect on norms, societal values and power relations in online communication.

References

Bakhtin, M. (1981). *The Dialogic Imagination: Four Essays*. Austin, TX: University of Texas Press.

Berera, J. (2019). *Ridurre al silenzio per annientare: una breve analisi del fenomeno del* mansplaining. Unpublished BA thesis. University of Bergamo.

Bridges, J. (2017). Gendering Metapragmatics in Online Discourse: 'Mansplaining man gonna mansplain…'. *Discourse, Context & Media*, 20, 94–102.

Buerkle, C. W. (2019). Adam Mansplains Everything: White-Hipster Masculinity as Covert Hegemony. *Southern Communication Journal*, 84(3), 170–182

Coesemans, R., & De Cock, B. (2017). Self-Reference by Politicians on Twitter: Strategies to Adapt to 140 Characters. *Journal of Pragmatics*, 116, 37–50.

Giaxoglou, K. (2018). #JeSuisCharlie? Hashtags as Narrative Resources in Contexts of Ecstatic Sharing. *Discourse, Context, and Media*, 22, 13–20.

Hart, B. (2014). RIP "mansplaining": How the Internet Killed One of Our Most Useful Words. *Salon*. Retrieved September 5, 2023 from http://www.salon.com/2014/10/20/rip_mansplaining_how_the_internet_killed_one_of_our_most_useful_words/

Hays, C. B. (2008). The Silence of the Wives: Bakhtin's Monologism and Ezra 7 – 10. *Journal for the Study of the Old Testament*, 33, 59–80.

Heyd, T., & Puschmann, C. (2017). Hashtagging and Functional Shift: Adaptation and Appropriation of the #. *Journal of Pragmatics,* 116, 51–63.

Kaplan, I. (2018, October 20). Stephen Colbert Accuses Trump of Trying to 'mansplain the Midterms' to Female Voters. *Rolling Stone*. Retrieved September 5, 2023 from https://www.rollingstone.com/tv/tv-news/stephen-colbert-trump-mansplain-the-midterms-female-voters-745095/

Kidd, A. G. (2017). *Mansplaining: The Systematic Sociocultural Silencer*. University of North Georgia. Retrieved September 5, 2023 from https://core.ac.uk/works/71156508

Kinney, A. (2017). Your Global Mansplaining Dictionary in 34 Languages. *The Establishment*. Retrieved September 5, 2023 from https://theestablishment.co/your-globalmansplaining-dictionary-in-34-languages-a5e44bf682ba

Lutzky, U., & Lawson, R. (2019). Gender Politics and Discourses of #mansplaining, #manspreading, and #manterruption on Twitter. *Social Media + Society*, 5(3).

Martin, J. R., & White, P. R. R. (2005). *The Language of Evaluation: Appraisal in English*. London: Palgrave Macmillan.

Matley, D. (2018a). 'Let's see how many of you mother fuckers unfollow me for this': The Pragmatic Function of the Hashtag #sorrynotsorry in Non-Apologetic Instagram Posts. *Journal of Pragmatics*, 133, 66–78.

Matley, D. (2018b). 'This Is Not a #humblebrag, This Is Just a #brag': The Pragmatics of Self-Praise, Hashtags and Politeness in Instagram posts. *Discourse, Context & Media,* 22, 30–38.

McArthur, T. (1981). *Longman Lexicon of Contemporary English.* Harlow: Longman.

Morikawa, E. A. (2019). *This Is What a Feminist Tweets Like: "Women's Language" and Styling Activist Identities in a #YesAllWomen Twitter Corpus*. Unpublished PhD thesis. The Graduate Center, City University of New York.

Page, R. (2012). The Linguistics of Self-Branding and Micro-Celebrity in Twitter: The Role of Hashtags. *Discourse & Communication*, 6(2), 181–201.

phosphate. 2013. On Statistics. *Fandom Wank Blog*. Retrieved September 5, 2023 from https://web.archive.org/web/20130518221612/http://www.journalfen.net/community/fandom_wank/1156737.html?thread=179210113

Rothman, L. (2012, November 1). A Cultural History of Mansplaining. *The Atlantic*. Retrieved September 5, 2023 from https://www.theatlantic.com/sexes/archive/2012/11/a-cultural-history-of-mansplaining/264380/Rayson, P. (2008). From Key Words to Key Semantic Domains. *International Journal of Corpus Linguistics*, 13(4), 519–549.

Scott, K. (2015). The Pragmatics of Hashtags: Inference and Conversational Style on Twitter. *Journal of Pragmatics*, 81, 8–20.

Sifton, S., & Barret, G. (2010, December 18). The Words of the Year. *New York Times*. Retrieved September 5, 2023 from https://archive.nytimes.com/www.nytimes.com/2010/12/19/weekinreview/19sifton.html

Solnit, R. (2008, April 13). The Archipelago of Arrogance. *Tom Dispatch. A Regular Antidote to the Mainstream Media*. Retrieved September 5, 2023 from http://www.tomdispatch.com/blog/174918/tomgram%3A_rebecca_solnit%2C_the_archipelago_of_arrogance

Solnit, R. (2014). *Man Explain Things to Me*. Chicago / Turabian: Haymarket Books.

Themadscientis. (2008, May 19). Women Who Hate Dean Hating Women Hating … Wait. *Fandom Wank Blog*, Retrieved September 5, 2023 from http://www.journalfen.net/community/fandom_wank/1156737.html?thread=179210113

Zappavigna, M. (2018). *Searchable Talk: Hashtags and Social Media Meta-Discourse*. London, England: Bloomsbury.

Online Software

ScrapeStorm. Available at: https://www.scrapestorm.com/

SocialBearing.com. Available at: https://socialbearing.com

USAS. Available at: http://ucrel.lancs.ac.uk/usas/

WMatrix4. Available at: https://ucrel-wmatrix4.lancaster.ac.uk/wmatrix4.html

Websites

Corbyn versus May on International Women's Day: https://www.youtube.com/watch?v=QCEJ6y5heq4

Appendix

Key semantic domains:

SEMTAG	O1.	%1.	O2.	%2.	LL	LogRatio[9]	Definition
Z99	1514	21.72	5684	0.58 +	7680.24	5.23	Unmatched
S2.1	82	1.18	875	0.09 +	265.35	3.72	People: Female
C1	77	1.10	896	0.09 +	237.44	3.60	Arts and crafts
S2.2	83	1.19	1829	0.19 +	165.37	2.68	People: Male
Q2.2	117	1.68	5794	0.59 +	92.00	1.51	Speech acts
S1.2.4+	14	0.20	103	0.01 +	54.51	4.26	Polite
I1	48	0.69	2197	0.22 +	42.68	1.62	Money generally
Q3	30	0.43	1105	0.11 +	35.76	1.94	Language, speech and grammar
S1.2.3+	9	0.13	102	0.01 +	28.17	3.64	Selfish
X3.2	26	0.37	1139	0.12 +	24.65	1.69	Sensory: Sound
L1+	6	0.09	51	0.01 +	21.83	4.05	Alive
Y2	15	0.22	480	0.05 +	21.02	2.14	Information technology and computing
T1.1	5	0.07	35	0.00 +	19.91	4.33	Time: General
A3	2	0.03	0	0.00 +	19.82	9.14	Being
A13	2	0.03	0	0.00 +	19.82	9.14	Degree
G1.2	15	0.22	554	0.06 +	17.82	1.93	Politics
A5.2+	14	0.20	513	0.05 +	16.79	1.94	Evaluation: True
S7.3	3	0.04	9	0.00 +	16.36	5.55	Competition
X2	3	0.04	12	0.00 +	14.89	5.14	Mental actions and processes
A5.1+++	12	0.17	428	0.04 +	14.87	1.98	Evaluation: Good
S1.1.4+	3	0.04	17	0.00 +	13.06	4.64	Deserving
P1	29	0.42	1928	0.20 +	12.82	1.08	Education in general
Y1	11	0.16	415	0.04 +	12.73	1.90	Science and technology in general
S1.2	3	0.04	22	0.00 +	11.70	4.26	Personality traits
S1.2.6-	8	0.11	264	0.03 +	10.84	2.09	Foolish

9 The Log Ratio is an effect size and represents how 'big' the difference between two corpora is for a particular keyword statistic (http://cass.lancs.ac.uk/log-ratio-an-informal-introduction/ [24/7/2020].

SEMTAG	O1.	%1.	O2.	%2.	LL	LogRatio	Definition
A2.2	27	0.39	1891	0.19 +	10.50	1.01	Cause&Effect/ Connection
A5.1---	3	0.04	29	0.00 +	10.23	3.87	Evaluation: Bad
S3.2+	1	0.01	0	0.00 +	9.91	8.14	Relationship: Sexual
G2.1-	8	0.11	290	0.03 +	9.72	1.96	Crime
E2+	30	0.43	2255	0.23 +	9.63	0.91	Like
I3.2	2	0.03	10	0.00 +	9.15	4.82	Work and employment: Professionalism
S1.2.4-	4	0.06	74	0.01 +	9.14	2.93	Impolite
T2-	21	0.30	1442	0.15 +	8.59	1.04	Time: Ending
S2	33	0.47	2728	0.28 +	7.86	0.77	People
X2.4	14	0.20	889	0.09 +	6.87	1.15	Investigate, examine, test, search
N5---	2	0.03	20	0.00 +	6.70	3.82	Quantities: little
E2	2	0.03	20	0.00 +	6.70	3.82	Liking
S3.2	10	0.14	549	0.06 +	6.58	1.36	Relationship: Intimacy and sex
A1.5.2+	3	0.04	61	0.01 +	6.38	2.79	Useful
T4+	4	0.06	113	0.01 +	6.37	2.32	Time: Early
Q4.3	10	0.14	562	0.06 +	6.30	1.33	The Media: TV, Radio and Cinema
K5.2	4	0.06	115	0.01 +	6.26	2.29	Games
G2.2-	7	0.10	338	0.03 +	5.73	1.55	Unethical
X2.3+	7	0.10	341	0.03 +	5.65	1.53	Learning
E4.1+	12	0.17	782	0.08 +	5.56	1.11	Happy
A2.1-	3	0.04	72	0.01 +	5.56	2.55	No change
G3-	1	0.01	3	0.00 +	5.45	5.55	Anti-war
X5.1-	2	0.03	29	0.00 +	5.40	3.28	Inattentive
A13.2	14	0.20	1015	0.10 +	4.97	0.96	Degree: Maximisers
T3---	4	0.06	143	0.01 +	4.94	1.98	Time: New and young
S7.3+	3	0.04	82	0.01 +	4.94	2.37	Competitive
S7.4+	13	0.19	930	0.09 +	4.78	0.98	Allowed
Q4	4	0.06	147	0.01 +	4.78	1.94	The Media
S1.1.2+	8	0.11	471	0.05 +	4.61	1.26	Reciprocal
X7-	3	0.04	88	0.01 +	4.60	2.26	Unwanted
S7.2-	1	0.01	5	0.00 +	4.57	4.82	No respect
N3.7+++	1	0.01	5	0.00 +	4.57	4.82	Long, tall and wide
A15+++	1	0.01	5	0.00 +	4.57	4.82	Safe
A11.1++	1	0.01	5	0.00 +	4.57	4.82	Important

SEMTAG	O1.	%1.	O2.	%2.	LL	LogRatio	Definition
X9.1-	3	0.04	90	0.01 +	4.50	2.23	Inability /unintelligence
A1.3-	1	0.01	6	0.00 +	4.25	4.55	No caution
A10+	20	0.29	1730	0.18 +	4.04	0.70	Open; Finding; Showing
K1	15	0.22	1201	0.12 +	3.97	0.82	Entertainment generally
X9.2+	9	0.13	603	0.06 +	3.91	1.07	Success
X8+	15	0.22	1213	0.12 +	3.85	0.80	Trying hard
O4.2	1	0.01	8	0.00 +	3.75	4.14	Judgement of appearance
S5-	6	0.09	340	0.03 +	3.72	1.31	Not part of a group
K5.1	12	0.17	914	0.09 +	3.71	0.89	Sports
A5.2-	4	0.06	180	0.02 +	3.65	1.65	Evaluation: False
B3	13	0.19	1024	0.10 +	3.63	0.84	Medicines and medical treatment
S8-	5	0.07	260	0.03 +	3.62	1.44	Hindering
A1.3+	4	0.06	181	0.02 +	3.62	1.64	Cautious
X2.6+	5	0.07	261	0.03 +	3.60	1.43	Expected
X3.2-	3	0.04	115	0.01 +	3.40	1.88	Sound: Quiet
A1.8+	7	0.10	457	0.05 +	3.23	1.11	Inclusion
A11.1+++	2	0.03	56	0.01 +	3.21	2.33	Important
I3.2-	1	0.01	12	0.00 +	3.03	3.55	Unprofessional
N3.4	4	0.06	205	0.02 +	2.97	1.46	Measurement: Volume
Q1.2	33	0.47	3398	0.35 +	2.91	0.45	Paper documents and writing
X3.4+	1	0.01	13	0.00 +	2.89	3.44	Seen
N3.6	2	0.03	67	0.01 +	2.66	2.07	Measurement: Area
X3.3	2	0.03	69	0.01 +	2.58	2.03	Sensory: Touch
S7.1++	1	0.01	17	0.00 +	2.43	3.05	In power
N3.3+	3	0.04	148	0.02 +	2.37	1.51	Distance: Far
E2++	2	0.03	76	0.01 +	2.29	1.89	Like
S1.2.1+	2	0.03	78	0.01 +	2.22	1.85	Informal/Friendly
I3.2+	3	0.04	154	0.02 +	2.22	1.46	Professional
X4.1	12	0.17	1066	0.11 +	2.19	0.67	Mental object: Conceptual object
E3-	11	0.16	959	0.10 +	2.16	0.69	Violent/Angry
A4.2+	12	0.17	1082	0.11 +	2.06	0.64	Detailed
S8+	20	0.29	2020	0.21 +	1.98	0.48	Helping
Q4.2	6	0.09	447	0.05 +	1.98	0.92	The Media: Newspapers etc.

SEMTAG	O1.	%1.	O2.	%2.	LL	LogRatio	Definition
X2.2+	48	0.69	5481	0.56 +	1.97	0.30	Knowledgeable
N5++	24	0.34	2514	0.26 +	1.91	0.43	Quantities: many/much
E4.2-	2	0.03	88	0.01 +	1.88	1.68	Discontent
S7.2+	2	0.03	94	0.01 +	1.71	1.58	Respected
A2.2-	1	0.01	27	0.00 +	1.66	2.38	Unconnected
S1.2.2-	1	0.01	29	0.00 +	1.55	2.28	Generous
X2.2-	4	0.06	281	0.03 +	1.54	1.00	No knowledge
S5+	24	0.34	2602	0.26 +	1.51	0.38	Belonging to a group
T2+++	1	0.01	31	0.00 +	1.45	2.18	Time: Beginning
S6-	2	0.03	106	0.01 +	1.40	1.41	No obligation or necessity
N3.2++	2	0.03	108	0.01 +	1.36	1.38	Size: Big
E4.1-	5	0.07	400	0.04 +	1.33	0.82	Sad
A2.1+	19	0.27	2031	0.21 +	1.32	0.40	Change
E3+	3	0.04	207	0.02 +	1.21	1.03	Calm
S7.1	1	0.01	37	0.00 +	1.19	1.93	Power, organising
S7.1+	27	0.39	3064	0.31 +	1.17	0.31	In power
Q4.1	7	0.10	635	0.06 +	1.17	0.64	The Media: Books
S3.1	8	0.11	752	0.08 +	1.14	0.58	Personal relationship: General
S1.2.5+	2	0.03	119	0.01 +	1.13	1.24	Tough/strong
X2.6-	1	0.01	39	0.00 +	1.11	1.85	Unexpected
F2++	1	0.01	39	0.00 +	1.11	1.85	Excessive drinking
N6+++	7	0.10	650	0.07 +	1.06	0.60	Frequent
N3.7+	4	0.06	320	0.03 +	1.06	0.82	Long, tall and wide
S1.1.3+	7	0.10	660	0.07 +	0.99	0.58	Participating
G2.2+	3	0.04	225	0.02 +	0.97	0.91	Ethical
F2	10	0.14	1022	0.10 +	0.92	0.46	Drinks and alcohol
A1.9	3	0.04	229	0.02 +	0.92	0.88	Avoiding
N5.1-	9	0.13	908	0.09 +	0.90	0.48	Part
G2.1	15	0.22	1639	0.17 +	0.89	0.37	Law and order
E1	2	0.03	137	0.01 +	0.82	1.04	Emotional Actions, States And Processes General
A15-	2	0.03	140	0.01 +	0.78	1.01	Danger
G2.2	1	0.01	51	0.01 +	0.75	1.47	General ethics
W3	7	0.10	699	0.07 +	0.74	0.50	Geographical terms
K2	6	0.09	586	0.06 +	0.71	0.53	Music and related activities

SEMTAG	O1.	%1.	O2.	%2.	LL	LogRatio	Definition
A1.5.2-	1	0.01	54	0.01 +	0.68	1.38	Useless
B2-	9	0.13	959	0.10 +	0.64	0.40	Disease
A11.1-	2	0.03	153	0.02 +	0.61	0.88	Unimportant
Z3	22	0.32	2633	0.27 +	0.55	0.24	Other proper names
S9	10	0.14	1106	0.11 +	0.54	0.35	Religion and the supernatural
S7.4-	1	0.01	61	0.01 +	0.54	1.21	Not allowed
S1.1.1	7	0.10	746	0.08 +	0.50	0.40	Social Actions, States And Processes
Q2.1-	1	0.01	63	0.01 +	0.50	1.16	Speech: Not communicating
T2+	12	0.17	1386	0.14 +	0.44	0.29	Time: Beginning
A5.3-	4	0.06	401	0.04 +	0.41	0.49	Evaluation: Inaccurate
E2-	3	0.04	286	0.03 +	0.40	0.56	Dislike
N3.7	3	0.04	292	0.03 +	0.36	0.53	Measurement: Length & height
E6+	3	0.04	292	0.03 +	0.36	0.53	Confident
A4.2-	1	0.01	74	0.01 +	0.34	0.93	General
N5--	1	0.01	75	0.01 +	0.32	0.91	Quantities: little
A11.2+	2	0.03	184	0.02 +	0.31	0.62	Noticeable
I1.3+	1	0.01	79	0.01 +	0.28	0.84	Expensive
A1.4-	1	0.01	80	0.01 +	0.27	0.82	Unlucky
T3+	5	0.07	561	0.06 +	0.24	0.33	Time: Old; grown-up
A1.2+	2	0.03	195	0.02 +	0.24	0.53	Suitable
X3.5	1	0.01	86	0.01 +	0.21	0.71	Sensory: Smell
G1.1	9	0.13	1084	0.11 +	0.21	0.23	Government
I2.1	9	0.13	1086	0.11 +	0.20	0.22	Business: Generally
W5	1	0.01	88	0.01 +	0.19	0.68	Green issues
N3.5+	1	0.01	88	0.01 +	0.19	0.68	Weight: Heavy
O4.5	4	0.06	452	0.05 +	0.18	0.32	Texture
X9.2-	2	0.03	207	0.02 +	0.17	0.45	Failure
X9.1+	7	0.10	842	0.09 +	0.17	0.23	Able/intelligent
X2.5-	1	0.01	95	0.01 +	0.14	0.57	Not understanding
N3.7-	1	0.01	104	0.01 +	0.08	0.44	Short and narrow
O4.1	7	0.10	890	0.09 +	0.07	0.15	General appearance and physical properties
T3++	1	0.01	108	0.01 +	0.06	0.38	Time: Old; grown-up
O4.2-	5	0.07	628	0.06 +	0.06	0.17	Judgement of appearance: Negative

SEMTAG	O1.	%1.	O2.	%2.	LL	LogRatio	Definition
T3-	12	0.17	1580	0.16 +	0.05	0.10	Time: New and young
N5.2+	6	0.09	771	0.08 +	0.05	0.13	Exceed; waste
I4	2	0.03	245	0.02 +	0.04	0.20	Industry
A6.2-	2	0.03	242	0.02 +	0.04	0.22	Comparing: Unusual
A5.1++	4	0.06	507	0.05 +	0.04	0.15	Evaluation: Good
A1.4+	1	0.01	115	0.01 +	0.04	0.29	Lucky
O4.6-	2	0.03	247	0.03 +	0.03	0.19	Temperature: Cold
A12-	8	0.11	1056	0.11 +	0.03	0.09	Difficult
A1.4	3	0.04	379	0.04 +	0.03	0.16	Chance, luck
A5.4-	2	0.03	254	0.03 +	0.02	0.15	Evaluation: Unauthentic
A5.1-	5	0.07	656	0.07 +	0.02	0.10	Evaluation: Bad
A15+	1	0.01	120	0.01 +	0.02	0.23	Safe
A1.1.2	4	0.06	524	0.05 +	0.02	0.11	Damaging and destroying
S6+	41	0.59	5698	0.58 +	0.01	0.02	Strong obligation or necessity
N3.3	2	0.03	260	0.03 +	0.01	0.12	Measurement: Distance
K3	2	0.03	264	0.03 +	0.01	0.09	Recorded sound
E5-	3	0.04	398	0.04 +	0.01	0.09	Fear/shock
A11.1+	7	0.10	955	0.10 +	0.01	0.05	Important
X5.1+	1	0.01	140	0.01 +	0.00	0.01	Attentive
M5	2	0.03	269	0.03 +	0.00	0.07	Flying and aircraft
K4	2	0.03	269	0.03 +	0.00	0.07	Drama, the theatre and show business
A4.1	17	0.24	2356	0.24 +	0.00	0.02	Generally kinds, groups, examples

Ashleigh Feltmate
Independent scholar
ashleigh.feltmate@gmail.com

Chapter 10 #WhyIDidntReport: How contracting the dialogic background builds safe spaces for victims

Abstract: This study analyses face-threatening acts and engagement formulation to track alignment and solidarity within a group of tweets related to the #WhyIDidntReport hashtag. The main finding is that Twitter users employ dialogically contractive formulations to exclude others with counter positions from engaging in the conversation of the thread.

Keywords: Twitter, hashtags, appraisal theory, digital activism, critical discourse analysis.

1. Introduction

As I write this introduction, I wonder how much the social media platform Twitter has changed to best cater this chapter to my potential audience; after all, this research could be read a week after publication or several years. When I began research on this project, a large portion of the literature I read as background information always mentioned Twitter's 140-character limit which is now a constraint of the past because as of September 2017, the platform announced that they were increasing the character limit of tweets to 280. For this reason, I want to preface this chapter with a statement: social media platforms are constantly updating, looking for ways to enhance the user experience, design, or how their service operates behind the scenes. As such, social media communication is a difficult path to navigate for researchers as our work could be made obsolete before we have the opportunity to publish it.

In the literature, scholars have argued over Twitter's role in social movements and whether it is "ideal for carrying out revolutions" (Murthy, 2013, p. 101). Murthy (2013) covers both sides of this debate and arrives at the nuanced conclusion that Twitter's weak-tie networks between users can "disseminate real-time information about an activist movement, or to recruit participants" but that a researcher requires much context to judge any movement that results from any social media communication (Murthy, 2013, p. 103). Given the continuously growing and prominent rallying movements in the form of hashtags on Twitter like #BlackLivesMatter and #MeToo, I argue that this social media has become an incredibly appealing platform where users discuss important social issues and individuals are encouraged to share their opinions and attitudes with other people. The focus of this chapter is the hashtag #WhyIDidntReport which functioned as a new discursive space for Twitter users to discuss the social stigma around the reporting of sexual assault and created a space for individuals to take stances and build in-group solidarity. Though this hashtag functions as a safe space for victims to share their experiences and receive support from like-minded individuals, at the same time it allows for individuals of the counter position – who believe that victims are liars until sufficient evidence is provided which proves otherwise – to come together and reaffirm their stance too. While there may be other groups of people with different stances using this hashtag, these two groups of individuals are particularly interesting because they stand in direct opposition to each other, and yet, from my brief exploration of the hashtag, did not have much interaction with one another. Overall, I believe this research to be important because there is a need for on-going analysis concerning *digital activism* on social media, how social media raises questions within the framework of Systemic Functional Linguistics, and how marginalised communities convey their attitudes and opinions on these platforms to rally support for movements like #MeToo.

This research asks the following questions: How do Twitter users who interact with the hashtag #WhyIDidntReport negotiate alignment within the dialogically complex background of the discourse it creates? As well, how does this alignment relate to the user solidarity within this discourse? I hypothesise, based on my interpretation of the theoretical resources I use, that individuals who composed friendly and supportive tweets will use formulations that expand the dialogic background rather than contract it. However, I also hypothesise that individuals from the unfriendly group of tweets will use formulations that contract the dialogic background to keep individuals of the opposite stance out of their conversations.

This chapter is structured as follows: first, I introduce the relevant contexts necessary for interpreting the data, including Twitter and hashtags, Bonilla and Rosa's (2015) work on *digital activism*, the larger #MeToo movement, and the hashtag movement of interest for this study, #WhyIDidntReport. I then explain the theoretical framework and methodology for this project, including the analytic tools I use as well as the data collection and data analysis process. After this are the results from coding the tweets with the tools for elements such as engagement formulations, face-work, politeness strategies, alignment, stance, and solidarity. A discussion section follows this where I detail my interpretation of the results, highlighting the abundance of contractive formulations in the data and how this relates to the hashtag and the Twitter participants; this section also explains the limitations of this study. Finally, I conclude this chapter by providing an overview of the project as well as reflecting on how I am extending the results of this study into my current research as a young academic interested in social media critical discourse studies (SM-CDS), digital humanities, and Twitter.

2. Background

2.1. Twitter and hashtags

As the popularity of social media grows as a mode that allows people from across the world to connect and exchange messages, so do the strategies participants implement to make online communication faster, easier, and more accessible. One convention that is attributed to the microblogging and social media networking website Twitter – but has made its way to other platforms like Facebook and Instagram – is the hashtag. This convention receives its name from the fact that British English refers to the number sign as the *hash* sign and that this sign functions as a tag or index marker (Oxford University Press, 2019). A hashtag can be any lexical entry in any language, like a single word (*#Obama*), a phrase (*#ImpeachmentHearings*), or an abbreviation (*#CDN* for *Canada* or *Canadian*), so long as the user places the hash (#) sign in front of this entry and ensures there are no interrupting spaces between letters or words. Interestingly enough, hashtags were not a part of the original design plan of Twitter, and instead "grew out of a proposal by Messina (2007) to introduce a system to tag and track content on the site" (Scott, 2015, p. 12). These first hashtags were called *channel tags* and allowed users to eavesdrop on other conversations about a specific topic; hashtags did not become an official feature of Twitter until 2009, three years after the platform was founded. Another feature of hashtags is that if "a large number of people post tweets containing the same hashtag within a short space of time," the hashtag is given the status of *trending* (Scott, 2015, p. 12). When a hashtag receives the status of *trending*, it is, in effect, advertised to users on the website's *trends* list to encourage browsing and because of this, conversations that include a hashtag are easily searchable. However, as scholars have previously described, hashtags have a variety of functions and meanings when used, including, but not limited to, serving as metadata, or data about data (Zappavigna 2011, 2015), becoming discursive spaces for sharing and interaction (Zappavigna, 2011; Bonilla & Rosa, 2015; Scott, 2015), and allowing individuals to evaluate their morals and stances (Evans, 2016; Giaxoglou, 2018t; Rightler-McDaniels

& Hendrickson, 2014). These three functions are all significantly important for #WhyIDidntReport, however, the latter two functions – the creation of discursive spaces and the evaluation of stances – will be a prominent focus in the discussion section of this chapter.

2.2. Digital activism

Before explaining the backgrounds of the important hashtags for the contextual framing of this chapter, I find it relevant to cover Bonilla and Rosa's (2015) discussion on social media platforms emerging as powerful sites for what they call digital activism. They speak from an anthropological point of view that questions whether a hashtag on Twitter, like #Ferguson, can function as a field site in the way it has been traditionally viewed. Within this conversation, Bonilla and Rosa (2015) note that from the approaches of linguistic anthropology and social movements, a hashtag like #Ferguson "serves as an indexing system in both the clerical sense and the semiotic sense" (p. 5). This clerical sense is commonly referred to as *searchability* in the literature – as I discussed above – because Twitter users can quickly find other tweets related to news or events through hashtags. Hashtags are also semiotic because they are a sign that represents a meaning that might not be reflected within the tag with which they are paired. For example, while #Ferguson textually indicates the city in Missouri, the hashtag allows individuals to "performatively frame" what the tweet is "really about" (Bonilla & Rosa, 2015, p. 5). Another powerful feature of hashtags, as Bonilla and Rosa (2015, p.5) explain, is that they "have the intertextual potential to link a broad range of tweets on a given topic or disparate topics" which creates a chain of potential interaction for participants, bringing many smaller conversations together in one sphere. Lastly, and most importantly with regards to this chapter's contents, this discussion points out that Twitter and hashtags have created a place where marginalised groups who would have no power in face-to-face interaction have a way to talk back to powerful people. With these four aspects in mind – searchability, semiotics, intertextuality, and talking back to individuals in positions of power – Bonilla and Rosa (2015) construct #Ferguson as having several intertwining functions that work together to help spread messages quickly and effectively to a targeted audience.

2.3. #MeToo movement

To understand the impact of #WhyIDidntReport, it is necessary to know about the long history of the #MeToo movement which serves as the larger context for this new hashtag. Tarana Burke first used "Me Too" in 2006 which started the movement against sexual harassment and sexual abuse and aims to assist "a growing spectrum of survivors[,] help each individual find the right point of entry for their unique healing journey[, and] disrupt the systems that allow sexual violence to proliferate in our world" (*Get to Know Us: History & Inception*). However, "Me Too" as a hashtag did not spread virally until 2017 when "Alyssa Milano encouraged women to tweet it to publicise their experiences" of sexual harassment in response to the sexual harassment allegations towards Harvey Weinstein (Smartt, 2017). *The New York Times* first published Milano's story on October 5th, 2017 which detailed "the story of accusations of sexual harassment against the Hollywood producer Harvey Weinstein" (Renkl, 2017). Ten days after the story was released, Milano encouraged women to tweet their experiences and this sparked a flood of messages containing #MeToo across social media within minutes of it being posted. With no indication of slowing down, the picture this hashtag painted was clear: victims were tired of staying quiet and they intended to use social media to unite and effectively communicate their messages.

2.4. #WhyIDidntReport's significance

While gathering relevant information for this research, I realised that the significance of #WhyIDidntReport is twofold; not only does it serve as another wave of support for the #MeToo Movement, but it also has importance as a reaction to the current climate and attitudes surrounding the action of reporting sexual assault. Understanding this significance requires an explanation of the inspiring events that led to the creation and trending status of the #WhyIDidntReport hashtag. Early in the week of September 16th–22nd, 2018, Christine Blasey Ford (henceforth Ford), an American professor of psychology, came forward with a letter where she accused Judge Brett M. Kavanaugh (henceforth Kavanaugh), President Donald Trump's Supreme Court nominee (henceforth Trump), of sexual assault when they were teenagers; Kavanaugh denied this allegation (Fortin, 2018). In an interview on Thursday, September 20th, Trump was asked about the Kavanaugh hearings and the allegations made against him and in his response, Trump "cast aspersions" on Ford, attacking the claims she had made within the letter (Wolfson, 2018). Following this, on Friday, September 21st, Trump shared similar sentiments on his Twitter account[1], which exists as Figure 10.1 in the analysis section. This initiation from Trump sparked a resurgence in the already popular #MeToo Movement and rallied survivors of

1 As of January 8th, 2021, Twitter permanently suspended Donald Trump's personal Twitter account.

sexual assault to come together under the new hashtag #WhyIDidntReport to share their own stories (Fortin, 2018). As of the following Sunday (September 23), "there had been 675,000 tweets" with the hashtag (#WhyIDidntReport, 2018). At the time of writing this chapter, Twitter users continue to share their stories with the hashtag because it provides a safe community where victims can – possibly for the first time – talk about what they went through.

3. Theoretical framework

Critical discourse analysis (CDA) – more recently referred to as Critical Discourse Studies (CDS) – is a group of approaches concerned with "studying social phenomena which are necessarily complex and thus require a multidisciplinary and multi-methodical approach" (Wodak & Meyer, 2015, p. 2). For these approaches, the term *discourse* embodies text, talk, conversations, documents, and much more; put simply, *discourse* is language in use. One of the aims of CDA is to increase our understanding of how discourse shapes "social processes, social structures and social change" which means that the discourse that people investigate does not necessarily have to be negative or an "exceptionally 'serious' social or political experiences or events" (Flowerdew & Richardson, 2017, p. 1; Wodak & Meyer, 2015, p. 2). One important feature of discourse that CDA practitioners need to be aware of is that it always originates from a particular context and therefore cannot be separated from it during analysis. This context connects to society and brings attention to two other important concepts for CDA: *power* and *ideology*. Machin and Mayr (2012) describe *power* as coming "from privileged access to social resources such as education, knowledge[,] and wealth" which then provides individuals "authority, status[,] and influence" so that they "dominate, coerce[,] and control" people who are not as privileged and systematically oppressed. Machin and Mayr (2012) define *ideology* as "a broader meaning to refer to belief systems" that individuals and collectives hold; it is important to remember that like the discourse CDA practitioners investigate, not all ideologies are harmful. Ideology and power are intertwined because privileged individuals reinforce the ideologies that construct the discourses that build our societies. This reinforcement and construction often happen implicitly through language and therefore CDA strives to unravel this complex relationship between discourse, power, and ideology to enact social change.

For many years, Twitter users have created hashtags (e.g., #BlackLivesMatter, #MeToo, #WhyIDidntReport) that allow marginalised members of society to discuss and critique the power imbalances and the harmful ideologies that are both embedded and compose society. Though society reinforces structures of power that strengthens a divide between the positions of those centred in power, and those marginalised as other, hashtags provide a channel to discuss and address this divide, which destabilises the structures and might create a new site where individuals are more balanced to push for change. Because of these new sites, I argue that the discourse which individuals make in conjunction with hashtags is incredibly important to analyse if we are to understand how people are presently advocating for social change. In the case of #WhyIDidntReport, victims of sexual assault feel that the hashtag is a safe space to share their personal and traumatising experiences; while the possibility for harm does exist, I argue that the positive aspects outweigh the negative ones. By sharing their stories, victims provide several reasons – fears of being ridiculed, not believed, assaulted again – as to why they did not report their assailant to the police; or perhaps they did report and the response the police gave belittled them. This action emphasises the effects of the harmful ideology that positions victims as liars which exists throughout society and keeps victims silent, protects criminals and allows those in positions of power to reinforce this ideology.

3.1. Analytic resources

As I introduced in an earlier section, the theoretical concepts that construct the analytic framework of this research are *face*, politeness strategies, and *engagement*. To begin, Goffman (1967) explains how participants interact in group settings as well as how they manage *face* in these interactions. *Face* is one's self-image which is dependent on factors such as the rules and values of society as well as social interaction. He also discusses the three levels a participant may respond with when their actions have created a threat to *face*. This threat can be thought of as an individual's attempt to damage another person's self-image which can be achieved by discrediting like when Trump points out that if Ford were sexually assaulted, surely the police would have stepped in. However, since no charges were laid in the past, Trump is effectively calling Ford a liar and attacking her *face*. Goffman (1967) also explains the kinds of *face-work* – how people manage *face* – that exist, and more precisely, the two different processes that participants use to maintain equilibrium amongst all other participants: avoidance strategies and corrective strategies. The main takeaway from Goffman (1967) is that through techniques of managing *face-work*, Twitter users can build a positive image of self, stance, and alignment. By analysing the tweets of, for example, Trump and his followers, we can also see how they promote themselves through destroying the *faces* of victims, like Ford. The hashtag #WhyIDidntReport also helps restore the *face* of individuals with whom they align, where victims protect their identities but also support (rather than destroy) others' *faces*. The inclusion of positive and negative politeness strategies in this analytical framework enhances the implications of the theoretical concept of *face*.

Brown and Levinson's (1987) work on politeness strategies is a critical part of this project because reporting assault is, in their terms, going *on record* to expose the situation. The terms *on record* (the act of clearly communicating one's intention) and *off record* (the act of ambiguously communicating one's intention) are important because they tie into the ideas of positive and negative politeness in interactions and face-threatening acts (FTAs) (Figure 10.1). As Brown and Levinson (1987) discuss, face-threatening acts are those acts that have the potential to damage the *face* of the addressee. In social interaction, the optimal choice is to not threaten another's *face*; however, if a threatening situation arises, there are multiple routes the act can go. Brown and Levinson's (1987) work helps to address one reason why many victims do not go *on record* (as shown in countless stories from the tweets of this hashtag): often victims are ridiculed, dismissed, and police may not take them seriously when they report and as such this exemplifies that victims do not go *on record* for their safety. However, it is possible for hashtags on Twitter to provide a sense of safety because of the discursive space that a group of like-minded people creates. Related to this, Twitter is inherently going *on record* and though a victim sharing their account of sexual assault is scary due to the fear of dismissal, it is these brave individuals that highlight the complexity of the situation. The act of solidarity that comes from this act of going *on record* in the tweets collected for this research is not spontaneous; rather, it is a reaction to Trump's attempt to shame and discredit Ford which happened both in his interview and in his tweet. The reality in our society of shame and discredit is why victims do not want to report; at the same time, it also makes these individuals' actions even more powerful because they are not only going *on record* for themselves but also to draw attention to this harmful ideology that exists in society.

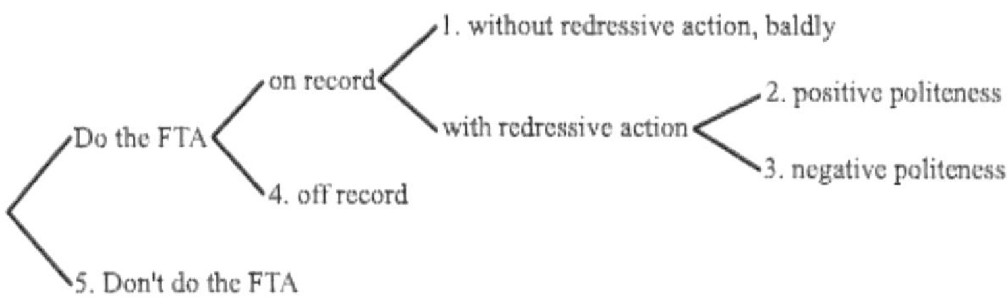

Figure 10.1. Brown and Levinson's (1987) FTAs, recreated

Though the above discussions regarding the concept of *face* provide a helpful way to analyse what can happen during interactions, it is important to keep in mind that *face* is heavily reliant on the context of the situation and rather than accounting for this, these authors posit their points as universals of interaction. For example, to reveal if an individual has committed a face-threatening act, it is necessary to consider what they are reacting to. For this reason, I used Martin and White (2005) in this research because their system of appraisal is situated within the approach of systemic functional linguistics (SFL). With its conception in the 1960s by Michael Halliday, SFL is "a very useful descriptive and interpretive framework for viewing language as a strategic, meaning-making resource" (Eggins, 2004, p. 2). There are a few crucial differences that set the SFL approach apart from other approaches to language, such as generative or functional frameworks. The first difference is the emphasis on the semiotic system where language users select from an abundance of available choices to realise meaning. Another important element of this approach is that because language is used in context, it realises its meaning in context too, and therefore it is critical to analyse the text within its context to reveal its full meaning. Lastly, within a text, whether it be a speech, a novel, or a tweet, there exist the interpersonal, ideational, and textual metafunctions that work together to create meaning. For Martin and White (2005), appraisal is situated in the interpersonal metafunction of SFL which involves the representation of social relations, like the relationship between the writer/speaker and reader/listener and looks at how the clauses function as exchanges between these parties. For this project, I focused on the category of *engagement* that Martin and White (2005) describe in their appraisal model because their classification of engagement formulations allowed for the interactions between participants to not only be compared against the larger dialogic background but also different groups within those utterances that are heteroglossic. The main advantage that this system has over the others that I previously discussed is that because every utterance occurs within the dialogistic background, everything is contextually specific. The element of context is important – especially in a study like this – because it is difficult to pry the utterances away from the context they are naturally embedded in, such as #WhyIDidntReport. Naturally, all tweets related to this hashtag have something to say about the situation regarding the act of reporting sexual assault and the stigma surrounding this act because this is what the hashtag is a reaction to.

Martin and White's (2005) engagement system is comprised of many divisions of choice that a speaker can make with the first being between utterances that are monoglossic and heteroglossic. Within Martin and White's

(2005) system, monoglossic utterances do not recognise other alternatives in the dialogic background (e.g., *Twitter is a microblogging service*). On the other hand, heteroglossic utterances do recognise alternative voices and positions in the background; however, how the speaker recognises the utterance varies and depends on their intentions. Martin and White (2005) distinguish this classification of heteroglossic utterances even further by grouping those that expand the background (in their terms, *entertain* and *attribute*) and those that contract it (*disclaim* and *proclaim*). While this chapter is concerned with whether Twitter users expand and contract the dialogic background, I also considered the types (and subtypes) of these overarching formulations so that I could more comprehensively analyse the speakers' utterances in the data. Below I provide examples for all types (and subtypes) of the formulations discussed in Martin and White (2005).

Entertain: *I heard that Twitter increased its character limit.*

Attribute:

- Acknowledge: *My friend said that Twitter increased its character limit.*
- Distance: *It is rumoured that Twitter increased its character limit.*

Disclaim:

- Negation: *You do not need to use hashtags in every tweet that you write.*
- Counter: *Although they were told otherwise, they continued to use hashtags in most tweets that they wrote.*

Proclaim:

- Concur: *Naturally, hashtags on Twitter have multiple functions.*
- Pronounce: *There is no doubt that hashtags on Twitter have multiple functions.*
- Endorse: *This study has demonstrated that hashtags on Twitter have multiple functions.*

Although a descriptive breakdown of these four formulations (and their subtypes) cannot be provided here due to limits of space, it is also important to know that each one has a different primary function, as well as a relation to the dialogic backdrop and implications for solidarity and authorial voice. An interesting feature I noticed regarding the categories of expansion and contraction is that there are utterance types that mirror and differ from one another in how they control the dialogic background. For the attribute and proclaim formulations, the speaker associates their message to an external voice; however, this voice will either acknowledge other positions (attribute: *Mr. Mandela said the Group of Eight nations have a duty to help battle the scourge of AIDS*, p. 111) or be highly warrantable and therefore suppress other voices (proclaim, endorsement: *The report demonstrates that the British prisoners have "no substantial complaints" about their conditions,* p. 126). Depending on a speaker's intention, as well as their stance toward the message they are conveying, the recipient will feel welcomed or threatened in the dialogic space and will be more or less likely to align with the narrative from what they infer about a speaker's intention. The action of alignment is also dependent upon the recipient's stance on the matter; if the two stances compete with one another, or if the speaker cannot convince them to subscribe to their stance, the listener is likely to disalign from them. A breakdown of these systems can be found below (Tables 10.1 and 10.2).

Table 10.1. Martin and White's (2005, p.100) system for classifying how utterances recognise dialogistic alternatives

Classification of Utterances	
Monoglossic (dialogistic alternatives are not recognised)	**Heteroglossic** (dialogistic alternatives are recognised)
• **Traditionally seen as truth statements**	• **Dialogistic background is diverse**
• **Makes no reference to other voices**	• **Entertains many points of view/voices**
• ***The banks have been greedy.***	• ***In my view the banks have been greedy.***

Table 10.2. A system for classifying how Martin and White's (2005) heteroglossic utterances interact with the backdrop of positions and voices

Heteroglossic Utterances			
Dialogically expansive formulations (allows for alternative positions and voices)		**Dialogically contractive formulations** (restrict alternative positions and voices)	
Entertain: the voice positions the utterance in its subjectivity, and therefore represents it as but one of many possibilities.	**Attribute:** the voice positions the utterance "in the subjectivity of an external voice," and therefore represents it as but one of several voices.	**Disclaim:** the voice of the utterance "positions itself at odds with, or rejecting" another voice.	**Proclaim:** the voice represents the utterance as highly warrantable, and therefore "sets itself against, suppresses or rules out" other voices.

Although this system allows for utterances to be placed in tidy boxes, I stress two elements that need to be kept in mind. Firstly, an utterance cannot always fit in a nice and neat box; in fact, it might straddle the boundary between two different dialogic formulations, or perhaps not fit into any at all. Secondly, I must consider how the text type Martin and White (2005) form their system on and the one of focus for this analysis have very important differences. Many of the examples used to explain the engagement formulations are either from extracts written in a formal style (government websites, newspapers, letters, lectures, advertisements) or come from instances of verbal communication (interviews or speeches). However, Twitter is a textual mode that also has specific elements which make it unique, including but not limited to abbreviations of phrases (*imho* means *in my honest opinion*) and emojis. Also, as discussed previously, hashtags create discursive spaces that allow Twitter users to align with others, whether that be sharing their personal stories about assault or voicing their opinions on the atmosphere surrounding reported assault; through this alignment, they can also convey their stance surrounding the movement. While Martin and White's (2005) system for classifying utterances within a dialogically active background helps us understand how people communicate these feelings as well as create safe spaces with those whom they might not regularly talk together on the internet, it is also important to keep in mind how the discourse I analyse differs from that which the authors constructed the system on and therefore be aware of possible difficulties that might arise during analysis.

4. Methodology

The research I report in this chapter comes from a larger study – my undergraduate thesis – where I originally analysed how Twitter users who talked about the event of #WhyIDidntReport successfully embedded illocutionary force into their tweets without resources such as prosodic cues and facial and other gestures. As the data for this project had to be manageable for one person (myself) to conduct in-depth analysis on, I selected thirty-one tweets for analysis whose data collection process and method I describe below. Also, while I coded the data for other strategies in the original study (the turn-taking organization, acts of going *on* or *off record*, face-threatening acts, and emoji modulation), this chapter is concerned with the analysis and findings of the engagement formulations, or when a tweet did not contain enough content to accurately discern a formulation, its alignment and solidarity.

4.1. Data

For this project, I used three different methods to collect tweets for analysis which resulted in the collection of tweets from three different Twitter threads. The first method was to go where many responses were being generated relating to the movement. This common point was Trump's tweet that was made after his interview concerning Ford's accusation of Kavanaugh (Figure 10.4). Although this initial tweet does not include #WhyIDidntReport, responses to this tweet do use it, along with other related hashtags such as #IdidntReport, #EnoughIsEnough, and #BelieveSurvivors. Because of the level of response, it received from an alternate dialogic position, this tweet, as well as two response threads, were chosen for analysis. Secondly, conversations within the movement that were not direct replies to Trump's thread were also examined. These tweets were retrieved by searching the hashtag and selecting what was the most popular tweet (counting by likes, retweets, and hashtags) at that time. While I do not know how quickly it gained popularity because I selected it for analysis on September 27, the fact that it remained in the "top" section of Twitter's search also serves as a good gauge of its popularity. From this tweet, three separate threads, along with their branching off threads, were chosen for analysis. Lastly, Twitter users who were being uncooperative or unhelpful to the movement were also of interest to this study. Finding tweets of this nature was difficult for two main reasons. First, *#WhyIDidntReport* contained many tweets of encouragement from both survivors and supporters. This in and of itself is a very good event to witness, but also made it difficult for this portion of the analysis. Secondly, to find tweets of this nature, the search field had to be constrained to those tweets including the hashtag as well as the keywords *didn't happen*. Luckily Twitter's filtering system helps make constrained searches like this easier, but there was still one final problem: tweets of this unhelpful stance did not have much interaction going on within them. One could argue this fact shows that this movement is about the dialogic alternative raising its voice against the norm, however, this is not for discussion here. Despite the limited tweets that could be selected, one was found that had a lot of interaction and it plus its branching threads were selected for analysis.

4.2. Method

For my analysis, I coded the selected tweets for the analytic resources that I described previously as strategies that Twitter individuals use to engage with other people on the platform and to negotiate their alignment and solidarity. Because I performed an in-depth analysis of the Twitter threads and needed a system to track the features I annotated throughout the discourse, I organised the tweets in tables so that threads that replied to other tweets could be viewed side by side. Another way to track the annotations I made for the analytic resources was to assign each coding tool a different colour. With this study, I analysed each engagement formulation separately for what it revealed before combining these findings and forming my interpretation of the data which I provide in the discussion section. I chose these tools with the intent of revealing how Twitter users negotiate their values of alignment and solidarity during interactions that related to #WhyIDidntReport. More specifically, I hope that an analysis of these tools shows how individuals – both those who push for change and those who oppose it – use dialogically contractive formulations in their messages to exclude others with counter positions from engaging in the conversation of the thread.

5. Results and discussion

One way I approached interpreting the findings was to generate frequency totals for each type of formulation described in the analytic resources section of this chapter. Though the reoccurring patterns I found in this small sample of data cannot be generalised to the entire #WhyIDidntReport hashtag, I believe it is meaningful to report my findings because the discourse of the three different threads I analysed patterned similarly to each other regarding user negotiation of alignment and solidarity.

5.1. Engagement formulations

Through my interpretation of the data, I identified thirty-seven engagement formulations within the thirty-one tweets. The reason why there are more formulations than tweets is that some tweets – for example, Trump's tweet (Figure 10.2) – have multiple engagement formulations operating within them. Another aspect of the data is that the formulations of *counter* and *negation* – bundled under the *deny* formulation – co-occurred with one another three times (italicised numbers in Table 10.3). Overall, Twitter participants used the contractive formulations of *proclaim* and *deny* more often than expansive ones. Contractive constructions consisted of twenty-nine of the total formulations (78.4 %) whereas I found only eight expansive formulations in this data set (21.6 %). Of the contractive formulations, more speakers used those that Martin and White (2005) classify as deny (Figure 10.2, *no doubt*); I found this type in fourteen of the thirty-one tweets (45.2 %) and it comprises seventeen of the thirty-seven formulations I recorded (45.9 %).

(1) ***10:14 AM - 21 Sep 2018*** @realDonaldTrump: [I have no doubt that (pronouncement, negation)], [if the attack on Dr. Ford was as bad as she says (counter)], charges would have been immediately filed with local Law Enforcement Authorities by either her or her loving parents. I ask that she bring those filings forward so that we can learn date, time, and place!
76K direct replies, 25, 792 Retweets, 109, 593 likes

Figure 10.2. Engagement formulations in Trump's tweet

Table 10.3. Occurrences of formulations within the Twitter threads

Formulation	Sub-formulation	Tweets[2]
Proclaim	Pronouncement	1, 1.2.3, 1.2.1.1, 1.2.1.1.1, 2, 2.2, 2.2.1.1, 3, 3.1, 3.1.2.1
	Endorsement	
	Concur	1.2, 2.1
Deny	Counter	*1*, 1.1.1.1, 1.2.3, *1.2.2.1*, 2, 2.1, 3.1.2, 3.1.1.1.1, 3.1.1.1.1.1
	Negation	*1*, 1.1, 1.1.1, 1.2, 1.2.3, *1.2.2.1*, 2.2.1.1.2.1, 3.1.1
Entertain		1.1.2, 1.1.1.1, 1.2, 1.2.2.1, 3.1.1.1
Attribute	Acknowledge	1.2.1, 3.1.2
	Distance	3.1.1.1

Table 10.4. Frequencies of engagement formulations

Formulation	Sub-formulation	Total (*T*)[a]	%	Total (*F*)[b]	%
Proclaim	Pronouncement	10	32.5	10	27
	Endorsement	0	0	0	0
	Concur	2	6.5	2	5.4
Deny	Counter	9	29	9	24.3
	Negation	8	25.8	8	21.6
Entertain		5	16.1	5	13.5
Attribute	Acknowledge	2	6.5	2	5.4
	Distance	1	3.2	1	2.7

Note a: (T) is the total frequency within tweets, calculated out of thirty-one.
Note b: (F) is the total frequency within formulations, calculated out of thirty-seven.

2 Tweets are numbered for purposes of anonymity.

In Figure 10.2 (also tweet 1 in the data), Trump used *no doubt* to introduce the possibility that Kavanaugh did sexually assault Ford, only to reject this statement by saying that if her story were true, surely the authorities would have done something about it. This denial is realised through *no doubt* having scope over the entire *if the* construction. However, because *no doubt* is in the same construction with *charges would have been laid*, Trump can deny all possibilities of Ford's claim being true. Related to this, I examined a reply to Trump's tweet – which I do not show in this chapter verbatim to protect the user's identity – where the individual also used the deny formulation in their response. In their tweet (labelled 1.1 in my data), the participant used the negotiation structure *I never… he never…* to show the audience – who is both Trump and anyone else who reads this tweet – that they have experienced multiple accounts of the problem that Trump addressed and excluded in his tweet. This construction places the speaker in an authoritative position where they try to correct any misunderstandings people may have. These denials contract the dialogic space as they do not allow for the possibility of voices other than those that match with their own to also contribute to the discussion.

Considering all contractive formulations in the data, as well as the sub-types, *pronouncements* – which fall under the *proclaim* type – are the most frequent as I identified them in ten tweets (one in each); this resulted in a total of 27 percent of the total formulations. Tweet 1.2.1.1 shows an example of this – once again, I do not show the tweet verbatim to protect the user – where the individual used another proclaim formulation (in tweet 1.2 in this thread they used a proclaim: concur) to directly confront the position that Trump and his supporters (the third party) push. The statement *[i]t's time for society to change* exemplifies this confrontation as society refers to the entire population, including Trump and his supporters who deny the issue. Pronouncements are contractive as the speaker positions against the diversity and challenges alternative positions. Interestingly enough, I found no engagement formulations of the endorsement type (a sub-type of the proclaim formulation) in this data set. Of the expansive formulations, I identified five that belonged to the *entertain* category and three that I classified as the *attribute* type. Expansive formulations consist of 21.6 % of all the formulations I identified in the data and according to their placement in the tweets (Table 10.3) they occur only in the first thread (replies to Trump) and the third thread (consisting of Trump's supporters). I discuss the presence and frequency of these formulations relating to the larger discourse below.

5.2. Two separate camps

Within the three main threads analysed for this project, I found that speakers aligned to one of two competing voices. The first, found in tweets from the first and second thread, encompasses Twitter users who are victims of sexual assault or are supporters of this group. Together, these individuals resist the belief which is presupposed in Trump's tweet that women are liars, and in doing so, aim to create supportive spaces for those people who are in need. For this resistance group, the counter position they argue against is the belief that women are liars and because of this belief, they are not taken seriously when they report instances of sexual assault. Certain speakers in the first two threads hold this negative position but this stance is mostly found in the third thread. This group – especially those individuals of the third thread – works to keep individuals of the first group out of their conversations through their use of engagement formulations. As reported in the previous section, contractive patterns are more common in this data than those which are expansive; more specifically, those which pronounce or counter the alternative position.

This initially came as a surprise, as I expected – at least in those threads that display support – to see participants using expansive formulations to open the dialogic space for other positions. However, the results show that there is very limited room for alternative positions.

Speakers either support victims or try to disempower them. From this, I suggest that these two groups have no intention of opening the dialogic space to one another's positions. Instead, they work only within their narratives to rule out counter positions. Within this division, the two groups also try to point out the "flaws" in each other's positions, albeit tweets of the supportive group are more present in the background than those which fuel the flawed belief encouraged by Trump. Through their discourse, participants effectively engage with others who subscribe to similar positions as well as build alignment and solidarity in their groups.

As I highlighted earlier, some utterances cannot be easily classified as one particular engagement formulation. This is true of the phrase *I don't understand how someone could […]* that an individual used in tweet 2.1 (this thread was largely comprised of victims and supporters) as it functions as both to proclaim (concur) and to disclaim (counter). The *I don't understand construction* is similar in meaning to the *how could you* formula which represents how the speaker cannot process the action of the other individuals (*someone*). It is particularly this combination of the two (*I don't understand how someone could*) that makes it impossible to categorise this tweet with one formulation. The proclaim (concur) move works to disclaim as the negation implies a positive-stakes stance against people who can do *X*, which is a proclaim-like move. It associates this disclaim by countering people who also reflect such behaviour. In this way, it is the negative association that brings in the positive alignment with this group of participants.

Facework is at the forefront of importance to this analysis as it is through this concept that we reach another small understanding of #WhyIDidntReport. Firstly, Trump directly attacks Ford's *face* through his stance taken in both the interview he did and his tweet. This attack on her *face* started the movement and the hashtag #WhyIDidntReport is the opposing side's attempt at calling Trump out on his face-threatening act. Additionally, the two different groups of individuals – those that support the victims and those that support Trump's stance – managed *face* through avoidance strategies to maintain equilibrium. These defensive and protective strategies allowed each group to avoid as much interaction with each other as possible and resulted in the dialogically contractive background that I observed. For the two groups identified in this chapter (victims/supporters and deniers), I found through an analysis of engagement formulations in their discourse that speakers were able to effectively build solidarity with others who held the same position. These formulations – which mostly contract the dialogic background – form a cluster within these tweets, creating an opportunity for others to share their stories (alignment) in such a way that a similar position is indirectly acknowledged (solidarity). I found that there was little room for alternative voices in the threads I analysed, which worked in favour of the group as this contributed to the building of a larger discursive safe space (#WhyIDidntReport) for victims to share their stories and to receive the support they long needed in a society that often works against them.

5.3. Limitations

Lastly, I find it prudent to discuss the limitations of not only this analysis but also this project. As mentioned previously, the results of this study are only a part of the project I completed for my undergraduate thesis in 2019. From the time I submitted my thesis for grading to the present, where I currently write this chapter, it has been roughly two years. My original project had many holes in its foundation and though during my two years of graduate studies I have had the time to reflect, read more relevant literature, and expand my knowledge, I think it is important that I address these areas of discrepancy for any concerned reader.

When I began this project and decided to use Martin and White's (2005) engagement formulations as one method of analysing the data, I had no prior knowledge of SFL. At the time, I was not aware of how important it would be to understand the SFL approach before using Martin and White's model. While I have learned a lot about SFL during my time in graduate courses since conducting this study, I must say that the analysis presented in this chapter is from a time when I knew nothing about this approach and as such, I suspect that it is lacking in certain areas. For example, I did not know about the metafunctions of SFL nor how important the interpersonal metafunction is to engagement and appraisal system; with this knowledge, I would have been better situated within the context of this framework and could have applied this to my data analysis. Another area that limits my findings is that I did not use Martin and White's (2005) entire appraisal system as part of my analytic tools and because of this, I feel as though the results I found are not complete. Due to time constraints, I only analysed the data for engagement formulations and did not consider the second subsystem that Martin and White (2005) detail in the same chapter: graduation, or how speakers can up- or down-scale the engagement value of their proposition for intensity or precision (in their terms, force or focus). I know this inclusion would have been beneficial to this analysis as perhaps it would have shown that one group was more intense or precise in their engagement when compared to the other. Though there are flaws in this research, I am still baffled by the overwhelming number of contractive formulations used in the data and as such, deem it worthwhile to present this finding, even if it is small.

6. Conclusion

Throughout this chapter, I have done my best to explain my central goal for this research project as well as highlight the challenges I faced as a young researcher analysing social media data. Sexual assault victims often feel threatened and disregarded when retelling their accounts in face-to-face interaction; as such, Twitter's increased distance between speakers allows victims to not only protect themselves when vulnerable but also share their experiences in a safe space. As the data showed, individuals used more dialogically contractive formulations than those which expanded the background, and this provided a small understanding of how these people convey alignment and stance with the #WhyIDidntReport movement. For both groups of people – those who resist the belief that women are liars and those who agree with this – the engagement formulations allowed users to open up the dialogic space for like-minded individuals to participate in the conversation while excluding those people who did not agree with their position. While the engagement with the #WhyIDidntReport hashtag forces those individuals, who subscribe to the belief that "all women are liars" to contradict themselves, this too aids in the spread of the message for those who advocate for change in society.

Because of this study, I have become more interested in how sexual assault victims use Twitter as a safe space to share their accounts that can result in social change. In the same area of research that draws on corpus-assisted discourse studies (CADS) within a social media context, my next project seeks to examine the strategies that Twitter participants use to discuss a community-based incident of sexual harassment with the broader objective of uncovering what the hashtag as a tool means for instances of digital activism. However, this type of research raises questions regarding how to best protect the identities of the Twitter users whose tweets I analyse because a person with malicious intent who wants to cause harm can easily take a verbatim tweet used as an example and search for it on the microblogging service. As such, researchers that use this type of data must take every precaution to protect user's identities, especially for those individuals who could face harm in situations of unequal power. Though we can learn a lot from the discourses that occur on social media platforms, as well as witness the societal change that these discourses are evoking, I believe it is also crucial that we be mindful of how our research practices and presentation of our findings represent these movements so that we do not restrain or negatively impact their progress.

References

Bonilla, Y., & Rosa, J. (2015). #Ferguson: Digital Protest, Hashtag Ethnography, and the Racial Politics of Social Media in the United States. *American Ethnologist,* 42(1), 4–17.

Brown, P., & Levinson, S.C. (1987). Politeness: Some Universals in Language Usage. In A. Jaworski & N. Coupland (Eds.), *The Discourse Reader* (2nd ed., pp. 312–323). Routledge.

Eggins, S. (2004). *An Introduction to Systemic Functional Linguistics* (2nd ed.). London: Continuum.

Evans, A. (2016). Stance and Identity in Twitter Hashtags. *Language@Internet,* 13(1). Retrieved September 5, 2023 from https://www.languageatinternet.org/articles/2016/evans

Flowerdew, J., & Richardson, J. E. (2017). Introduction. In J. Flowerdew & J. E. Richardson (Eds.), *Handbook of Critical Discourse Analysis* (pp. 1–10). Routledge.

Fortin, J. (2018, September 23). #WhyIDidntReport: Survivors of Sexual Assault Share Their Stories after Trump Tweet. *The New York Times.* Available at https://www.nytimes.com/2018/09/23/us/why-i-didnt-report-assault-stories.html

Get to Know Us: History & Inception. (2020, July 16). *Me Too*. Retrieved September 5, 2023 from https://metoomvmt.org/get-to-know-us/history-inception/

Giaxoglou, K. (2018). #JeSuisCharlie? Hashtags as Narrative Resources in Contexts of Ecstatic Sharing. *Discourse, Context & Media*, 22, 13–20.

Goffman, E. (1967). On Face-Work: An Analysis of Ritual Elements in Social Interaction. In *Interaction Ritual: Essays on Face-to-Face Behaviour* (pp. 5–45). Doubleday.

Machin, D., & Mayr, A. (2012). *How To Do Critical Discourse Analysis: A Multimodal Introduction*. London: SAGE.

Martin, J. R., & White, P. R. R. (2005). Engagement and Graduation: Alignment, Solidarity and the Construed Reader. In *The Language of Evaluation: Appraisal in English* (pp. 92–160). London: Palgrave Macmillan.

Murthy, D. (2013). *Twitter: Social Communication in the Twitter Age*. Polity Press.

Oxford University Press. (2019). Hash, n.3. In *OED Online*, Oxford: Oxford University Press. Available at www.oed.com/view/Entry/389023

Renkl, M. (2017, October 19). The Raw Power of #MeToo. *The New York Times*. Retrieved September 5, 2023 from https://www.nytimes.com/2017/10/19/opinion/the-raw-power-of-metoo.html

Rightler-McDaniels, J. L., & Hendrickson, E. M. (2014). Hoes and Hashtags: Constructions of Gender and Race in Trending Topics. *Social Semiotics*, 24(2), 175–190.

Scott, K. (2015). The Pragmatics of Hashtags: Inference and Conversational Style on Twitter. *Journal of Pragmatics*, 81, 8–20.

Smartt, N. (2017, December 20). *Sexual Harassment in the Workplace in a #MeToo World*. Forbes Community Voice. Retrieved September 5, 2023 from https://www.forbes.com/sites/forbeshumanresourcescouncil/2017/12/20/sexual-harassment-in-the-workplace-in-a-metoo-world/

Trump, D J [@realDonaldTrump]. (2018, September 21). *I Have No Doubt That, If the Attack on Dr. Ford Was as Bad as She Says, Charges Would Have* [Tweet]. Twitter. Retrieved September 5, 2023 from https://twitter.com/realDonaldTrump/status/1043126336473055235

Wodak, R. & Meyer, M. (2015). Critical Discourse Analysis: History, Agenda, Theory, and Methodology. In R. Wodak & M. Meyer (Eds.), *Methods of Critical Discourse Analysis* (pp. 1–13). London: SAGE.

Wolfson, S. (2018, September 21). #WhyIDidntReport: Sexual Assault Victims React to Trump's Attack on Ford. *The Guardian*. https://www.theguardian.com/society/2018/sep/21/whyididntreport-sexual-assault-victims-trump-kavanaugh-ford.

Zappavigna, M. (2011). Ambient Affiliation: A Linguistic Perspective on Twitter. *New Media & Society*, 13(5), 788–806.

Zappavigna, M. (2015). Searchable Talk: The Linguistic Functions of Hashtags. *Social Semiotics*, 25(3), 274–291.

Marco Mazzone

University of Catania, Italy

mazzonem@unict.it

Chapter 11 Political correctness and taboos: A psychological-developmental model

Abstract: I try to take seriously Butler's suggestion that we should refrain from looking at verbal offences on the one hand, and Politically Correct (PC) norms on the other, in terms of the magical view of performatives: as if they could not fail, whatever the circumstances of their utterance. I analyse this first by considering some reasons to think that the power of words is sometimes overestimated. Then, I look at the explanations of magic in anthropology to provide an appropriate notion of "magic (performative)": a hybrid entity, encompassing both an affective-symbolic component and a claim to objective description (with the related causal efficacy). Finally, I provide reasons to think that this "primitive" way of thinking is still alive deep down our well-educated minds.

Keywords: magic, performative, Politically Correct, verbal offense, harm.

1. Introduction

In this paper, I intend to analyse the issue of political correctness – more precisely, of political correctness norms (PCNs), that is, the norms intended to regulate linguistic behaviour in the service of political correctness – as a special case of tabooing.

More precisely, I want to address a couple of essentially psychological issues related to taboos. My research questions are (a) the extent to which PCNs are a form of tabooing in the sense that is described in the traditional anthropological literature (in other words, whether they may be described as a form of primitive thought, as it were), and (b) how we should understand in psychological terms such primitive forms of tabooing.

A preliminary definition of "taboo" might be something like: things (words, but also actions) that are "thought to be ominous or evil or somehow offensive to supernatural powers", such that "to violate a taboo automatically [causes] harm" (Burridge, 2014, p. 2). As may be seen, there are two components to this definition. First, the violation of the taboo is responsible for causing harm. Second, harm is not consequence of (the violation of) natural laws or conventional rules: it is rather an effect of something being evil and offensive to supernatural powers. In a sense, the offense (the violation) itself is taken to have supernatural power, since it is able to cause harm *due to the fact* that it infringes a supernatural moral order. The offense – so to speak – directly affects this supernatural order.

I will proceed as follows. First, I will provide an argument, though not a very strong one indeed, to the effect that PCNs may be a form of tabooing in the sense described above. Then I will review some relevant anthropological literature in search of a framework to understand the faith in the magical power of words. Finally, I will present a developmental psychological model proposed by Erik Erikson, in order to theoretically frame the phenomenon under consideration. The general idea is that more primitive ways of reasoning are not suppressed by the emergence of more sophisticated ones, but the former are instead incorporated into the latter so that they still affect our ordinary belief formation.

This is far from implying that PCNs are always to be understood as taboos. My general claim is, instead, that we should try to draw a line between the normative policies that are justified by the circumstances and the ones that are at risk of displaying what we shall call (with Judith Butler) a "magical view" of performatives.

2. PCNs, Judith Butler, and some evidence

In her book *Excitable speech*, Judith Butler (1997) analyses both verbal offenses and PCNs from the perspective of their common performative nature. Performatives have the power to produce social consequences: as John Austin (1962) put it, while constative utterances only describe independent states of affairs, performative utterances have the power to *create* (social) states of affairs. However, according to Butler, the proponents of PCNs may tend to overestimate this power, to the point that it is sometimes thought of as "sovereign power, power figured as emanating from a subject, activated in a voice, whose effects appear to be the magical effects of that voice. In other words, power is understood on the model of the divine power of naming, where to utter is to create the effect uttered" (Butler, 1997, p. 32).

In this sense, Butler explicitly speaks of a "magical view" of performatives, according to which these are endowed with "magical efficacy" (Butler, 1997, p. 21). In contrast to that view, Butler argues that verbal offenses – and performatives in general – may fail, since their efficacy depends on objective constraints that may apply or not in any given circumstance.

Are there reasons to think that Butler is right when she attributes a magical view of performatives to (some) supporters of PCNs? I want to provide here some reason to accept a weaker claim, that is, the claim that the proponents of PCNs tend to largely overestimate the power of words. If this is the case, then we might want to understand why, and the belief in the magical efficacy of words might provide precisely such a psychological explanation: that is, proponents of PCNs tend to overestimate the power of words *because* they are not entirely free from the influence of magical thought. This explanation might then gain support from our further considerations about primitive thought and its survival within our civilised thought. So, let us start from the overestimation claim.

This is a common allegation to political correctness (e.g., Friedman, 2018). According to O'Neill's (2011, p. 284), PCNs' supporters put their focus exclusively on words at the detriment of intent and context. But intent and context are essential to how verbal offenses work, which explains why presumed offensive words may fail to be such or be reappropriated with completely different purposes (e.g., Butler, 1997, p. 161) when they are uttered in different contexts with different intentions. This also explains why presumed neutral words, which are proposed as an alternative to offensive ones, cannot stay neutral for long. They are exposed to a negative semantic shift which depends on the fact that they are *used* as insults:

> [...] where does the alleged rudeness of the term *retarded* originally come from? If not from the term's literal meaning, it must come from its delivery: the tone and context in which it is delivered. If people use the term *mentally retarded* as an insult to refer to others with scorn through a spiteful tone of voice or in an insulting context, the term will certainly be offensive. It is offensive in these cases precisely because it is intended to be and because its delivery reveals this intention. (O'Neill, 2011, p. 281)

In other words, O'Neill's point is that the substitution of alleged neutral terms for the offensive ones is ineffective because, contrary to the assumptions of (some) PCNs' supporters, words *by themselves* have neither the power to offend nor that to prevent offenses. O'Neill accuses political correctness of "dishonesty" since, in its relentless search for neutral terms, it is forced to adopt ever more inaccurate euphemisms. In the political debate this point has sometimes been expressed as a charge of hypocrisy. However, speaking of dishonesty and hypocrisy misses the well-intentioned attitude which underlies PC preferences (I will come back to the moral dimension in Section 4 below). The real point is whether those moral intentions are (partially) ill-grounded, due to overestimation of the power of words – both their power to offend and their power to prevent offenses.

In sum, if O'Neill is right, we should refrain from attributing magical power to offensive words as if they produced harmful effects independently of intent and context. For the same reason, it is an illusion to think that hateful speech can be prevented by normative prescriptions about which words to use. Words in themselves do not have such unconstrained power.

That the offensive power of words tends to be overestimated by political correctness supporters is also suggested by literature surveying empirical evidence: for instance, Jay (2009) provides reasons to put limitations on the claim that offensive words can harm people, while Lilienfeld (2017) analyses the notion of "microaggression" in recent psychological literature finding that "strong claims" about their offensive power are made based on "inadequate evidence" (but for a more favorable assessment of the efficacy of PCNs, see Maass et al., 2014).

3. Anthropology and the explanation of magic

In anthropology, the debate on how to explain the power of magic dates back to the beginning of the 20th century, when "the intellectualist explanations of magic by Tylor and Frazer were opposed by their critics, Durkheim, Mauss, and Levy-Bruhl" (De Lara, 2000, p. 119). The more specific issue of how words in particular acquire magical power has further been addressed by equally famous contributions such as Ogden and Richards (1923), Malinowski (1923), Evans-Pritchard (1933, 1934), Cassirer (1953), Tambiah (1968), Beattie (1970).

Making a long story short, the intellectualist view claims that magic has to be understood in terms of intellectual or cognitive beliefs, and therefore that it aspires to be "science" but unfortunately it is mistaken science – science gone wrong. On the other hand, Levy-Bruhl (1936) among others has opposed this view based on his notion of "mystical thought", which is to be intended not in terms of intellectual beliefs but in terms of what he called an "affective and intellectual complex" where the affective component is dominant. Key to this view is the idea that there is a sharp dualism between the empirical and the mystical approach, so that, insofar as primitive cultures are engaged in magic and rituals, they are not pursuing science at all: they are not interested in causal connections but in similarity relations. The advantage of this position with respect to the intellectualist one is that it is less Western- and modernist-centric (in other words, it does not anachronistically attribute to primitive cultures our scientific framework); but it is so at the cost of assuming a relativistic dualism which leaves little room for reciprocal understanding. It is as if primitive cultures were never interested in pursuing knowledge without the interference of affections, on the one hand, and, on the other, as if we civilised people were always able to avoid that interference.

Such a rigid dualism is somehow preserved in a further position, the symbolic view proposed by Beattie (e.g., 1970; see also Tambiah, 1968, 2017). According to him, the "mystical" and the "pre-logical" described by Levy-Bruhl apply to beliefs that are not founded in experience but "in the potency of symbols and symbolic procedures, and to the associations of ideas in terms of metaphor rather than of real identity", and therefore it is important to distinguish the symbolic and the practical, scientific ways of thinking (Beattie, 1970, pp. 258–9).

In a sense, the symbolic view is a reinterpretation of the "affective and intellectual complex" proposed by Levy-Bruhl, in terms of an essentially linguistic phenomenon. Interestingly, in this line Tambiah (2017) interprets ritual acts and magical rites in terms of performative acts in Austin's sense. Performatives are not based on objective truth, they create a *sui generis* kind of reality. As a consequence,

> it is inappropriate to subject these performative rites to verification, to test whether they are true or false in a referential or assertive sense or whether the act has effected a result in terms of the logic of "causation" as this is understood in science. (Tambiah, 2017, p. 468)

However, there is a problem with this application of the notion of performative. In fact, it is one thing to expect that performative acts are able to create social reality, it is quite another to presume that they have power over diseases or other physical conditions, as primitive cultures seem to do. The point is precisely that primitive mentality seems inclined to extend the power of performatives outside their legitimate (socio-institutional) scope – which brings us back to Butler.

In fact, the position of Tambiah appears to be circular when compared with Butler's consideration that one can adopt a magical view of performatives. With this consideration in mind, the claim that magical rites can be understood in terms of performatives seems either misleading or trivial: it is misleading in that the notion of performative, if applied without any qualification, cannot explain precisely what is specific to magical uses; and it is trivial because, provided that we appropriately restrict our considerations to magical uses of performatives, we hardly have a non-circular explanation – it is not very informative to say that magical rites are *magical* uses of performatives.

A more nuanced, and more convincing, approach than the previous ones is that of Evans-Pritchard (1933, 1934). It makes room for the intuition that belief in magic is not entirely foreign to us "civilized people": it is in fact a way to make symbolic sense of reality by performatively imposing a social status to certain states of affairs, but, in contrast with the symbolic view of Beattie and Tambiah, Evans-Pritchard insists that the performatives at issue cannot be entirely separated from empirical concerns and therefore, to a variable extent from one case to another, they may attest to a confusion between beliefs and desires. In other words, magical rites involve for sure performatives endowed with symbolic effects but, to some extent, those performatives are also believed to have a non-symbolic (empirical) power over reality.

In sum, according to the view proposed by Evans-Pritchard, magic is not simply a failed attempt to make science in our sense, but it is neither a manifestation of a purely symbolic attitude towards reality. Rather, it is a symbolic practice which is however open to cause mistaken beliefs, as if mere metaphors could provide us with objective descriptions of (and direct power over) target domains of reality (diseases etc.).

4. The psychological developmental model

Given the above interpretation of mystical thought as a confusion between the symbolic and the scientific view of the world – between metaphors and actual causal laws – we might wonder whether this is something to which we civilised people are subject, too.

I want to conclude by briefly considering a developmental model of identity formation proposed by Erik Erikson, which provides an affirmative answer to this question (that is, it describes the self as a layered structure where "ancient" and "modern" components coexist), and at the same time extends our previous considerations in the direction of moral thinking. In fact, as far as PCNs are concerned, the question of whether words have or not unconstrained power and efficacy is just one side of the issue; the other side is the underlying moral attitude involved.

Erikson (1968) proposes a three-stage model of identity development according to which the adult *ethical* stage is preceded by the children's *moral* stage and then the adolescents' *ideological* stage – where each stage is not just replaced by the appearance of the next, it is rather absorbed and persists deeply into it.

With regard to the first stage, the moral one, Erikson focuses on a parallel between childhood and primitive mentality. The moral orientation is claimed to be based on a primitive logic, "predicted on superstitions and irrational inner mechanisms" (Erikson, 1968, pp. 259–69). The conscience of the child is described as "primitive, cruel and uncompromising" (idem: 119), and its superego is characterised as an "archaic [...] primitive [... structure which] remains a rigidly vindictive and punitive agency of 'blind morality'" (Erikson, 1968, p. 210). What is relevant for our purposes is the insistence on primitive logic and superstition, an archaic attitude that might account for the attribution of magical efficacy to words. Also, as noticed by Cote and Levine (1987, p. 297), in this model the child attributes an "all-or-nothingness quality to normative thought that denies the relevance of ambiguous circumstances". This sort of normative attitude shows up in certain forms of polarization within the political correctness debate, where considerations of the contextual circumstances as to whether something is offensive are entirely dismissed, resulting in moral overreaction which prevents dialogue. The simple use of certain words is perceived – so to speak – as what we called "a violation of the supernatural moral order".

In contrast to the moral stage, the ideological stage reflects "awareness of a world in which various authorities exist" (Cote & Levine, 1987, p. 298). But while plurality of ideas is acknowledged in principle, in fact adolescents' adherence to ideologies aims at identity construction, which leads to the adoption of entirely asymmetric attitudes toward their own and others' views: a totalising acceptance of the former goes together with the use of the latter as something to position against. As a consequence, what is lacking at this stage is the awareness – which is characteristic of adulthood at its best – that no one belief system "is flawless or covers all contingencies" and that other ideas "are not to be considered invalid simply because of a perceived 'differentness' " (idem: 299). These considerations might explain why political correctness is prone to shift from a mechanism for inclusion (of minorities) to one of exclusion. It might be a consequence of the natural dynamics of ideological positioning: the construction of (group) identity requires the negative characterization of outgroups, that is, it implies that there must be someone who is (morally) wrong (more on this in Mazzone, 2018, 2020).

Interestingly, according to Erikson only tentatively and incompletely adults overcome the two previous stages, and since pre-adult morality is assumed to be primitive and tribal, this might explain – among other things – why we tend to attribute magical power to words. These considerations would also be consistent with Evans-Pritchard's idea that there is no sharp line between primitive cultures and scientifically oriented ones: the appeal of magic is deeply rooted in our cognitive and moral structure.

To be sure Erikson's model is not uncontroversial, which is one reason why, after all, my argument for PCNs as a form of tabooing is less strong than it should. However, there is growing evidence in favor of the general lines of the argument: first, the tribal roots of our morality have been convincingly documented (e.g., Haidt, 2012); second, the literature on motivated reasoning has shown how preferences tend to affect beliefs, in a way that is reminiscent of Levy-Bruhl's "affective and intellectual complex" (Epley & Gilovich, 2016); third, there is robust evidence of the power of superstition on our well-educated minds (e.g., Vyse 2014).

5. Conclusion

In the overall – let me emphasise it – what I have tried to show is that *some instances* and *some applications* of PCNs might be seen as a form of tabooing in the traditional sense, that is, as manifestations of more primitive ways of thinking that are present in every stage of human development, both in ontogeny and in historical development. More precisely, I have tried to show that some views of political correctness overestimate the power of words, and that this overestimation might be explained by the persistence in modern humans of more primitive ways of thinking. This – it must be clear – does not imply that PCNs cannot be useful and even morally advisable in the appropriate circumstances.

This consideration is not just a diplomatic disclaimer, it has actual theoretical import. I do not intend to provide a general explanation of either politically correct or offensive speech. I am not supporting, in particular, Pinker's (2007) explanation of emotionally charged language in terms of primitive magic and tabooing, nor am I suggesting that these notions might explain slurs in general – an interpretation of Pinker (2007) that is critically discussed in Piazza (2019, pp. 29–30). I agree with Piazza that the "power of magic" explanation of slurs would leave entirely unexplained the social structure that endow them with performative efficacy. First of all, we should mention what Butler (1997) calls the "citational" character of slurs (that is, the fact that by uttering them one is reviving a past history of offensive uses) and also the fact that slurs draw a line between ingroup and outgroup – they cause affiliation and exclusion/aggression at the same time. Moreover, offensive speech presupposes an intention to offend, which manifests itself through cues such as the tone of voice and an offensive context (as remarked in the above quotation by O'Neil, 2011).

However, while explanation of offensive speeches merely in terms of faith in primitive magic would fail to account for the features that, in the appropriate circumstances, endow them with *actual* performative effects, on the other hand when those circumstances do not apply, to believe nevertheless in the efficacy of words per se is at risk of being a form of magical thinking. The same holds for PCNs: their efficacy cannot be taken for granted irrespective of intent and context (remember O'Neill's account of how politically correct words can be used as insults). When we do, there are reasons to think that we are adhering to a magical view of performatives.

References

Austin, J. L. (1962). *How to Do Things with Words*. Oxford: Oxford University Press.

Beattie, J. H. M. (1970). On Understanding Ritual. In B. R. Wilson (Ed.), *Rationality* (pp. 240–68). Oxford: Basil Blackwell.

Burridge, K. (2014). Taboo Words. In Taylor, J. R. (Ed.). *The Oxford Handbook of the Word* (pp. 270–283). Oxford: Oxford University Press.

Butler, J. (1997). *Excitable Speech: A Politics of the Performative*. New York: Routledge.

Cassirer, E. (1953). *Language and Myth*. New York: Dover Publication.

Cote, J. E., & Levine, C. (1987). A Formulation of Erikson's Theory of Ego Identity Formation. *Developmental Review*, 7(4), 273–325.

De Lara, P. (2000). Wittgenstein and Evans-Pritchard on Ritual: Twenty-Two Reasons to Believe Wittgenstein Was an Anthropologist. *Journal of the Anthropological Society of Oxford*, 31(2), 119–132.

Epley, N., & Gilovich, T. (2016). The Mechanics of Motivated Reasoning. *Journal of Economic Perspectives*, 30(3), 133–40.

Erikson, E. (1968). *Identity. Youth and Crisis*. New York/London: Norton & Co.

Evans-Pritchard, E. E. (1933). The Intellectualist (English) Interpretation of Magic. *Bulletin of the Faculty of Arts*, King Fuad 1st University, I(2), 1–21.

Evans-Pritchard, E. E. (1934). Levy-Bruhl's Theory of Primitive Mentality. *Bulletin of the Faculty of Arts*, King Fuad 1st University, Il(2), 1–26.

Friedman, J. (2018). *Politicamente corretto: il conformismo morale come regime*. Milano: Meltemi.

Haidt, J. (2012). *The Righteous Mind: Why Good People Are Divided by Politics and Religion*. New York: Vintage.

Jay, T. (2009). Do Offensive Words Harm People? *Psychology, Public Policy, and Law*, 15(2), 81–101.

Lilienfeld, S. O. (2017). Microaggressions: Strong Claims, Inadequate Evidence. *Perspectives on Psychological Science*, 12(1), 138–169.

Lévy-Bruhl, L. (1936). *Primitives and the Supernatural*. London: George Allen & Unwin.

Maass, A., Suitner, C., & Merkel, E. (2013). Does Political Correctness Make (Social) Sense? In J. P. Forgas, O. Vincze & J. László (Eds.), *Sydney Symposium of Social Psychology. Social Cognition and Communication* (pp. 331–345). New York, NY, US: Psychology Press.

Malinowski, B. (1923). The Problem of Meaning in Primitive Languages. In C. K. Ogden & I. A. Richards (Eds.), *The Meaning of Meaning* (pp. 296–336). London: Kegan Paul, Trench, Trübner & Co.

Mazzone, M. (2018). La Performatività e i suoi Vincoli: lo 'Stadio Ideologico' nell'Animale Umano. *Reti, Saperi, Linguaggi: Italian Journal of Cognitive Sciences*, 1, 191–202.

Mazzone, M. (2020). Performativity and the Ideological Construction of the Self. The Age of Narcissism and (Possibly) Beyond. In A. Pennisi & A. Falzone (Eds.), *The Extended Theory of Cognitive Creativity. Interdisciplinary Approaches to Performativity* (pp. 115–131). New York: Springer.

Ogden, C. K., & Richards, I. A. (1923). *The Meaning of Meaning*. London: Kegan Paul, Trench, Trübner & Co.

O'Neill, B. (2011). A Critique of Politically Correct Language. *The Independent Review*, 16(2), 279–291.

Piazza, F. (2019). *La parola e la spada. Violenza e linguaggio attraverso l'Iliade*. Bologna: il Mulino.

Pinker, S. (2007). *The Stuff of Thought: Language as a Window into Human Nature*. New York: Viking.

Tambiah, S. J. (1968). The Magical Power of Words. *Man*, 3(2), 175–208.

Tambiah, S. J. (2017). Form and Meaning of Magical Acts: A Point of View. *Journal of Ethnographic Theory*, 7(3), 451–473.

Vyse, S. (2014). *Believing in Magic. The Psychology of Superstition*. New York: Oxford University Press.

ŁÓDŹ STUDIES IN LANGUAGE

Vol. 1 Barbara Lewandowska-Tomaszczyk / Patrick James Melia (eds.): PALC'99: Practical Applications in Language Corpora. Papers from the International Conference at the University of Łódź, 15-18 April 1999. 2000.

Vol. 2 Lou Burnard / Tony McEnery (eds.): Rethinking Language Pedagogy from a Corpus Perspective. Papers from the Third International Conference on Teaching and Language Corpora. 2000.

Vol. 3 Barbara Lewandowska-Tomaszczyk / John Osborne / Frits Schulte: Foreign Language Teaching and Information and Communication Technology. 2001.

Vol. 4 Piotr Cap: Explorations in Political Discourse. Methodological and Critical Perspectives. 2002.

Vol. 5 Ewa Waniek-Klimczak / Patrick James Melia (eds.): Accents and Speech in Teaching English Phonetics and Phonology. EFL perspective. 2002.

Vol. 6 Barbara Lewandowska-Tomaszczyk / Kamila Turewicz (eds.): Cognitive Linguistics Today. 2002.

Vol. 7 Barbara Lewandowska-Tomaszczyk (ed.): PALC 2001: Practical Applications in Language Corpora. 2003.

Vol. 8 Corpus Linguistics by the Lune. A Festschrift for Geoffrey Leech. Edited by Andrew Wilson, Paul Rayson and Tony McEnery. 2003.

Vol. 9 Barbara Lewandowska-Tomaszczyk (ed.): Practical Applications in Language and Computers. PALC 2003. 2004.

Vol. 10 Imagery in Language. Festschrift in Honour of Professor Ronald W. Langacker. Edited by Barbara Lewandowska-Tomaszczyk and Alina Kwiatkowska. 2004.

Vol. 11 Seana Coulson / Barbara Lewandowska-Tomaszczyk (eds.): The Literal and Nonliteral in Language and Thought. 2005.

Vol. 12 Piotr Cap (ed.): Pragmatics Today. 2005.

Vol. 13 Jacek Waliński / Krzysztof Kredens / Stanisław Goźdź-Roszkowski (eds.): Corpora and ICT in Language Studies. PALC 2005. 2007.

Vol. 14 Krzysztof Kosecki (ed.): Perspectives on Metonymy. Proceedings of the International Conference "Perspectives on Metonymy", held in Łódź, Poland, May 6-7, 2005. 2007.

Vol. 15 Barbara Lewandowska-Tomaszczyk / Tomasz Płudowski / Dolores Valencia Tanno (eds.): The Media and International Communication. 2007.

Vol. 16 Krzysztof Kredens / Stanisław Goźdź-Roszkowski (eds.): Language and the Law: International Outlooks. 2007.

Vol. 17 Barbara Lewandowska-Tomaszczyk (ed.): Corpus Linguistics, Computer Tools, and Applications – State of the Art. PALC 2007. 2008.

Vol. 18 Barbara Lewandowska-Tomaszczyk / Katarzyna Dziwirek (eds.): Studies in Cognitive Corpus Linguistics. 2009.

Vol. 19 Barbara Lewandowska-Tomaszczyk / Marcel Thelen (eds.): Meaning in Translation. 2010.

Vol. 20 Łukasz Bogucki / Krzysztof Kredens (eds.): Perspectives on Audiovisual Translation. 2010.

Vol. 21 Piotr Stalmaszczyk (ed.): Turning Points in the Philosophy of Language and Linguistics. 2011.

Vol. 22 Stanisław Goźdź-Roszkowski: Patterns of Linguistic Variation in American Legal English. A Corpus-Based Study. 2011.

Vol. 23 Kamila Ciepiela (ed.): Identity through a Language Lens. 2011.

Vol. 24 Stanisław Goźdź-Roszkowski (ed.): Explorations across Languages and Corpora. PALC 2009. 2011.

Vol. 25 Krzysztof Kosecki / Janusz Badio (eds.): Cognitive Processes in Language. 2012.

Vol. 26 Alina Kwiatkowska (ed.): Texts and Minds. Papers in Cognitive Poetics and Rhetoric. 2012.

Vol. 27 Paul A. Wilson (ed.): Dynamicity in Emotion Concepts. 2012.

Vol. 28 Piotr Pęzik (ed.): Corpus Data across Languages and Disciplines. 2012.

Vol. 29 Mikołaj Deckert: Meaning in Subtitling. Toward a Contrastive Cognitive Semantic Model. 2013.

Vol. 30 Łukasz Bogucki: Areas and Methods of Audiovisual Translation Research. 3rd Revised Edition. 2019.

Vol. 31 Janusz Badio / Kamila Ciepiela (eds.): Language, Action, Interaction. 2013.

Vol. 32 Barbara Lewandowska-Tomaszczyk / Krzysztof Kosecki (eds.): Time and Temporality in Language and Human Experience. 2014.

Vol. 33 Iwona Witczak-Plisiecka (ed.): Cognitive and Pragmatic Aspects of Speech Actions. 2014.

Vol. 34 Małgorzata Anna Kamińska: A History of the *Concise Oxford Dictionary*. 2014.

Vol. 35 Łukasz Bogucki / Mikołaj Deckert (eds.): Accessing Audiovisual Translation. 2015.

Vol. 36 Joanna Jabłońska-Hood: A Conceptual Blending Theory of Humour. Selected British Comedy Productions in Focus. 2015.

Vol. 37 Krzysztof Kosecki / Janusz Badio (eds.): Empirical Methods in Language Studies. 2015.

Vol. 38 Katarzyna Stadnik: Chaucer's Choices. Through the looking-glass of medieval imagery. 2015.

Vol. 39 Paulina Pietrzak / Mikołaj Deckert (eds.): Constructing Translation Competence. 2015.

Vol. 40 Małgorzata Fabiszak / Karolina Krawczak / Katarzyna Rokoszewska (eds.): Categorization in Discourse and Grammar. 2016.

Vol. 41 Marcel Thelen / Gys-Walt van Egdom / Dirk Verbeeck / Łukasz Bogucki / Barbara Lewandowska-Tomaszczyk (eds.): Translation and Meaning. New Series, Vol. 1. 2016.

Vol. 42 Łukasz Bogucki / Barbara Lewandowska-Tomaszczyk / Marcel Thelen (eds.): Translation and Meaning. New Series, Vol. 2, Pt. 1. 2016.

Vol. 43 Łukasz Bogucki / Barbara Lewandowska-Tomaszczyk / Marcel Thelen (eds.): Translation and Meaning. New Series, Vol. 2, Pt. 2. 2016.

Vol. 44 Przemysław Łozowski / Katarzyna Stadnik (eds.): Visions and Revisions. Studies in Theoretical and Applied Linguistics. 2016.

Vol. 45 Marek Kuźniak / Bożena Rozwadowska / Michał Szawerna (eds.): From Motion to Emotion. Aspects of Physical and Cultural Embodiment in Language. 2016.

Vol. 46 Anna Rędzioch-Korkuz: Opera Surtitling as a Special Case of Audiovisual Translation. Towards a Semiotic and Translation Based Framework for Opera Surtitling. 2016.

Vol. 47 Mateusz Sajna: Video Game Translation and Cognitive Semantics. 2016.

Vol. 48 Kamila Ciepiela (ed.): Identity in Communicative Contexts. 2016.

Vol. 49 Mikołaj Nkollo: The Entrenchment of the 'unus alterum' Pattern. Four Essays on Latin and Old Romance Reciprocal Constructions. 2016.

Vol. 50 Paweł Rydzewski: Backness Distinction in Phonology. A Polish Perspective on the Phonemic Status of *y*. 2016.

Vol. 51 Piotr Pęzik / Jacek Tadeusz Waliński (eds.): Language, Corpora and Cognition. 2017.

Vol. 52 Janusz Badio (ed.): Events and Narratives in Language. 2016.

Vol. 53 Mikołaj Deckert (ed.): Audiovisual Translation – Research and Use. 2017. 2nd Expanded Edition 2019.

Vol. 54 Michał Szawerna: Metaphoricity of Conventionalized Diegetic Images in Comics. A Study in Multimodal Cognitive Linguistics. 2017.

Vol. 55 Artur Gałkowski / Monika Kopytowska (eds.): Current Perspectives in Semiotics. Signs, Signification, and Communication. 2018.

Vol. 56 Artur Gałkowski / Monika Kopytowska (eds.): Current Perspectives in Semiotics. Text, Genres, and Representations. 2018.

Vol. 57 Łukasz Bogucki / Piotr Cap (eds.): Exploration in Language and Linguistics. For Professor Piotr Stalmaszczyk on the Occasion of His 60th Birthday. 2018.

Vol. 58 Michał Kornacki: Computer-assisted Translation (CAT) Tools in the Translator Training Process. 2018.

Vol. 59 Marcin Walczyński / Piotr Czajka / Michał Szawerna (eds.): On the Verge between Language and Translation. 2018.

Vol. 60 Łukasz Bogucki / Paulina Pietrzak / Michał Kornacki (eds.): Understanding Translator Education. 2018.

Vol. 61 Marcin Walczyński: Psycho-Affective Factors in Consecutive Interpreting. 2019.

Vol. 62 Kamila Ciepiela (ed.): Language, Identity and Community. 2019.

Vol. 63 Olga Łabendowicz: Audiovisual Translation in Poland. Changing Audiences. 2019.

Vol. 64 Enrique Bernárdez / Joanna Jabłońska-Hood / Katarzyna Stadnik (eds.): Cognition in context. New insights into language, culture and the mind. 2019.

Vol. 65 Montse Corrius / Eva Espasa / Patrick Zabalbeascoa (eds.): Translating Audiovisuals in a Kaleidoscope of Languages. 2019.

Vol. 66 Barbara Lewandowska-Tomaszczyk / Valeria Monello / Marco Venuti (eds.): Language, Heart, and Mind. Studies at the intersection of emotion and cogni-tion. 2020.

Vol. 67 Marta Chodkiewicz: Understanding the Development of Translation Competence. 2020.

Vol. 68 Urszula Paradowska: Developing Information Competence in TranslatorTraining. 2021.

Vol. 69 Luca Valleriani: Upper-class English in Natural and Audiovisual Dialogue. 2021.

Vol. 70 Michał Kornacki and Gary Massey (eds.): Contextuality in Translation and Interpreting. Selected Papers from the Łódź-ZHAW Duo Colloquium on Translation and Meaning 2020–2021. 2022.

Vol. 71 Monika Kopytowska / Artur Gałkowski / Massimo Leone (eds.): Thought-Sign-Symbol. Cross-Cultural Representations of Religion. 2022.

Vol. 72 Bartosz Pietrzak: The Concept of Honor in the Language of Early Arabic Poetry. A Cultural Linguistic Study. 2022.

Vol. 73 Aleksandra Beata Makowska: Terminology and phraseology in research papers in the domains of new technologies. A cognitive corpus-based perspective. 2024.

Vol. 74 Emanuela Campisi / Ester Di Silvestro / Marco Venuti (eds.): Strategies of Inclusion and Exclusion in online and offline Interaction. 2024.

www.peterlang.com

www.ingramcontent.com/pod-product-compliance
Ingram Content Group UK Ltd.
Pitfield, Milton Keynes, MK11 3LW, UK
UKHW041825031026
15587UKWH00002B/572

9 783631 852149